Business Journey
to the East

An East–West Perspective
on Global-is-Asian

Praise for the Book

Professor Wee and Mr Combe have provided a very insightful treatise on how to do business in Asia, especially China. I have no doubt that this book will prove to be an extremely useful guide to those who want to understand China better. There has been a lot of misunderstanding about China and the Chinese race as a whole. This book provides useful tips to Western businessmen to understand China better and, in the process, allows them to pay less tuition fees. A must-read for those who want to know China and Asia better.

~ **Zhang Zhong-liang**, Chairman and Group CEO,
China Precision Technology Ltd

An excellent fusion of Western and Asian learning on how to build a sustainable business in Asia. This is a must-read for any company serious about understanding Asia.

~ **Bob Herbold**, Managing Director,
Herbold Group LLC and former Chief Operating Officer,
Microsoft Corporation, USA

The Master has done it again. This time, Professor Wee Chow-Hou partners Fred Combe to produce a significant and insightful book on the differences and similarities in Asian and Western approaches to managing business relationships, operations, and difficult situations. For those of us who want to know more about the subtle nuances of the Asian mind and what it takes to build a lasting relationship and thus achieve success, this book is a must-read.

~ **Professor Tsui Kai Chong**, Provost,
SIM University, Singapore

Wee and Combe's book offers an insider's perspective on why Western companies cannot afford to maintain the status quo when doing business in Asia. *Business Journey to the East* takes a practical look at real strategies that executives can leverage to develop the transcultural leadership skills that are essential to doing business in this region.

~ **J. Frank Brown**,
Dean of the International Business School,
INSEAD, France

The Asian ways of doing business are often talked about yet regularly misunderstood. Only masters like Professor Wee and Fred Combe can clear our thoughts with breakthrough insights into how to manage complex business situations. Their rich experiences, embodied in this book's easy-to-understand language, make *Business Journey to the East* a must-read for executives working in this area of global significance.

~ **David K. Tse**,
Chair Professor of International Marketing and Director,
Chinese Management Centre,
Hong Kong University, Hong Kong

People skills are the vital ingredients for success in Asia. Building relationships should come first, doing business should come second. *Business Journey to the East* reinforces these imperatives and is essential reading for all those looking to succeed in the new Asia.

~ **Stephen Daintith**, Chief Financial Officer,
Dow Jones, USA

This is a profoundly perceptive analysis of modern business from the perspective of an established academic and a seasoned practitioner. Professor Wee and Mr Combe make a powerful argument for the relevance of integrating the best of the East and West in doing business in Asia. They write with assurance and wit derived from their expert knowledge of the Chinese language and history, combined with the breadth of their business consulting and experiences in the East and West. This is an indispensable book for all engaged in business in Asia.

~ **Kwee Liong Seen**, Executive Director,
Pontiac Land Pte Ltd, Singapore

With the tremendous pressure on driving business growth, winning in Asia today is a buzz word for any global corporation. All speak of the incredible opportunities, yet few understand the complexities, the ambiguities, and the challenges of navigating the extremely diverse and unique business environment in Asia. Wee and Combe have put together an objective, experience-based guide to doing business in Asia. It not only narrates actual experiences but puts it in clear cultural context, tapping into Wee's many treatises on Sun Zi's *Art of War*. Finally it allows the reader to envision and identify with each unique chapter as if he were living it. *Business Journey to the East* is simple, unassuming, straightforward, and practical. Read this book and have the pleasure of having Wee and Combe as your guide to understanding how to do business in Asia.

~ **Benjamin Q. Avancena**, International Vice-President,
Johnson & Johnson Medical Device and Diagnostics, North Asia

Business Journey to the East is a must-read for everyone doing business in China. While challenges facing businessmen go beyond the East–West cultural divide, Professor Wee Chow-Hou and Fred Combe have authored a book with refreshing insights gleaned from great philosophers on why Asians and Westerners think and deal differently. Blending theoretical sophistication and keen observation on contemporary scenarios, this book will attract a great deal of attention, not only in Western countries, but throughout East Asia as well. In particular, it helps to put the Asian style of entertainment—drinking binges and karaoke—in perspective. The oft-discussed themes in literature on cross-cultural communication, "face" and *guanxi*, are given a treatment that they deserve in this book and business executives will certainly benefit from adopting a multilevel relationship structure to managing "face," the hallmark of human relationships in Asia. *Business Journey to the East* is a book that anyone with a deep business interest in China can sink their teeth into, learn from, and thoroughly enjoy!"

~ **Andy Lim**, Chairman,
Tembusu Partners Pte Ltd

Ever tried walking through a glass wall, getting yourself a bloody nose, and doing it all over again? For over 40 years, I have seen Western companies (and their expatriate managers) struggle to find the answers to how to think global but beat local in Asia. Now that following the people also means following the money, many more will make the attempt. This book is a unique distillation of scars and victories, with insights into and practical guidance on how to see the glass walls, make them disappear, and win Asian "mind share" for your business.

~ **Nihal Kaviratne**, CBE Former Chairman,
Unilever Indonesia

This is the book that every serious CEO, senior executive and MBA student should read and devour. Professor Chow-Hou Wee and Fred Combe have managed to present a coherent strategic picture of their East–West perspectives and research on the numerous strategic cultural dimensions which can be used to build a successful global business. This book is easy to read and is designed for literally everyone involved in business development in Asia, and provides you with excellent guidelines to avoid making mistakes while developing greater insight into doing business in Asia.

~ **Willie Wong**, Co-Founder & Group Chairman,
Frontken Corporation Berhad (listed in Malaysia)
Director, Ares Green Technology Corporation (listed in Taiwan)

Professor Wee and Combe have highlighted some of the important factors which are significant for doing businesses in Asian countries. Understanding the concept of "face," the boundary between bribery and gift-giving, how to avoid corruption, and learning to socialize through karaoke sessions are all important factors in doing business in Asia. Today, as the world is becoming interconnected, it is crucial to explore different cultural challenges, and appreciate and respect diversity. This book also gives a thorough perspective on leadership with plenty of real-world, concrete examples and advice for you to recognize the ways of doing businesses in the fast emerging Asia.

~ **Professor Kwok-Kee Wei**, Dean, Faculty of Business and
Professor (Chair) of Information Systems
City University of Hong Kong, Hong Kong

Business Journey to the East is a most comprehensive book on doing business successfully. From the East to the West, from theory to everyday practice, from tactical to strategic, this book offers tremendous insights into doing the right things in Asia. While there are many ways to being successful, there are also many ways to do things wrong. *Business Journey to the East* will give you answers to what to do and what not to do, and on how leadership is perceived in the East, how you achieve your (mutual) goals, how you earn and develop the famous *guanxi*, and how important "face" is in every aspect of Eastern culture. This book is based on extensive personal and professional experience, and also takes into account the wisdom of history; it includes a broad cultural context as well as ancient Eastern war strategies. This is a book that will increase your successes in Asia—and that will let you enjoy the unique Eastern business environment.

~ **Roland Diggelmann**, Managing Director,
Region Asia Pacific, Roche Diagnostics Asia Pacific Pte Ltd

This book is a must-read not just for Westerners but also Asians because it provides a unique road map to understanding how business is conducted in Asia, how the relationship between leaders and followers works in the region and how lost opportunities in the past can be recovered in the future. It carefully describes the inner thinking of the rich and resourceful Asian culture and how it has affected business models, practices, and relationships in Asia. Never before, as far as I can recollect, has any published book gone into such fine detail and presented the authors' brilliant observations and expertise in such an organized fashion, offering Westerners and Asians alike such insight into and understanding and appreciation of an often misunderstood culture and market.

~ **James Lu**, Executive Director,
Hong Kong Hotels Association, Hong Kong

After the "stretch" growth goals are set and the strategy is agreed upon, the hard work of executing a plan in Asia begins. Asian and expatriate managers alike are challenged by the same key issues —how to make decisions, how to get commitment to act, how to communicate change, how to reward performance and punish failure, and how to avoid the 1,001 mistakes when operating in business and social cultures that are at times significantly different from Western norms. In a world where many authors are afraid to discuss culture, Wee and Combe have done an admirable job, as both experienced practitioners and academics, to give their answers to the difficult questions. This is the kind of book that you read carefully and then pull out every few months to help craft a response to a new, difficult situation.

~ **Charles M. Ormiston**, Managing Director,
Bain & Company S.E. Asia, Inc.

Asia is a complex fabric of cultural, religious, and racial diversities. Being the most densely populated continent with thousands of years of civilization, it poses tremendous challenges for many who intend to do business in Asia. With the rapid economic growth and social and political transformation within the last several decades or so, no investor in this region can ignore its dynamism and its roots. Professor Wee Chow-Hou and Fred Combe have successfully produced this timely gem that so succinctly outlines the Oriental traditions and practices which are intertwined with business and the lives of Asians. This book definitely serves more than its purpose for those intending to expand their global businesses. It is not only another good book about Asia but a "guide and manual" for those who see "Global is Asian" for the coming century.

~ **Lai Fatt Sian**, Dean,
Faculty of Accountancy and Management
Universiti Tunku Abdul Rahman, Malaysia

Because Asian markets are rising very quickly, or because a larger chunk of manufacturing is being shifted to the East, Western companies face numerous challenges. To operate in Asia, attract and retain local talent, negotiate with suppliers and distributors, and compete effectively with emerging brands, Western employers cannot take for granted that their Asian managers will easily fit into their corporate culture. As this book shows, managers and staff in Asia have a different attitude to authority and a unique form of respect for leadership, and while trust and good relations are universally needed, they take a unique form in Asia. Exploring the roots of these cultural differences in Asian classics on philosophy and strategy, and drawing on the authors' extensive experience of dialogues between cultures, this book provides invaluable guidelines to understanding the true meaning of key concepts such as "face," *guanxi*, and more.

~ **Christian Koenig**, Director,
ESSEC Business School Asian Center, Singapore

This is a new, highly interesting book by Professor Chow-Hou Wee and Mr Fred Combe that amalgamates Chinese cultural knowledge with Western economic scholarship and transports deep insights and precious advice for the business practitioners all over the world.

~ **Harro von Senger**, Professor of Sinology,
Faculty of Philosophy,
Albert-Ludwigs-University Freiburg im Breisgau, Germany

Business Journey to the East

An East–West Perspective
on Global-is-Asian

Chow-Hou Wee • Fred Combe

Singapore • Boston • Burr Ridge, IL • Dubuque, IA • Madison, WI • New York
San Francisco • St. Louis • Bangkok • Kuala Lumpur • Lisbon • London • Madrid
Mexico City • Milan • Montreal • New Delhi • Seoul • Sydney • Taipei • Toronto

The *McGraw·Hill* Companies

Education

Business Journey to the East
An East–West Perspective on Global-is-Asian

McGraw-Hill Education (Asia) would like to thank Pearson Education South Asia Pte Ltd for reproduction of selected quotes extracted from *Sun Zi Bingfa: Selected Insights and Applications* by Wee Chou-Hou (ISBN 9789810675917). These quotes appear on the following pages of this publication: xv, 1, 27, 32, 34–36, 39–48, 51, 73, 93, 119, 143, 169, 189, 198, 199, 213, 231, 237, 261, 269, 291, 309, 319, 327, 333, 338, 341, 365.

All quotes from *Working GlobeSmart* by Ernest Gundling have been modified and reproduced by special permission of the Publisher, Davies-Black Publishing, a division of CPP, Inc., Mountain View, CA 94043. Copyright 2003 by Davies-Black Publishing. All rights reserved. Further reproduction is prohibited without the Publisher's written consent. These quotes appear on the following pages of this publication: 22, 112.

1 2 3 4 5 6 7 8 9 10 CTF ANL 20 09

When ordering this title, use **ISBN 978-007-127802-7** or
MHID 007-127802-8

Printed in Singapore

Contents

Contents

多算胜，少算不胜，
duo suan sheng   shao suan bu sheng

而况于无算乎！
er kuang yu wu suan hu

吾以此观之，胜负见矣。
wu yi ci guan zhi   sheng fu jian yi

With thorough and detailed planning, one can win.
With less thorough and detailed planning,
one cannot win.
How much more certain is defeat when one
does not plan at all!
From my observations of how planning is done,
I can already predict victories from defeats.

(Sun Zi Bingfa 孙子兵法, *Lines 1.48 to 1.51 of
Chapter 1 on Detailed Assessment and Planning,*
计 *(ji))*

Preface

East and West Must Meet

With the rise of Asia over the last 20 years, many Western companies have rushed into investing in the region. Yet, more companies have failed than succeeded in Asia because they simply do not invest enough in equipping their Western-trained managers with the appropriate cultural skills, knowledge, and emotional intelligence to work and relate with their Asian counterparts. Similarly, many Asian managers fail to succeed within Western organizations because they lack the desire and motivation to get involved in the corporate politics of how these organizations operate. With increased globalization and the gradual "flattening" of the globe, there is an urgent need to prepare managers to face the greater challenges of the future. As the "journey to the east" takes on greater momentum, familiarization with how things are done and understood in Asia becomes even more important in order to succeed in doing business there.

As stated in a 2004 article by the Association of Executive Search Consultants (AESC): "Despite nearly two decades of corporate globalization efforts, many organizations still struggle to find managers who are comfortable and effective in the increasingly global economy. Most suffer both from a lack of cultural awareness when dealing with employees and partners overseas and from a lack of experience managing increasingly complex processes over long distances."

We realized that an extraordinary amount of waste was being created by companies and individuals in Asia as a result of failed investment projects, breakdowns in business relationships, loss of talented Asian management, unsuccessful personal development plans, and badly managed careers.

For those companies and individuals who got it right, however, they gained an enormous competitive advantage: approval for new investments ahead of competition, a powerful alliance of supportive stakeholders, an exciting and motivated pipeline of Asian managers, and management boards enriched with senior Asian leaders. It is clear that diversely educated and experienced top management teams give corporations an edge, enhancing their ability to manage globalization and strengthening their financial performance.

What surprised us most, though, was the lack of preparation, training, and development undertaken by Western companies and their managers, particularly their senior leaders, in building sustainable businesses and organizations in Asia. They may have excellent training and development programs, outstanding career development processes, great corporate affairs and public relations structures, and Asia as their top global investment opportunity, yet they have placed little focus and priority in getting the basics right, in preparing and developing their leadership teams to succeed in Asia.

Even scarier was the sad realization that many companies and individuals are making this mistake repeatedly in Asia. They have become serial offenders. Not only are they ill-prepared and becoming frustrated with the lack of progress, they have failed to accept and share the lessons of the past. Too often, they take out the old leadership team and replace it with an equally untrained and underdeveloped new leadership team. It is no surprise when things get stuck again.

As Mary Teagarden, a professor of global strategy at Thunderbird, the Garvin School of International Management, states:

> *"What is essential in a global environment is the ability to work with individuals, groups, organizations, and systems that are unlike our own. We must also understand what differentiates people and what unites them. Understanding that tension—how are we alike and how are we different—is a critically important starting point."*

It is clear that organizations need to ensure that managers have had the opportunity to build a basic understanding of the new cultures in which they will be immersed—with a particular focus on appreciating how behaviors differentiate. These managers must demonstrate a belief that differences matter and an openness to new and different ideas.

Managing Contradictions

The root cause of many problems in doing business in Asia lies in the many contradictions that challenge Western thinking in Asia. Throughout this book, you will come across one contradiction after another, you will appreciate ambiguity as an accepted norm in Asia, and you will discard the conventional logic of our engrained Western mindset. However, the contradictions are not created solely by Asian culture, the West itself is behaving in a contradictory pattern.

The following are some examples of key contradictions:

1. Asia represents the most exciting growth opportunity today for Western multinationals and investors, yet few understand and appreciate Asia for its history, diversity, and culture.

2. The same companies continue to reallocate and increase investment in Asia without equipping their Western-trained managers with the correct skills and emotional intelligence to work with and relate to their Asian counterparts.

3. The West believes it is controlling the destiny of Asia while it is increasingly under the control of a resurging Asia.

4. The West tends to view the marketplace as an opportunity to be exploited while Asia tends to view it as a war to be contested.

5. The West wants to do more business with Asia, yet views it as the biggest threat to its economic competitiveness.

6. The West lobbies hard and furiously for market liberalization in Asia, yet retreats to economic nationalism and trade sanctions when faced with Asian encroachment on home soil.

We have been witnessing these contradictions for many years with increasing alarm, surprise, and sadness. Finally, we decided that something had to be done. While we are certain that there are many books on Asian culture and values, we are equally convinced there are very few books designed to help accelerate and sustain Western business success in Asia. As such, we began our quest to uncover the rich knowledge that would help unleash the energy and the full potential of any company or individual wishing to succeed in Asia.

In this pursuit, we were mindful that the "ideal book" would be one that can combine the experiences of the practitioner's world and the analytical perspectives of an academic. Hence, when both of us met each other, it was like a divine arrangement from above. Our views clicked instantaneously and, to our pleasant surprise, our perspectives of how business has been done in Asia quickly converged. Comforted by the uniformity of our views on similar topics and excited by the prospect of unleashing the joint energy and wisdom of one Asian and one Westerner on an East-meets-West project, we quickly agreed to become partners and decided on the quest together.

Challenges in Writing this Book

Advising people on doing business in Asia is like writing a book on "How to succeed in Europe"! Given the long history of Europe, there is no simple way to explain to anyone that there is a common, generic way to be successful. As any American or Asian tourist visiting Europe today will tell you, Europe is more like a huge modern day theme park than a structured, united community of states. Crossing the border into another country is like moving into another new themed ride. The costumes and food are different, the languages and behaviors are very pronounced, and the houses and road signs are anything but uniform!

Writing about Asia is a similar story; the task is perhaps even more complex. For a start, how do you define what is Asian? After all, Asia as a region can stretch from Istanbul in the west to Japan in the east, from Mongolia in the north to Indonesia in the south. For the purpose of this book, and largely because of the dominant role of China today, we are defining Asians as largely the group of people who have been heavily influenced by Chinese culture, traditions, customs, habits, and thinking. They include those living in China, those who have migrated to other parts of Asia over the years (for example, Hong Kong, Taiwan, Thailand, Singapore, Indonesia, Myanmar, Cambodia, the Philippines, and Vietnam), as well as those who have been under strong Chinese or Confucian influence over the years (for example, Japan and Korea). Of course, we acknowledge that such a definition is incomplete and may not satisfy every reader of this book. We also concede that such a broad definition may hamper our generalization of comments and observations. Nonetheless, we will sharpen it by using specific examples and references. In addition, from time to time, we will make references to other Asians (for example, Indians) when we have useful and meaningful experiences to share.

We are very conscious that it can be easy to descend into meaningless stereotyping in a book such as this. We are sure there will be many Asians, as per our definition, who will not agree with everything that is said in this book. We are looking, however, to identify the collective consciousness of Chinese-influenced Asia, so that Westerners can more quickly understand how to do business with these people. Diversity requires versatility and sensitivity in business relationships and these skills do not come naturally to Westerners.

The intention of this book is to explore the challenges that confront companies, leaders, and individuals who want to succeed in Asia. It will be interspersed with anecdotes, personal experiences, views from both Asian and Western leaders, and views from government and religious leaders. It will explore the many contradictions of working and operating in Asia. It intends to challenge a few sacred cows, desensitize a few awkward taboos and challenge strongly held views and theories. More importantly, it will show that contradictions in life and business in Asia are perfectly fine, so long as they can be recognized and understood. It is when they lead to misunderstanding, confusion, and chaos that serious consequences can occur.

While it is true that unlike his Western counterpart, the Asian corporate strategist does not document nor institutionalize strategic and corporate planning in great detail, strategic thinking and strategizing are actually deeply ingrained in his mindset. Specific strategies and stratagems to deal with all kinds of life situations have been developed, refined, and studied for thousands of years, especially in Chinese history. This book will help the Western mind to develop its own strategic thinking to either challenge or complement the Asian mind game.

We are continuously learning how to do business successfully in Asia. We hope this book will be able to help you as well. It is like the following Chinese saying: If we all have the right attitude and openness, then our chances of success are greater.

当 你 （ 学 生 ） 想 学 习 的 时 候 ，
dan ni (xue sheng) xiang xue xi de shi hou

老 师 自 然 会 出 现 。
lao shi zi ran hui chu xian

When you (the student) are ready to learn,
the teacher will appear.

Indeed, as a way to provoke thinking and reflection, we have deliberately chosen to begin each chapter with a Chinese quotation from *Sun Zi Bingfa*, the most well known Chinese military treatise in the world. It is also a book that has influenced much of the strategic mindset of the typical Asian and especially the Chinese strategist.

Chow-Hou Wee
Fred Combe

Acknowledgments

We would like to thank our many "teachers" over the years who have helped us understand and excel in Asia. By contributing their comments and views to help shape the outcome of this book, the following people are also very much our teachers: Ehsan Malik, J.D. Bandaranayake, Janak Hirdaramani, Satish Shankar, Pradeep Pant, Ken Balendra, Charles Ormiston, Charles Wigley, Andrew Clark, and Nihal Kaviratne.

We would also like to thank our family members and other friends who have encouraged us tremendously. The contributions of the editorial services of the publisher are also gratefully acknowledged.

Finally, we like to thank the United Overseas Bank Limited (UOB) for sponsoring the launch of this book.

Enjoy this book!

故善战者，致人而不致于人。

gu shan zhan zhe   zhi ren er   bu zhi yu ren

Thus, the person adept in warfare seeks to control and manipulate his enemy instead of being controlled and manipulated.

(Sun Zi Bingfa, 孙子兵法, Line 6.3 of *Chapter 6 on Weaknesses and Strengths,* 虚实 *(xu shi))*

The New Asian Challenge

Myth or Reality?

The First Wave of the Asian Challenge

Many readers will remember how Japan emerged as an economic threat to the West in the 1980s. Books were written on how Japan could possibly topple the West in terms of economic and trade domination. At that time, Japan was the leader of the Asian pack, supported by four Asian tigers—Hong Kong, Singapore, South Korea, and Taiwan.[1] Indeed, it was a time when the export initiatives of these Asian economies posed a credible threat to Europe and the United States. It was also during that period—from the late 1970s up to the 1990s—that many Asian-manufactured products became well known in the world. From the sloppy, cheap, and low-quality imitation goods of the 1950s and 1960s, Japanese companies were able to build their products and brands to world-class standards and quality by the 1980s. It was during the 1980s that Western

Europe and the United States felt the Japanese threat most as many of the Japanese exports began to displace the local industries.

Today, Japanese brands such as Lexus, Matsushita, Sony, Nikon, Canon, Toyota, Seiko, and Sharp are quality names recognized by households and corporate boardrooms worldwide. The Japanese success story has been replicated by the South Koreans and the Taiwanese. They, too, have managed to build products and brands that meet world-class standards. Hyundai, Samsung, LG, and Acer are well-recognized brands around the world today. By building world-class products and brands, the Koreans and the Taiwanese, just like the Japanese, are able to export their products to the rest of the world. More importantly, as economic competition increases, they are able to locate their factories and plants overseas and continue to compete effectively through lower costs.

Interestingly, while the economic threats posed by Japan and the four Asian tigers were serious, they did not cause the demise of Western economies. Instead, the United States and many European countries responded aggressively to the threat and rose to the challenge. Many innovations, new and improved products, and technology emerged from the West, and Western economies began to reassert themselves. Thus, despite the threats, the West has been very successful in exporting its products, services, ideas, cultures, movies, and lifestyles to Asia and the rest of the world.

In particular, many Western brands were hailed as luxury products and became status symbols. Even the ordinary fast food from McDonald's, Kentucky Fried Chicken, and Burger King have been marketed and positioned as lifestyle and middle-income products. So too is Starbucks, whose coffee is viewed as a middle-class lifestyle product.

Indeed, if one were to scan the world's luxury products and services that are marketed in Asia, one would find that they are largely dominated by Western brands. In fact, Asians crave for brands like Louis Vuitton, Cartier, Patek Philippe, Mercedes, Rolex, and BMW and worship them as status symbols.

Hollywood movies and television shows from the West further reinforce this belief of Western supremacy.[2] Their influence and popularity have been very pervasive and widespread across Asia. Not surprisingly, the West is tempted to believe that despite their rise, China and the rest of Asia will not pose any serious threats. After all, despite decades of strong economic growth after the Second World War, Japan did not quite challenge the supremacy of the West. Yes, its products did make tremendous inroads into Europe and America, but the Japanese culture and way of life hardly influenced Western societies. Instead, many young Japanese tried to emulate Western music and culture.

These are indeed very tempting propositions. However, they are flawed on several counts. First, it is important to note that it is only the young Japanese who tend to emulate the West, not all Japanese. More significantly, when these young Japanese join the corporate world, they begin to embrace more of their traditional values and culture. As such, despite decades of Western influence, Japanese culture, social values, customs, and traditions have remained largely intact. This is because the Japanese, like most Asians, tend to protect their cultural traditions much more than Westerners, and such traditions can go back thousands of years. They are proud of the fact that their ancestors were intellectuals and master builders when many Europeans were still very primitive, and the United States was yet to be discovered. However, they recognize that Western countries moved ahead of Asia in the second millennium,[3] and it is important that Asians learn from the West in areas where they are weak, while not swallowing everything that the West dishes out to them.

Second, it is not completely true that the Japanese have not made any cultural inroads into the West. One only needs to notice the number of sushi and Japanese restaurants in Europe and America to realize that it is not entirely a one-way street.[4] Moreover, as Japanese companies continue to set up their factories and operations in Western countries, Japanese management will also gradually exert its influence.

Third, the rise of Asia today is not confined to Japan and the four Asian tigers. It is much more pervasive and significant in that the two most populous countries in the world—China and India—have entered the race. In fact, these two countries were always there in the past, but very much at the bottom of the totem pole. The big difference is that they both have now awakened, especially in the case of China. More importantly, compared to the Japanese, the Chinese and obviously Indians,[5] are much more skilful in mastering the English language and other Western languages, which allows them to assimilate faster into European and American societies.[6] This also means that they will learn about Western systems and cultures much faster.

China as the Dragon Head of Asia

One of the most significant events that happened last century had to be the opening of China to the Western world in 1978. Prior to this, the bamboo curtain was shut, and China was never an economic threat to the rest of the world. Deng Xiaoping (邓小平) changed all that.

It was Napoleon who once said, "China is like a sleeping giant.[7] If she is asleep, let her sleep on. For when she awakes, she will rock the world." Well, the giant has awakened! Since China began to welcome foreign trade and investment 30 years ago, its rate of growth has been simply spectacular. With its entry into the World Trade Organization on December 11, 2001, it has also learned to play by international rules and is fast becoming a global economic player. The hosting of the Beijing 2008 Olympics spurred its economic development even further. Some commentators describe it as China's "coming-out party," a turning point in world affairs.

Very few educated people can still be unaware of the rising economic and strategic power of Asia, and China in particular. The Chinese have gone on a massive shopping spree of international assets, most notably stakes in major US banks suffering from the subprime crisis. There are now more than 100 billionaires (US$) in China, second only to the United States.

Barring any significant political or cultural turmoil, China is set to enter another golden era that may even surpass any other period in its 5,000 years of history. Despite some social problems,[8] China is on course to become a global economic superpower. Since its opening in 1978, China has been growing at an average of 8 to 12 percent per year. For its size, it does not take one too long to figure out the importance and significance of the growth of the Chinese economy.[9] By the end of 2006, China was already ranked as the fourth largest economy in the world,[10] after the United States, Japan, and Germany. At its current rate of growth, it may even overtake Germany by 2009, Japan by 2025, and the United States by 2045.

Certainly, owing to its large population of 1.3 billion, the per capita income of the Chinese will take a long while to catch up with these countries. For example, even if China were to overtake the United States in terms of total GDP by 2045, its per capita income will likely be less than one-fifth that of the United States. However, one must not forget that there will be more than 300 million Chinese living in the big cities by then. These 300 million Chinese will, on average, have per capita incomes that may rival the United States, Japan, and Germany by then. By all counts, 300 million is not a small number, which, in aggregate, can be likened to a "super consumer nation" that is bigger than each of the other three countries mentioned. However, it is a reality that China's people will grow old before they get rich.

By 2010, 70 percent of global manufacturing will be done in Asia. China is now the world's largest manufacturing center, one of the biggest importers of energy-related resources, the largest exporter of countless products, attracts the most direct foreign investments, and the list goes on. Indeed, the Chinese impact has already been felt rapidly around the world. We maintain that even if you choose not to do business in China today, the Chinese will come to you. This is evident by the increasing number of Chinese tourists "flashing" their appreciating *renminbi* (人民币) in various parts of the world,[11] the increasing number of Chinese companies seeking public listing in overseas stock markets,[12] and the increasing incidence of acquisitions undertaken by Chinese companies abroad.

As of June 2008, the total foreign exchange reserves of China had already surpassed US$1.4 trillion. This was in stark contrast to the United States, which had debts of about US$1 trillion for the same period, and continues to suffer a huge trade deficit with China. Not surprisingly, the United States has become more and more defensive in its posture with China.

With its rise as an economic superpower, China's political and cultural clout is likely to increase correspondingly. As it is, in the realm of sports, the Chinese have dominated the world in table tennis and badminton since the 1960s.[13] In recent years, the impact and influence of the Chinese in the world of sports have extended to swimming, diving, basketball, athletics, and even tennis.[14] More Chinese athletes are making their presence felt in the world arena. In the realm of culture, Chinese acrobatic shows, orchestras, music, paintings and artifacts have also begun to show their impact around the world.

Regretfully, China has never been easily or completely understood. It is an old civilization, with a recorded history that stretches back for several thousands of years. Its political experience has been characterized by centuries of complexity. China must be viewed as a large, complex feudal castle unto itself, whose position, scale, history, and centuries-old habits of mind and heart have inevitably shaped it into a very different architecture from the preconception held by most in the West. Chinese and Western systems have been noted more for their differences than their similarities.

There are many concepts that challenge the Westerner's mind. The business environment of Chinese society, for example, cannot separate the "system" and the "market" —they are allied and intertwined. The concept of "ownership" remains cloudy, and there is a clear bias toward entities, rather than individuals, as entrepreneurs. The challenge of dealing with China is not about size and scale alone, but also about understanding the different interests that arise from the country's history. If you want to imagine how China might look 50 years from now, think of a highly advanced and well-managed Confucian social market, similar to Singapore today, but on a giant, stupefying scale.

Few Westerners are even close to being fully aware of China's obvious impact. The West needs to pull back from the simplistic notion that China's rise is a free-marketer's dream of a low-cost giant workshop and factory for the Western world. China is a land of paradoxes and contradictions, which can easily hide the giant forces of change. The irony is that American and European companies are "unwittingly" teaching Chinese companies how to gain competitive advantages against them in the global marketplace. As foreign investors stake their own prosperity on China's economy, they are actually pushing the country into a position where it can eventually play rule-maker.

Of course, the West still maintains its lead in science, technology, innovation, design, and brand creation and development. For example, China spent US$60 billion on R&D in 2005, compared to US$282 billion in the United States and US$104 billion in Japan. However, the gap may be narrowing faster than the West thinks, especially when the Chinese economy continues to gain momentum. In addition, with their immense accumulated wealth,[15] Chinese companies are beginning to flex their muscles through acquisitions, effectively creating the possibility to leapfrog themselves in all areas of competition. They have also begun to realize the importance of creating world-class brands. At the lower end, some Chinese car manufacturers (e.g. Geeley) and electronics companies (e.g. Haier) are already making their impact on the world through their brands.

Following the Dragon Head

Spurred by the relentless development in China, another sleeping giant, India, has also awakened. In particular, it has become an important information technology (IT) outsourcing center for many multinational corporations (MNCs) from the West. Owing to its strengths in IT and strong command of the English language, India is also providing many other customer-related services (e.g. customer call-center services) for its global clients.

Other than China and India, Vietnam is also fast getting onto the economic growth engine. Despite suffering from severe recovery problems arising from the last Asian financial crisis, other Asian countries like Thailand, Indonesia, Malaysia, and the Philippines are also keen to strengthen their economic development.

It is clear that the global center of gravity is moving eastward. The long dormant civilization of Asia is likely to re-emerge to regain the dominant position it held at the end of the 10th century A.D. when it was culturally and economically far more advanced than Europe.

Contrary to perception, the bulk of Asia's growth has become more intra-regional in nature and less reliant on the West. This is particularly so in recent years. Indeed, Asian consumers are beginning to spend more owing to rapid wealth creation. The current slowdown in the US economy and potential global recession will be partly offset by the growing and largely unrecognized power of Asian consumers.

Rising Asia will continue to reshape globalization, giving it less of a "Made in the USA" character and more of an Asian look and feel. At the same time, Asia will alter the rules of the globalizing process. By having the fastest-growing consumer markets, with more firms becoming world-class multinationals and embracing a higher degree of science and technology, Asia looks set to challenge Western countries as the focus for international economic dynamism. Our optimism is supported further by the following observations and trends.

Productivity Improvements

These will be brought about by implementing technologies and processes that have already been mastered elsewhere in the world. More importantly, much of this increased productivity has been brought in by the MNCs that have invested aggressively in China over the past 30 years. According to Peter Williamson, author of *Winning in Asia: Strategies for Competing in the New Millennium*, if Thailand or Malaysia were to reach the productivity levels of South Korea today, income levels would double. If they were to target US productivity levels, incomes would quadruple. Perhaps even more striking is the case of China. If China could reach the productivity levels that the US achieved in 2000, it would have a staggering market size that is 40 times larger than its current one![16]

Savings Rates

In general, East Asians are known to save more than 20 percent of their income while the Chinese save more than 30 percent. This excludes the possible billions of dollars that are not even kept in bank deposits.[17] With increased income over the last 20 years, Asians are beginning to spend more. And with increased savings, they are in a strong position to spend even more in the future. This dual trend of increased spending and savings is just beginning.

Workforce Growth

Owing to a younger population, Asia's workforce is expected to grow by more than 1 percent per annum over the next 15 years. In contrast, Europe will experience a decline in workforce growth while that of the United States will only increase marginally. What this means is that Asia's competitiveness and productivity will continue to increase faster than those of Europe and the United States.

Avoiding Pitfalls of the West

Many Asian countries have been astute observers of Western systems and societies. As such, they are likely to benefit more by avoiding the same mistakes as the West. For example, they are unlikely to shorten the working week, increase welfare benefits, or provide free medical services, etc.—programs that would erode their economic competitiveness. In particular, many Asian leaders have been trained in the West. As such, they are better equipped to integrate the best of the West with the traditional values and systems of their home country. Singapore is a good example. Its success has been premised largely on its ability to merge the best of Western management, legal systems, and governance with oriental values and cultures.

Knowing Asia

Today, Asia is seen as the world's best opportunity for growth. This is because since 2001, it has accounted for about half of the world's growth, and this share is likely to go up in the future. Not surprisingly, almost every serious global company is investing or plans to invest in Asia. Given this phenomenon, you would think that most global companies would be digging deep into Asia's history and culture to understand Asian consumers better. The past can give tremendous insight into how these consumers will behave in the future. Yet, shockingly, very few global companies actually do this. Asia is still so new to them, and few have invested enough in learning about the region's history and culture.

The expatriate managers that Western MNCs transfer to the region are often poorly equipped to deal with their new surroundings. Instead of taking some time out to speak to senior Asians about the history and culture of the country they are posted to, or taking a short course in Asian culture or reading up on it, they are often too keen to plunge into the action mode. They rush out into the market, meet their customers, evaluate their sales and marketing organizations, and launch new products, hoping to score big hits. As a result, they often hit the wall and face severe blockages along the way.

For the vast majority of educated Westerners, their ignorance of Asian history and geography gives them a poor start. In some ways it is hard to blame them. The education systems that most of them were brought up in focused mainly on the history of the Western world and very little on the Eastern world. They may know a little about the American War of Independence, the D-day landings, the Battle of Waterloo, Hannibal's crossing of the Alps, Christopher Columbus's discovery of the Americas, and Henry VIII and his six wives. However, they know virtually nothing of Asian history. Whatever they do know most probably relates to modern history: the nuclear bombs that fell on Japan, the Korean War, and the Vietnam War. When it comes to Asia's ancient history of empires and conquests, most of them will admit that their knowledge is very limited.

As Kishore Mahbubani, a Singaporean career diplomat, scholar, and author of *Can Asians Think?*, acknowledges, the 500-year-old cycle of Western domination of the world may be coming to an end. "Many Asians are pleased to wake up to the new realization that their minds and bodies are not inferior. Most Westerners cannot appreciate the change because they have never directly felt the sense of inferiority many Asians experienced until recently. Until a few decades ago, Western societies beckoned as beacons on the hill. Now, Asians have found a new confidence in themselves. They have the economic freedom to think, reflect, and rediscover their cultural heritage. They have a rich social, cultural, and philosophical legacy that they can draw on and use to evolve their own modern and advanced societies."

It is only a matter of time before Asian civilizations will reach the same level of development as Western civilizations. The major new reality in Asia is the genuine conviction and confidence among new Asian minds that their day will come even if they have to stumble once or twice more before they make it. Many Asian minds have now been exposed to the highest level of Western civilization, in the fields of science and technology, business and administration, arts, literature, and even sports. Many have clearly thrived at this level. The Asian mind, having been awakened, cannot be put to sleep in the near future. A new discourse will begin between East and West where Asian societies will start to successfully develop again. Given this stark reality, it is very important that the West develops the appropriate response to the new Asia.

Developing the Appropriate Response

Economic and business competition in the world is definitely not a level playing field. There are strong and weak players within countries, within regions, and within continents, and this trend will continue. Over time, the center of gravity will also shift, and this time around, it is shifting toward Asia. However, unlike wars, economic and business competition need not be a zero-sum game. By opening up borders, there is an opportunity to begin to iron out some of the unevenness as well as to create more win-win situations.

The instinctive response from the West, when under threat, is to create barriers of a protectionist nature. It is clear that protectionism and, to a lesser extent, ignorance are at the heart of these issues. Globalization does not only entail the movement and transfer of capital, investment, technology, and management across national borders. It also demands cultural and social inclusiveness, both of which can be sensitive and create a resistance to change and a sense of insecurity. Resistance to Dubai Ports World in the United States and Mittal Steel in Europe were recent examples of the West closing up. They also demonstrate the difficult re-adjustment faced by the West with the shifting of the global center of gravity toward Asia.

For many decades, the West has used international institutions, military power, and economic resources to run the world in ways that will maintain Western dominance, protect Western interests, and promote Western political and economic values. Suddenly, this dominance appears to be severely threatened with the rise of Asia. Globalization and, in particular, the rise in Asian confidence, prosperity, and success have thrown different cultures and civilizations into closer proximity with inevitable friction.

What we are beginning to see are the early symptoms of a re-balance between the East and the West. Kishore Mahbubani argues provocatively that the world will be a much richer place when Western minds stop assuming that Western civilization represents the only universal civilization. He says, "To prepare for the New World, we will have to discard conventional wisdom, break up old thought patterns and begin thinking along new mental corridors. Most Westerners cannot see that they have arrogated to themselves the moral high ground from which they lecture the world. The rest of the world can see this."

We sense that the West needs to wake up to the reality of a new Asia, to be more open and accepting of Asian investment in the West, and to embrace the diversity of thinking that Asia adds to civilization. Building moral and economic protectionist walls in the West will be a disaster for globalization and a resurgent East. Of course there will be friction.[18] In this shrinking globe of ours, as the East and the West come closer together, many ancient civilizations will interact in a direct fashion never seen before in the history of man.

The West needs to be more open-minded, to allow the Asians into their club, and to establish with their Asian counterparts a two-way street for the flow of ideas, values, and people. The greatest weakness of the West is that many Westerners still think and believe that they are driving down a one-way street—that Asia will gradually succumb to Western culture, Western thinking, and Western brands. In fact, and as mentioned earlier, there may be some basis for many Westerners to hold such a line of thinking. Based on our assessment, such a mindset, if perpetuated into the future, may develop into a complacency trap for the West. Let us elaborate.

Cultural and political dominance and supremacy only work if they can be supported by strong military and economic prowess. In the case of the United States, there is no doubt about its military supremacy today. However, who is to guarantee that such supremacy will continue forever, or, for that matter, for the next 100 years? One only has to recall the military prowess of past colonial masters like the Spaniards, the Portuguese, and the British. With the weakening of their economies, they simply could not sustain their military prowess. For example, the United Kingdom today is a mere shadow of its past greatness when it had its Commonwealth empire.

The New Challenges: Global-is-Asian

Globalization is not a new phenomenon, neither is it entirely led by the West, although that is how it is currently perceived. The Arabs, the Indians, and the Chinese have been taking their religions, cultures, and knowledge beyond their shores for centuries. That is how the three major religions—Judaism, Christianity, and Islam—spread from the Middle East. The Europeans took their languages and cultures to what is now known as the United States, a country to which most of the export of Western culture is currently attributed. Indeed, today's importers of culture are potentially tomorrow's exporters and vice versa. This is exactly the case for Asia.

Arising from its increasing economic influence, a new, more Asian cultural identity is now being exported to other countries. Korean television serials and pop singers are fast becoming the rage in Japan, China, and other Asian countries. Japanese *anime* has many fans in China. Chinese kung-fu and period movies, cultural, musical and acrobatic shows, and India's Bollywood song-and-dance epics are viewed throughout Asia. They are beginning to show their impact in the West as well. Not surprisingly, Hollywood has begun to reflect these Asian influences by including an increasing number of Asian movie stars in its films. There are now instances of joint East–West movie production, and Asian movie directors are gaining stature in Hollywood and the rest of the world.[19]

In the world of sports, other Asian countries have also joined China in exerting their presence in the global arena. Japan and South Korea, for example, can be counted among the top sporting nations of the world. India and Pakistan have traditionally excelled in sports like hockey and cricket, and Thailand and Taiwan have produced world-class snooker and billiard players. Indeed, the turning point was the 2008 Beijing Olympics. We are not surprised that China overtook the United States in the total number of gold medals, and that several other Asian countries like South Korea and Japan finished among the top 10 nations of the world in the overall medal tally.

It is clear that Asia will continue to surge forward, with the possibility of it taking over the lead within this century. All the signs of economic growth are there. The scope for Asian demand driven by a rapid growth in Asian income levels is enormous. To deal effectively with a rising and confident new Asia, the West will have to learn fast and shed its superiority complex.

As a start, the West will have to understand and know how to manage ambiguity, paradoxes, and contradictions and realize that the standard views of black/white or right/wrong may not be the same in Asia. Westerners need to start thinking like Asians to understand them better in order to succeed in the future. The principles of universal diversity and equal opportunity should be pursued aggressively. Just as we celebrated Western investment in Eastern Europe after the fall of the Berlin Wall, we should welcome Asian investment today in Europe and the United States.

The question is whether the rest of the world fully appreciates and understands this and, more importantly, knows what to do about it. Even for those MNCs that already have a head start and experience on the ground, the rules are changing fast. Peter Williamson, author of *Winning in Asia*, argues, "It is time for Western multinationals to understand the ever-improving local Asian competitors and how they will evolve in the future, with a new seriousness." It is clear that Asian companies, which combine "home team" advantage with tomorrow's world-class capabilities, pose a stiff challenge to Western multinationals, whose successful strategies to date may have to be fundamentally revised.

In 2006, there was an outpouring of nationalistic disdain in the West toward the proposed takeovers of assets too close to home by Asian companies. If you can recall, there was considerable political and media coverage at the time, with many politicians calling for protectionist measures. In short, it was a sudden realization that the one-way street of investment, West to East, was starting to reverse. The companies in the spotlight at the time did actually end up acquiring their targets: India's Mittal Steel took over Arcelor and Dubai World Ports successfully bought P&O.

It has been very interesting to observe the more recent muted and resigned reactions of the West to the investments made by Asian and Arab sovereign wealth funds in Western banks, reeling from the subprime crisis in the United States: GIC (Singapore) invested US$10 billion in UBS, Temasek (Singapore) invested US$4.4 billion in Merrill Lynch, ADIA (Abu Dhabi) invested US$7.5 billion in Citibank, and CIC (China) invested US$5 billion in Morgan Stanley. All of this happened between Thanksgiving and Christmas, when most people were preparing for and enjoying the season's festivities. This is just the start. There will be far more investments to shore up the balance sheets of the Western banks in 2008.

The year 2008 is therefore the defining moment in the shift of financial and economic power from the West to the East. While everyone understood implicitly that Asia had been financing the West's growing debt and consumer excesses, nobody truly realized the dependency until the crisis hit. On this occasion, there was little reaction or surprise. In times of crisis, people can easily lose their convictions and seek quick solutions. What is very clear though is that we are now entering a new phase in the change management process between the West and the East. Faced with hard facts, resistance to Asian investment is starting to fade considerably, and the early signs of acceptance are beginning to appear. What does this mean for all of us and how do we respond?

For those of us living and working in Asia, this creates more opportunities. It confirms the growth phase of investments from Asia into the West. While Asian companies are more self-confident and braver than in the past, this is still a new and uncomfortable zone. They need help to identify, acquire, and integrate potential targets in the West. They face the same cultural challenges that Western companies face in Asia, except in reverse, and this is just the beginning.

For those of us living and working in the West, the changes will be greater and emotionally more charged. It will challenge the comfort of our beliefs and values. Becoming prey rather than predator will create greater insecurity and more uncertainty than ever before. Those who are smart will identify the opportunities ahead of everyone else and position themselves well to take advantage of these. Dr Spencer Johnson's famous little book *Who Moved My Cheese?* puts it simply: We need to anticipate change, adapt to change quickly, enjoy change, and be ready to change quickly, again and again.

With the expansion of global business into Asia, having interpersonal skills attuned to cultural differences is no longer simply a matter of proper business etiquette, but a critical competitive advantage. Open communication is more difficult due to language and cultural barriers. It is also often difficult to understand the gaps between expectations and assumptions. Feedback is often indirect and may be delayed. Geographical differences limit the ease of tracking progress and results. There are often unfamiliar ways of doing business, which lead to misunderstandings.

We will be exploring these issues throughout the book. What is required are an open mind and a positive attitude to accept differences. If you are willing to change your mindset and behavior, you will be more successful in dealing with the paradoxes and contradictions of Asia. As Ernest Gundling, author of *Working GlobeSmart* states, "In a cross border context, core values such as trust, respect, listening, observation, empathy, flexibility, informed judgment, and persistence are the foundations for positive multicultural teamwork."

Asia is such an extraordinarily rich tapestry of land and cultures interwoven over many centuries of trading and wars that it is impossible to simplify into a few quick lessons. While it has clearly Asian roots, it has pockets of Western (Portuguese, Dutch, Spanish, English, French, and American) and Arabic influences as well. As such, it is almost impossible for us to claim that we have all the answers to the issues at hand. What we seek to do is to provide and share our experiences and anecdotes so that all of us will emerge richer in knowledge and understanding on how to do a better job when doing business in Asia.

We will also be investigating why we are so different—
Asians and Westerners—but before we get there, we
need to get to know someone who played a critical part
in shaping how many Asian corporate strategists think and
strategize—the military supremacist Sun Zi (孙子). In fact,
as mentioned in the Preface, we have deliberately chosen to
begin each of our chapters with a quote from *Sun Zi Bingfa*
as a way to stimulate thinking and reflection.

Endnotes

1. This was a label given by Western scholars. Interestingly,
   scholars from Asia labeled the same four Asian economies
   as the four little dragons, largely because of their historical
   linkages with China.
2. These shows, for example, *American Idol*, *CSI*, and various
   talk shows, are very popular in Asia. Many Asian productions
   even attempt to copy and emulate such shows from the West.
3. This occurred in many areas, including the political, social,
   cultural, literary, technological, and economic fronts. In
   particular, the advancements made by the Western world
   in the second millennium were most noticeable in the
   economic and technological realms.
4. Similarly, one can find many Chinese restaurants in Europe
   and America set up by those who migrated there. Chinese
   food has attracted many Western diners over the years,
   despite the relative "weakness" of China in the past.
5. Owing to India's colonial past as part of the British
   Commonwealth, Indians are already adept in the English
   language. In fact, English is the only language that can unite
   the countless dialects and local languages spoken by the
   people of India.
6. Just look at Silicon Valley in the United States and other
   science parks around the world where an increasing number of the scientists and technologists are either Chinese or
   Indian.

7. It is significant to note that even the overseas Chinese generally consider themselves metaphorically to be descendents of the dragon. Economies/countries with large ethnic Chinese populations regard China as the head of the dragon among them.

8. In late 2006 and 2007, growing social unrest was reported among farmers in rural China. Much of the unrest had to do with corrupt officials who worked with unscrupulous businessmen to forcibly acquire land for development. There were also instances where vagrants were lured and "kidnapped" at railway and bus stations and forced to work in slave-like conditions in coal mines and brick factories.

9. As an illustration, if China's per capita income in 2006 were to double overnight, the size of its economy would instantaneously overtake that of the United States. If China's per capita income were to be half that of the United States as of 2006, the Chinese economy would be two-and-a-half times the size of the United States.

10. Measured in terms of total Gross Domestic Product (GDP).

11. Recognizing the importance of these Chinese tourists, many airports around the world have begun to install Chinese directional signs and make announcements in *Putonghua* (Mandarin).

12. Like in the United States, Hong Kong, and Singapore.

13. Interestingly, the Chinese used table tennis to extend its influence into other areas, especially in the realm of politics. The "ping-pong" diplomacy of the Chinese began in the 1960s when then President Nixon of the United States made a historic trip to China.

14. The most famous Chinese basketball player as of 2007 has to be Yao Ming. Since his entrance into the American NBA league, he has gained tremendous stature and popularity.

15. As mentioned earlier, Chinese foreign exchange reserves exceeded US$1.33 trillion as of June 2007.

16. That is, as of 2006.

17. For example, the more rural Chinese are still fond of hiding their deposits in "secret places" at home such as under the mattress, in biscuit tins, etc. The more sophisticated urban and entrepreneurial Chinese have learned to park their monies overseas in various ways, including overseas safe deposit boxes.

18. For example, the United States has been pressurizing China to revalue its currency (*renminbi*) since late 2005. When the Chinese foreign exchange reserves exceeded US$1.33 trillion, an all-time high for all nations, in June 2007, the pressures from the United States grew even stronger, including the calls for more trade sanctions against the Chinese. There were also incidents whereby attempted acquisitions of US companies by the Chinese were "torpedoed" by politicians and lobbyists.

19. Good examples include Lee Ang and Zhang Yimou.

故上兵伐谋，其次伐交，
gu shang bing fa mou　　qi ci fa jiao

其次伐兵，其下攻城。
qi ci fa bing　　qi xia gong cheng

攻城之法为不得已。
gong cheng zhi fa wei bu de yi

Thus, the most supreme strategy is to attack the plans and strategies of the enemy. The next best strategy is to attack his relationships and alliances with other nations. The next best strategy is to attack his army. The worst strategy of all is to attack walled cities. Attack walled cities when there are no other alternatives.

(Sun Zi Bingfa, 孙子兵法, *Lines 3.8 to 3.12 of Chapter 3 on Strategic Attacks,* 谋攻 *(mou gong))*

2

Sun Zi Bingfa

Unlocking the Mindset of the Asian Strategist

The Influence of *Sun Zi Bingfa*

One of the most influential books that impacted significantly the mindset of Asian corporate strategists has to be the Chinese military classic called *Sun Zi Bingfa* (孙子兵法).[1] The significance and importance of *Sun Zi Bingfa* in influencing military thought and political thinking have seldom been questioned. For example, most top military academies around the world would include *Sun Zi Bingfa* as part of the curriculum for training top military commanders. Mao Zedong (毛泽东), the great communist ruler of China in the 20th century, was reputed to be a devout follower of *Sun Zi Bingfa*. The Japanese military strategists of the Second World War were widely known to use *Sun Zi Bingfa*. During the 1991 Persian Gulf War, quotations from *Sun Zi Bingfa* were cited regularly in the papers to support the strategies adopted by General Norman Schwarzkopf. Over the years, *Sun Zi Bingfa* has also found increased receptivity and applications in the business world. There are many reasons for this.

First, many Japanese, Korean, Chinese, Taiwanese, and Hong Kong corporate strategists are familiar with the *Sun Zi Bingfa* and are known to be inspired by its philosophy in the development of business strategies. In fact, there are more versions of the Japanese and Korean translations of *Sun Zi Bingfa* than in any other language. In addition, many Japanese and Korean chief executive officers (CEOs) and top executives will profess that they are familiar with the philosophy, and some would explicitly acknowledge that they use the philosophy in the development of business and corporate strategies.

Second, with the opening of China in 1978, many ancient Chinese classics have made a dramatic comeback in influencing corporate boardroom strategies and thinking and management practices. One only has to make a trip to a bookstore in China to notice the countless number of books attempting to relate these classics to the modern management setting. Given that China is a civilization that has existed for 5,000 years,[2] it is not surprising that many of these "secrets" could be embedded among these classics, awaiting to be discovered and expounded. Indeed, Chinese scholars and researchers have wasted no effort in trying to mine the gems among these classics, although many of them have also gone overboard in their attempt to relate them to business practices. Nonetheless, among the various Chinese classics, *Sun Zi Bingfa* remains the top favorite and most researched. Its wide acceptance should not come as too much of a surprise as the Chinese have often viewed doing business as warfare, as depicted by the saying, 商场如战场 ("the business field is like the battlefield").

Finally, strategies, strategic planning, and many other related management concepts such as organizing, teamwork, delegation, and empowerment have long been practiced by the army. Not surprising, many of these concepts have now found their way into the corporate boardroom. *Sun Zi Bingfa*, being the oldest known military treatise, probably provides the greatest inspiration, insights, and inputs into modern strategic thought and practices. This aspect will be elaborated on later.

Misconception and Misinterpretation of *Sun Zi Bingfa*

Regretfully, when *Sun Zi Bingfa* was first known to the Western world, it was not given the appropriate treatment. For example, the term *bingfa* (兵法) was inappropriately translated as "art of war." In reality, the term, *bingfa* (兵法), was used in ancient China to denote strategies and methods (*ce lue yu fang fa* 策略与方法), not the waging of wars (*zuo zhan* 作战), although Sun Zi did devote a chapter in his book to the waging of wars. The inappropriate translation was aggravated further by the failure to factor in the true meaning of *zi* (子), which actually denotes a philosopher. Indeed, *Sun Zi Bingfa* should be translated as *The Military Philosophy of Sun Zi*.

As a result of using the word "war" in the title of the book, many Westerners tend to view the Chinese as likely military conquerors and wagers of war.[3] On the contrary, one only needs to trace the 5,000 years of Chinese history to realize that the nation did not have the same kind of colonization mentality as Britain, Spain, France, and Portugal.[4] A detailed examination of *Sun Zi Bingfa* will reveal that Sun Zi was very concerned about the high costs of going to war, and the kinds of suffering that wars can inflict on a nation and its people.[5] To him, war should only be embarked upon as a last resort when all other alternatives have been exhausted. Thus, wars should be avoided at all cost. Instead, one should win by strategizing—clearly a nonviolent approach to resolving conflicts. This is further supported by the following quotations:

故 善 用 兵 者， 屈 人 之 兵 而 非 战 也，
gu shan yong bing zhe　 qu ren zhi bing er fei zhan ye

Thus, the adept in warfare are able to subdue the army of the enemy without having to resort to battles.

~ Line 3.18 of Chapter 3 on Strategic Attacks,
谋攻 (*mou gong*)

拔 人 之 城 而 非 攻 也， 毁 人 之 国 而 非 久 也；
ba ren zhi cheng er fei gong ye　 hui ren zhi guo er fei jiu ye

He (the adept in warfare) is able to capture the cities of others without having to launch assaults. He (the adept in warfare) is able to destroy and damage the states of others without waging protracted campaigns.

~ Lines 3.19 and 3.20 of Chapter 3 on Strategic Attacks,
谋攻 (*mou gong*)

The tendency to view the book as an advocacy of war has also caused much misunderstanding and an underestimation of the value and contribution of *Sun Zi Bingfa* (孙子兵法) to the business realm.[6] What is more important is not to ignore the "gems" that can be culled from the philosophy of Sun Zi. Rather, one should carefully develop such gems into useful concepts and practices in the business world.

Another important point to note is that this is a book on military philosophy, and not on the science of war. In other words, it is not a "how to" book. Rather, it is a book that provides concepts, ideas, thoughts, and principles without providing the reader with definite answers. In fact, the answers lie very much in the hands of the reader once he/she is able to find breakthroughs in understanding and mastering the ideas, concepts, thoughts, and principles behind Sun Zi's philosophy. This makes the applications of the philosophy much more dynamic and powerful in that they will not be limited by time or space.

Examples of Applications of Sun Zi's Philosophy in Business[7]

To give you a quick flavor of how Sun Zi's philosophy can be gainfully applied to business, we have randomly selected some quotes and given brief comments on their possible applications. To a large extent, the concepts discussed behind these quotes are also very much interrelated. These quotes, in our assessment, are also particularly pertinent to doing business in Asia. Of course, if one were to spend time on understanding and mastering the works of Sun Zi, one would be able to discover more lessons and applications that could be used in the realm of business. Indeed, the limit to the applications of *Sun Zi Bingfa* to the business world is only constrained by one's own creativity, thinking, and strategizing skills.

Importance of Planning and Strategizing

The importance of planning and strategizing was clearly emphasized in the opening chapter of Sun Zi's 13-chapter treatise when he said:

多算胜，　少算不胜，　而况于无算乎！

duo suan sheng,　　shao suan　bu sheng　　er kuang yu　wu　suan　hu

With thorough and detailed planning, one can win. With less thorough and detailed planning, one cannot win. How much more certain is defeat when one does not plan at all!

~ Lines 1.48 to 1.50 of Chapter 1 on Detailed Assessment
and Planning,
计 *(ji)*

Note that the emphasis is not on whether there is planning or no planning. Rather, it is on the thoroughness of the plan. In war, no general goes into battle without a plan. The one who enters the battlefield without a plan is a soldier. In the same way, no CEO can lead his company against his competitors without any business plans. Rather, victories or failures in the business world depend very much on how thorough and detailed the plans are. In fact, with the increased risks and uncertainties created by possible terrorist actions; health-related threats like bird flu; natural disasters like tsunamis, earthquakes, and fire; and the many other unpredictable events that can happen anytime and anywhere, the thoroughness of planning, including contingency planning, crisis planning, and scenario planning, has become more important than ever before. Here, it is important to point out that when a plan is very thorough and detailed, execution becomes a breeze. There will also be less panic and less likelihood of rash and regrettable actions.

Use of Intelligence

It is interesting to note that Sun Zi began his 13-chapter treatise with detailed assessment and planning, and ended it with a chapter on intelligence and espionage. To him, detailed planning cannot exist in a vacuum. Rather, it requires strong intelligence to support it:

故 明 君 贤 将， 所 以 动 而 胜 人，
gu ming jun xian jiang suo yi dong er sheng ren

成 功 出 于 众 者， 先 知 也。
cheng gong chu yu zhong zhe xian zhi ye

Thus, the enlightened ruler and the capable general are able to secure victories for their military campaigns and to achieve successes that far surpass those of many others. The reason is because of foreknowledge.

~ Lines 13.8 and 13.9 of Chapter 13
on Intelligence and Espionage,
用间 (*yong jian*)

What is more significant is that Sun Zi did not believe in the effects of supernatural forces, guesses, or superstitions on planning. Instead, he focused heavily on human intelligence, as supported by the following quotation:

先 知 者 不 可 取 于 鬼 神， 不 可 象 于 事，
xian zhi zhe bu ke qu yu gui shen bu ke xiang yu shi

不 可 验 于 度， 必 取 于 人， 知 敌 之 情 者 也。
bu ke yan yu du bi qu yu ren zhi di zhi qing zhe ye

This foreknowledge cannot be obtained from the spirits nor from the gods. It cannot be obtained by comparing with similar present or past events and situations. Neither can it be obtained from the study of astrology. This foreknowledge must be obtained from men (and women) who have knowledge of the situation of the enemy.

~ Lines 13.10 to 13.13 of Chapter 13
on Intelligence and Espionage,
用间 (*yong jian*)

In the same way, good corporate planning must be grounded with accurate data and information that are obtained from the market. Despite the advent of information technology (IT), we still need capable analysts to make sense and draw meaningful conclusions out of the massive amount of information. In other words, the people factor cannot be discounted in corporate strategic planning.

SWOT Analysis from an Outside-in Approach

Recognizing the importance of intelligence is one thing. Getting the right information to facilitate decision-making is a totally different matter. At times, a lot of data and information may be collected, but they are of little relevance and value. This is where Sun Zi gave another interesting perspective on what kind of intelligence would be critical to decision-making.

Many business strategists will be familiar with the concept of SWOT analysis. SWOT stands for strengths, weaknesses, opportunities, and strengths. SWOT analysis is typically used as one of the bases for deriving the core competency and business model of a company. Interestingly, the root of SWOT analysis can actually be found in the following saying of Sun Zi:

知 彼 知 己, 胜 乃 不 殆; 知 天 知 地, 胜 乃 不 穷。
zhi bi zhi ji   sheng nai bu dai   zhi tian zhi di   sheng nai bu qiong

---

Know the other side (the enemy), know yourself, and your victory will not be threatened. Know the weather, know the terrain, and your victories will be limitless.

~ Lines 10.56 and 10.57 of Chapter 10 on Terrain,
地形 (*di xing*)

To know the other side, which includes the enemy, is tantamount to trying to know the strengths and weaknesses of oneself relative to the other side (the enemy). To know the weather and terrain is tantamount to knowing the opportunities and threats that exist in the macro environment.[8] Indeed, the relevance and applications of this particular quote to the business world are simply too obvious to ignore. Let us make some comments about this quote to demonstrate our points.

First, Sun Zi used the term *bi* (彼), which means "the other side," instead of the word *di* (敌), which means "the enemy." This is because prior to the outbreak of war, the enemy is still not defined. At most, he can only be viewed as the other side. At times, owing to successful diplomacy and negotiation, war may not even break out. Therefore, at this stage of analysis, it is crucial not to view the other side as the enemy. Doing so would likely jeopardize any possibility of finding peaceful solutions. In essence, the enemy can easily be considered to be a subset of the other side, but the other side cannot be construed as the enemy until direct confrontation is declared.

In the same way, while there may be many companies competing in the same market, a company is not the competitor of another unless their products/services compete directly in the same market for the same customers. At times, it is even possible for companies that seemingly compete directly against one another in one market (e.g. in the domestic market) to join forces when tackling a different market (e.g. in an overseas market). After all, strategic alliances, joint-ventures, and other forms of cooperation among direct competitors are plentiful in the business world.[9]

More importantly, the other side, when used in the context of business, can refer to many other parties and stakeholders beyond that of the competitors. For example, the other side in business can also refer to customers, suppliers, agents, bankers, labor unions, employees, government agencies, and many other stakeholders that may directly or indirectly impact the business of the company. Clearly, these parties are not the "enemies" of the company.

Second, Sun Zi advocated the importance of analyzing the other side and oneself before attempting to analyze the weather and terrain. This is because the impact of weather and terrain is less consequential if the strengths of the other side (in this case, the potential enemy) are overwhelmingly strong such that the chances of victory are zero or near zero. In the same way, if a company does not have a product or service that can withstand competition,[10] its claim to having knowledge of the business infrastructure and market conditions as well as mastery of timing for doing business (business climate) will be of little help.

Third, within the statement of knowing the other side and oneself, it is significant to note that Sun Zi placed more priority and importance on knowing the other side first before knowing oneself. The logic is actually not difficult to understand. To begin with, whether one is strong or weak is not decided by oneself, but rather by the competitors. If there are many stronger competitors around, then one becomes relatively weaker. At the same time, what strategies should be used and whether they would be successful depend very much on the other side(s). Ironically, many companies are often contented with knowing themselves first, before knowing the competitors and other stakeholders around them. Indeed, this is the concept of knowing oneself to know one's core competency. In contrast, Sun Zi advocated that the better way to know oneself is from the outside-in approach. It is by knowing the other side that one gets to know oneself.

Finally, in analysis, more consideration should be given to the weather than the terrain. This is because the climate is always very dynamic and changing while the terrain is relatively static. Different weather conditions can drastically affect the terrain and its visibility and, in turn, affect the movement, deployment, and effectiveness of weapons and troops in war. In the same way, the infrastructure for business is always there and does not change overnight. However, the timing of the entry/launch of a product or service can determine whether it will be a success or a failure.

Be Proactive

In war, one has to be vigilant and combat-ready at all times. In other words, one has to be constantly proactive to ensure that one does not become history. Thus, Sun Zi said:

以 虞 待 不 虞 者 胜；
yi   yu   dai   bu   yu   zhe sheng

He who is proactive and well-prepared and awaits his unprepared enemy will win.

~ Line 3.48 of Chapter 3 on Strategic Attacks,
谋攻 (*mou gong*)

Sun Zi went further to say that:

故 用 兵 之 法， 无 恃 其 不 来， 恃 吾 有 以 待 也；
gu yong bing zhi fa   wu shi qi bu lai   shi wu you yi dai ye

---

Thus, in the conduct of war, one must not rely on the failure of the enemy to come, but on the readiness of oneself to engage him.

~ Line 8.22 of Chapter 8 on Variations and Adaptability,
九变 (*jiu bian*)

无恃其不攻， 恃吾有所不可攻也。
wu shi ji bu gong   shi wu you suo bu ke gong ye

One must not rely on the failure of the enemy to attack, but on the ability of oneself to build an invincible defense that is invulnerable to attacks.

~ Line 8.23 of Chapter 8 on Variations and Adaptability,
九变 *(jiu bian)*

Just like in war, a company cannot rely on the failure of its competitors to attack. Instead, it must constantly seek to be ahead of its competitors. This can be achieved by closely monitoring the activities of the competitors, studying the changing tastes and preferences of the consumers, harnessing changing technology, discerning the changing economic conditions, etc. It must constantly think and act ahead, and not simply react to events when they happen.

The First/Early Mover Advantage

The concept of first/early mover advantage that we commonly refer to in the realm of business is mentioned in *Sun Zi Bingfa:*

孙子曰： 凡先处战地而待敌者佚，
Sun Zi yue   fan xian chu zhan di er dai di zhe yi

后处战地而趋战者劳。
hou chu zhan di er qu zhan zhe lao

Sun Zi said: Those who arrive first at the battleground will have sufficient time to rest and prepare against the enemy. Those who arrive late at the battleground will have to rush into battle when they are already exhausted.

~ Lines 6.1 and 6.2 of Chapter 6 on Weaknesses and Strengths,
虚实 *(xu shi)*

Obviously, the battleground that Sun Zi referred to has to be a very important area for the contesting troops to occupy, and this is not much different from the concept of key markets that a business firm wishes to capture. In fact, Sun Zi even extended the first/early mover advantage to the realm of managing troops. This is because the first/early mover can create a great impact and affect the fighting spirit and morale of the remaining troops:

故 车 战， 得 车 十 乘 已 上，
gu che zhan   de che shi cheng yi shang

赏 其 先 得 者，
shang qi xian de zhe

Therefore, in chariot fighting, when more than ten have been captured, reward the first one who succeeds in doing so.

~ Line 2.32 of Chapter 2 on Waging War
作战 (*zuo zhan*)

Obviously, there are good reasons to do likewise in the business world. By rewarding the first person who demonstrates gung-ho performance, the CEO is signaling that he appreciates risk-taking and innovative and creative behavior. More importantly, the generous reward will serve to motivate and encourage the rest of the team members to do likewise.

Creating Your Own Victories

Another very inspiring concept advocated by Sun Zi is that of creating your own victories.[11] The following quotes are very telling:

故曰：胜可为也。
gu yue   sheng ke wei ye

敌虽众，可使无斗。
di sui zhong   ke shi wu dou

Thus I say: victories can be created by us. Although the enemy may have a much larger and stronger force, he can be prevented from engaging me.

~ Lines 6.44 and 6.45 of Chapter 6 on Weaknesses and Strengths,
虚实 (*xu shi*)

There are many ways suggested by Sun Zi to create one's own victories. Here, we would just like to highlight two possibilities. The first way is to choose areas where you have distinctive advantages over that of the enemy (competitor):[12]

进而不可御者，冲其虚也；
jin er bu ke yu zhe   chong qi xu ye

He is able to advance without any resistance because he attacks areas that are the weaknesses of the enemy.

~ Line 6.19 of Chapter 6 on Weaknesses and Strengths,
虚实 (*xu shi*)

故善攻者，敌不知其所守；
gu shan gong zhe   di bu zhi qi suo shou

Thus, the expert in offense attacks places where the enemy does not know how to defend.

~ Line 6.14 of Chapter 6 on Weaknesses and Strengths,
虚实 (*xu shi*)

Another way is to choose areas ignored by the enemy (competitor):

攻而必取者， 攻其所不守也；
gong er bi qu zhe   gong qi suo bu shou ye

To be certain to capture what you attack is to attack a
place where the enemy does not defend or where
his defense is weak.

~ Line 6.12 of Chapter 6 on Weaknesses and Strengths,
虚实 (*xu shi*)

In choosing areas in which one has distinctive or competitive advantages, there are likely to be competitors in the
market as well. In contrast, in choosing areas ignored by the
competitors, there are basically no competitors, and even
if there are, they are usually very weak. As such, competition hardly exists. In this case, even the weaker player will
have the chance to build up its strengths gradually over
time. More importantly, as there are no other competitors,
no comparison is available, so the likelihood of being
knocked out by the competition is almost zero! This is a
good example of how one can win by default—not because
one is good, but because there are no other contestants in
the market.

Flexibility and Adaptability

Another important lesson to learn from *Sun Zi Bingfa* is the
need to remain flexible and adaptable in implementation.
Take the case of war. Despite all the detailed planning and
intelligence, twists and turns, and sudden events and crises
will emerge when war begins. As such, while the overall
war plan may remain intact and on course, the tactics and
methods to achieve the final victory may have to vary and
change according to the battle situations on the ground. The
following quote illustrates this point:

故 其 战 胜 不 复 ， 而 应 形 于 无 穷 。
gu qi zhan sheng bu fu   er ying xing yu wu qiong

Therefore, the victory gained from each battle comes
about because strategies and tactics are never repeated.
Rather, they vary according to the circumstances with
countless possibilities.

~ Lines 6.55 and 6.56 of Chapter 6 on Weaknesses
and Strengths,
虚实 (*xu shi*)

Sun Zi went further to use water to demonstrate its
great adaptability and how an army must behave likewise
in battle:

夫 兵 形 象 水 ， 水 之 形 ， 避 高 而 趋 下 ；
fu bing xing xiang shui   shui zhi xing   bi gao er qu xia
兵 之 形 ， 避 实 而 击 虚
bing zhi xing   bi shi er ji xu
水 因 地 而 制 流 ， 兵 因 敌 而 制 胜 。
shui yin di er zhi liu   bing yin di er zhi sheng

The principle underlying military deployment may be
likened to water. It is the inherent characteristic of
flowing water to escape from high grounds and hasten
its movement downwards. In the same way, the
disposition and deployment of an army should be to
avoid strengths and attack weaknesses. Just as water
controls its flow according to the characteristics of
the terrain, an army should create its victory according
to the situations of the enemy.

~ Lines 6.57 and 6.60 of Chapter 6 on Weaknesses
and Strengths,
虚实 (*xu shi*)

In the same way, one must be adaptive and flexible in the conduct of business. In other words, to excel, a company must not only be discerning, but also be fast and opportunistic (like the flowing water). This is particularly true in Asia where opportunities abound, but they also disappear very quickly.

Strategies against Enemies and Competitors

Throughout the 13 chapters of his treatise, Sun Zi provided much food for thought, and one only needs to think, reflect, adapt, and apply the strategies to the realm of business. In particular, Sun Zi advocated many strategies that can be used against the enemy. These same strategies are equally relevant and applicable for use against business competitors. As an illustration, we have cited some examples that are found in Chapter 1 of *Sun Zi Bingfa*:

a) Using Methods and Tactics to Confuse the Enemy (Competitor):

故 能 而 示 之 不 能， 用 而 示 之 不 用，
gu neng er shi zhi bu neng   yong er shi zhi bu yong

近 而 示 之 远， 远 而 示 之 近。
jin er shi zhi yuan   yuan er shi zhi jin

Thus, when you are capable, feign that you are incapable. When you are able to deploy your forces, feign that you are unable to do so. When you are near the objective, feign that you are far away, and when you are far away from the objective, feign that you are near.

~ Lines 1.31 and 1.33 of Chapter 1 on Detailed Assessment and Planning,

计 (*ji*)

b) Exploiting the Vulnerabilities and Weaknesses of the Enemy (Competitor):

利 而 诱 之 ， 乱 而 取 之 ，
li   er   you zhi   luan er   qu   zhi

When the enemy is greedy for small advantages, offer baits to lure him. When the enemy is in a state of chaos and disorder, launch an attack and capture him.

~ Lines 1.34 and 1.35 of Chapter 1 on Detailed Assessment and Planning,
计 (*ji*)

怒 而 挠 之 ， 卑 而 骄 之 ，
nu   er   nao zhi   bei   er   jiao zhi

When the enemy is easily angered, seek ways to provoke and irritate him. When the enemy has a low opinion of you, encourage his arrogance even more.

~ Lines 1.38 and 1.39 of Chapter 1 on Detailed Assessment and Planning, 计 (*ji*)

c) Mastering Relative Superiority:

实 而 备 之 ， 强 而 避 之 ；
shi   er   bei zhi   qiang er   bi   zhi

When the enemy is strong and effective, be well-prepared and ready to confront him. When the enemy is far superior and highly ferocious, it is best to avoid him.

~ Lines 1.36 and 1.37 of Chapter 1 on Detailed Assessment and Planning,
计 (*ji*)

d) *Eroding the Capabilities of the Enemy (Competitor):*

佚而劳之，　亲而离之。
yi er lao zhi   qin er li zhi

When the enemy is well-rested, use methods to tire him.
When the enemy is in harmony and united, use schemes
to divide him (and his troops).

~ Lines 1.40 and 1.41 of Chapter 1 on Detailed Assessment
and Planning,
计 (*ji*)

e) *Capitalizing on the Un-preparedness of the Enemy (Competitor):*

攻其无备，　出其不意。
gong qi wu bei   chu qi bu yi

Attack the enemy where he is not prepared. Move, appear,
and strike where he least expects you.

~ Lines 1.42 and 1.43 of Chapter 1 on Detailed Assessment
and Planning,
计 (*ji*)

Conclusion

One of the most important lessons that one can learn from
Sun Zi Bingfa is that in war, one should neither be led nor
dictated to by the enemy. Similarly, in business competition,
a company should not blindly follow what the competitors
do. Instead, it must seek to have a clear understanding of
and insight into the competitors, the customers, the market

conditions, etc. It should always attempt to be proactive and different from its competitors.[13] In other words, it must constantly seek to be innovative and creative in the way it deals with its customers and competitors. Then, and only then, will it be able to outlast the competitors, and surpass them as well. The following quote from Sun Zi serves as a useful reminder to end this chapter:

故 善 战 者， 致 人 而 不 致 于 人 。
gu shan zhan zhe   zhi ren er bu zhi yu ren

Thus, the person adept in warfare seeks to control and manipulate his enemy instead of being controlled and manipulated.

> ~ Line 6.3 of Chapter 6 on Weaknesses and Strengths,
> 虚实 (*xu shi*).

Endnotes

1. While its exact origin and authorship have been debated, scholars of military history are unanimous that the book existed, and was probably written, around 400 B.C. to 320 B.C., about 100 years after the births of Confucius (孔子 *Kong Zi*) and Lao Tzu (老子 *Lao Zi*), two well-known Chinese philosophers. Thus, the book is over 2,400 years old. Readers who are interested in understanding more about *Sun Zi Bingfa* and its applications can refer to Wee, C.H. (2003), *Sun Zi Art of War: An Illustrated Translation with Asian Perspectives and Insights*, and Wee, C.H. (2005), *Sun Zi Bingfa: Selected Insights and Applications*. Both books are published by Prentice Hall of Pearson Education.

2. It is significant to note that in the history of mankind, many civilizations, cultures, races, societies, and nations have flourished as well as perished. Even the once great Soviet Union has now disintegrated. Interestingly, China

has remained relatively "intact" and has "survived" for more than 5,000 years. No doubt, over this long period, it had its own ups and downs, that is, dark ages and golden eras. If sustainability is the key yardstick to measure success, then China stands out in a class of its own. In particular, it has now clearly entered another very strong golden era of development.

3. As mentioned earlier, while the Chinese tend to view business as war-like in nature (that is, tending toward zero-sum outcome scenarios), this does not mean that they are wagers of war in the military realm. These two thoughts are not necessarily linked, and should not be lumped together.

4. The most ambitious historical campaign waged out of China was by Genghis Khan during the 13th century. Then again, Genghis Khan was actually a Mongolian warrior and conqueror who conquered China. Historically, China was known more for establishing business and trade ties with the rest of the world than waging military campaigns. Good examples include the Silk Route and the trade missions of Cheng Ho (an imperial eunuch) to Southeast Asia during the 15th century.

5. Read his Chapter 2 on waging war, 作战 (zuo zhan)

6. For example, some scholars argue that in war, you have to kill your enemy in order to win. In contrast, businesses are always based on win-win propositions. In reality, it is also possible to achieve a win-win outcome in war through strategizing and strategic alliances. On the other hand, when companies embark on forceful acquisitions and the destruction of competitors, the outcomes are definitely zero-sum in nature, which can be more "ruthless" than military campaigns.

7. Readers who are interested in finding out in greater detail how *Sun Zi Bingfa* can be applied to business can refer to Wee, C.H. *Sun Zi Bingfa: Selected Insights and Applications*. Singapore: Prentice Hall, Pearson Education (Southeast Asia), 2005.

8. In business, weather and terrain refer to the business climate (which includes the aspect of timing) and the infrastructure that affects business operations.

9. Good examples can be found in the airline, banking, and shipping industries.

10. Note that the company need not make the best product nor provide the best service. What is important is that the product or service must be able to compete in some way against other offerings in the market.

11. Interestingly, the Blue Ocean Strategy, as advocated by W. Chan Kim and Renee Mauborgne, is basically about creating your own victories in business.

12. In other words, these are areas in which you are much stronger than competitors.

13. Of course, a company must not seek to be different for difference sake. Instead, the different product/service features that it offers must be wanted/desired by the consumers.

故曰: 知彼知己, 胜乃不殆;

gu　yue　　zhi　bi　zhi　ji　　　sheng　nai　bu　dai

知天知地, 胜乃不穷。

zhi　tian　zhi　di　　　sheng　nai　bu　qiong

Thus it is said: Know the other side (the enemy), know yourself, and your victory will not be threatened;
Know the weather, know the terrain, and your victories will be limitless.

(Sun Zi Bingfa, 孙子兵法, *Lines 10.56 and 10.57 of Chapter 10 on Terrain,* 地形 *(di xing))*

CHAPTER 3

Double Glazing

Why Are We Different?

Introduction

One thorny issue that most Western companies have to deal with in Asia is the general perception by Asians that there are glass ceilings restricting the promotion of Asians into senior management positions. In a discussion with Nihal Kaviratne, former chairman of Unilever Indonesia, in mid-2006, he eloquently described the phenomenon, whether real or perceived, as something far more multidimensional. It was "not only ceilings, it was glass walls, social and cultural, and these were double-glazed—one put up by the Westerners and one put up by the Asians."[1]

This is an interesting analogy as it conveyed how differently Westerners and Asians look at each other.[2] Even though they may be working together in large organizations, their private lives can be very different and separate. By looking at each other through different panes of glass, it can create a superficial world, an almost pseudo-community of people linked only by the cause of work and very little else. Yet, we believe that this is not really what people want. Most people want to be part of a real community, where they can integrate with others of differing views and traditions.

Why are we therefore so different and what is holding us back from breaking down these double-glazed walls and ceilings?

Aristotle versus Confucius

To start, we need to go back into history to understand the philosophical foundations of both Western and Asian civilizations. Three important branches of philosophy originated in roughly the same time period of antiquity, circa 600–400 B.C.: the Athenian school, featuring philosophers like Socrates, Plato, and Aristotle; the Buddhist school; and the Chinese school featuring Confucius (孔子 *Kong Zi*) and Lao Zi (老子 *Lao Zi*), who, together with others, form the heart of Chinese philosophy.

In his book, *The Geography of Thought: How Asians and Westerners Think Differently and Why*, Richard Nisbett argues very clearly how both the West and Asia actually think and even see the world differently because of their different ecologies, social structures, philosophies, and educational systems. A lot of it boils down to how their approaches in life have been driven by Aristotle in the West and Confucius in the East. These have created very large differences in habits of thought.

Aristotle developed the importance and uses of critical thinking, setting the stage for centuries of philosophical inquiry, and invented logic. As such, Westerners have a strong interest in categorization, which helps them to know what rules to apply to objects, and how formal logic plays a role in problem solving. From a very early age, Westerners are taught to break apart problems and to fragment the world. Their culture is largely linear-oriented. This apparently makes complex tasks and subjects more manageable, but a large, hidden price is paid. They can no longer see the consequences of their actions. They also tend to think of themselves as unique individuals, with distinctive attributes and goals.

Interestingly, while much of Western philosophy begins with common sense but arrives at paradox, much of Chinese philosophy begins with paradox but arrives at common sense. The world seems more complex to Asians than to Westerners, and understanding events requires the consideration of many factors and issues that work in relation to each other. As Nisbett states, Asians have a "broad, contextual view of the world and their belief that events are highly complex and determined by many factors. The individualistic or independent nature of Western society influences their belief that they can know the rules governing objects and therefore control the objects."

Asian culture, and especially Chinese culture, has no clearly defined division between philosophy and religion. Take the case of Taoism, Confucianism, and Buddhism. While Taoism and Confucianism began as philosophies, and Buddhism began as a religion, the three have blended together over the years. For example, Lao Zi and Confucius began by preaching their philosophies as a way of life and how one could be a better person and citizen. Regretfully, the tendencies to idolize and worship ancient philosophers such as Lao Zi and Confucius have, over the years, veered tremendously toward mystifying and spiritualizing their works. As a result, instead of focusing on the gems of their philosophical thoughts and teachings, many people are misled by distorted interpretations and end up believing in legends rather than the truth. Today, one can see temples in China, Taiwan, Hong Kong, Singapore, Malaysia, and other countries with sizeable ethnic Chinese communities that are dedicated to worshipping Lao Zi and Confucius.

Conversely, other than focusing on the religious aspects, Buddhism is being taught as a philosophy and way of life. In some Asian countries, there are Buddhist schools, and even universities. To the Chinese, religious faith and philosophy are lived each day as a way of life.[3] The concept of *yin* (阴)—the feminine, dark and passive—and *yang* (阳)—the masculine, light and active—dominates many aspects of Chinese life and thought. In Chinese philosophy, everything has a positive and negative side: a black and white, a good and evil, a dark and a light, and a female and a male aspect. *Yin* (阴) and *yang* (阳) are the two contradictory forces that permeate the universe, and a person is not expected to opt for one over the other. Instead, he/she is expected to find his/her own balance between these two polar extreme phenomena in life.[4]

Confucius laid down the principles that became the foundation of social order of Chinese society even up till today. He taught that it was the duty of rulers to govern with benevolence and justice, and that it was the duty of the people to obey and respect their leaders. In Asia, and especially among Chinese societies, there is a cultural inclination for harmony, a preference for internal cooperation, and a sense of belonging to a community. There is more comfort with discipline and following instructions. Confucianism created a series of moral obligations among individuals. It made the individual feel very much a part of a large, complex, and generally benign social organism, where clear mutual obligations served as a guide to ethical conduct. Any form of direct confrontation, such as debate, was discouraged.

Asians feel good about themselves when they are in harmony with the wishes of the groups to which they belong and are meeting the group's expectations. Until recently, the idea of self-advancement ahead of family advancement was very foreign to Asians. This is in complete opposition to Westerners, who feel good about themselves when there is equality and the existence of similar rules, which allow them to focus on personal goals of success and achievement. Business in Asia is also very cultural and communication biased, with a very high percentage of nonverbal communication. Moreover, the communication of emotions or feelings is almost completely nonverbal. For Westerners, this can present a challenge as it is only through direct experience that they can start to understand nonverbal communication and gain cooperation from others to achieve results.

Asians, especially the Chinese, tend to see the world as one that is filled with changes and contradictions. They are better able to see relationships between events than Westerners. To a typical Chinese, every event is related to another event. To understand one, you need to understand the opposite, and the causal relationship as well (有因必有果 *you ying bi you guo*). As such, they are willing to entertain apparently contradictory propositions, which can help in getting closer to the truth.

With two very different cultural orientations, one derived from Aristotle, the other largely from Confucius, it is no wonder that confusion and misunderstanding exist in business between Westerners and Asians. Westerners believe they can control and stabilize the future through sound rationale and logic. This makes business planning a straightforward exercise. Asians, however, see contradictions and changes as key drivers. Thus, business planning becomes a more complex process as relationships between people, activities, and events ensure that little can be truly controlled.

Business Planning Exercises in Asia

We are sure many of you attend annual business planning meetings in Asia. These can often be drawn out and frustrating affairs. Normally a protracted numbers negotiation exercise, it is often portrayed to others as a critical strategic planning exercise. It becomes an annual parade for country managers to put on a dazzling performance, only to be soured by the bullying tactics of the regional board which merely wants to draw out an acceptable set of numbers to be presented, in turn, to its global board. However, it is the approach and handling of such exercises that really provide serious food for thought. Allow us to illustrate what we mean.

We have seen many high-performing and serious-minded Asian country managers using their "airtime" to explain the complexities of their markets, how changes (people, policies, etc.) in one part of the business might affect other parts, how this may cause competitors, customers, and suppliers to react, which, in turn, will create other changes, etc. All these interrelated factors and events ultimately mean that planning a set of numbers becomes virtually impossible, although in many instances, these Asian country managers will more than meet their performance targets. However, such a stance is not well received. It generally provokes major discomfort in a Western-dominated regional board. The regional board members would inevitably want to jump into solution-finding mode, using logic to create a satisfactory set of numbers. The Asian country manager is normally sidelined in the process, and eventually sits down disconsolately.

In contrast, if the country manager is a Westerner, he will normally present a crisp, clear, logical story with numbers and figures. While the numbers may not meet the target, they are explained with convincing reasons. There is very superficial discussion on external events that may seriously impact the performance. No detailed analysis of those consequences is either done or presented. Generally, as the plan is well presented, it is accepted with little challenge, and the Western country manager feels that the job has been well done. That same evening, while drinking and socializing at the bar, the usual postmortem analysis and comments would be that the Western country manager outperformed his Asian counterpart.

The reality is that this business process, a Western designed model, is overweight on Aristotle and underweight on Confucius. The danger is that the imbalance creates a final plan, which inadequately covers the "what ifs" and is not "owned" by the Asian management. As a result, commitment may be lacking too. More seriously, the underlying flaws and loopholes in the planning exercise may be overlooked and not addressed adequately. These will eventually cause an underachievement of the plan.

Of course, we are also underestimating the Asian country manager in this process. He is also aware that by being overweight on Confucius and underweight on Aristotle, he creates a sense of confusion and disorientation among the Westerners. He already has a set of numbers in his mind, which he is comfortable with. He probably escapes with a relatively safe target imposed by the regional board. As a result, the potential to outperform the target agreed upon is quite high.

On the other hand, if things do not quite go according to plan, he can always counterargue that the target is set and owned by the regional board, not him. Thus, by being elusive, less assertive and articulate, the Asian manager is often able to deliver better results than the plan. The Western country manager, on the other hand, by being so explicit, will have to "live or die" by his committed numbers. Indeed there is a contradictory (yin-yang) approach in the world of business planning!

Separating Fact from Fiction

Virtually everything people hear about Asia is true, and so is the opposite. Western thought is dominated by linear logic, as per Greek philosophy, whereas Chinese thinking is influenced by early philosophers, who saw a paradoxical balance of opposites in all things. Where Westerners tend to look for clear alternatives (option A instead of option B), Asians may examine ways to combine both option A and option B. This difference in approach may make a Westerner think that an Asian is being illogical, evasive, or devious, when the Asian believes he is being quite straightforward. The Western mind starts with the parts, breaks a complex matter into component parts, and then deals with them one by one with an emphasis on logical analysis. The Asian mind starts with the whole, treats all things as interconnected, and deals with them as a whole with an emphasis on all-inclusiveness and the mastery of wisdom. Bending rules is a way of life for Asians, particularly if the rules are bent out of loyalty to friends, family, or colleagues. Asians will focus on the unique circumstances of a particular situation and adapt rules to fit that situation. Learning to differentiate between the two approaches is probably the key challenge for Westerners in order to develop their cultural competence in Asia.

Dual Carriageway of Thought

Therefore, with more than two billion people in the world today being the heirs of ancient Chinese traditions of thought and one billion being the heirs of an intellectual inheritance from ancient Greece, you might feel that things need to change!

The key question for Westerners is whether they can concede that there are two different ways of thinking, that theirs is not necessarily superior, and that there would be incredible benefits from harnessing the alternative approach. This would create a fascinating fusion by blending Western individual leadership with Asian collective harmony. Unfortunately, we sense that in most cases, this is inadequately addressed in mantras such as "Think Global, Act Local." This effectively implies an acknowledgment that Asian local culture and knowledge are appreciated, so long as they are structured within a Western-influenced, global strategic framework. We prefer the subtlety of "Think Local, Learn Global." This suggests a two-way communication process, with no predetermined right or wrong way.

For Asians, the key question remains whether their minds will be able to develop the right blend of values that will preserve some of the traditional strengths of Asian values (attachment to the family as an institution, deference to social interests, thrift, conservatism in social mores, respect for authority, etc.) as well as absorb the strengths of Western values (the emphasis on individual achievement, political and economic freedom, respect for the rule of law as well as for key national institutions). This will be a difficult and complicated challenge for them as they can sometimes be torn between the two. They may feel uncomfortable with certain Western values, especially those that relate to a perceived excessive stress on the individual rather than the community, a lack of social discipline, and a too-great intolerance for eccentricity and abnormality in social behavior. They believe that Western countries would do better if they could learn some Asian values too.

Asian values have suffered unfairly from negative assessments by Western politicians and business leaders, some of which date back to the 1997–1998 Asian financial crisis. There were comments and criticisms that if some of the excesses of Asian values had been properly managed, the crisis might not have occurred. This is a rather simplistic and flawed analysis which, quite rightly, upset many Asian leaders. Nevertheless, Asian leaders have acknowledged that there is room for improvement. Lee Kuan Yew, the first prime minister of Singapore,[5] for example, acknowledges the advantages of certain institutions inherited from the West, particularly institutions related to the civil service and open competition. However, he also criticizes cronyism and corruption, which remain endemic in parts of Asia. He argues that this is not the result of Confucianism but of the debasement of Confucian values.

Most Westerners would agree that the so-called Confucian values, particularly the Confucian commitment to hard work, thrift, filial piety, and national pride, have encouraged rapid economic growth over the last 20 years. They would also agree that nepotism, favoritism, and corruption need to be weeded out in Asia.

What is clear is that Asia has no settled identity as yet. It is in the process of coming into being. The long and intense process of self-definition and self-understanding is just beginning, a term often described as the "Asianisation of Asia." As Asia grows in self-confidence, it tries to rediscover and promote its own roots by investigating the ancient civilizations that helped form it. Kishore Mahbubani goes one step further in his analysis. He believes that this is "an effort (by Asians) to define their own personal, social and national identities that enhances their sense of self-esteem in a world in which their immediate ancestors had subconsciously accepted the fact that they were lesser beings in the Western universe."

What is also clear is that there is an implicit resistance to the idea of a solely Western-driven globalization. Many people in Asia still believe that the past 500 years of Western military, political, and economic dominance have made the West intellectually and morally arrogant. With the resurgence of China, there is a sense that the tide is now turning in favor of Asia. Nevertheless, Asia does not expect its culture to be unchanging or uncontested. It also appreciates the obvious and multiple ways in which Western and global influences continue to transform behavior, lifestyle, and taste in the region.

Globalization may succeed where domestic forces have failed. More than half of the 500,000 foreign students in the United States come from Asia. Asian successes in the United States have demonstrated that Asia has potentially the largest pool of talent to share with the world. Ostensibly this is a loss to Asia. Many may not return immediately, but a large number of them will do eventually. These returnees will be the ones who will help the integration of both cultures.

False Harmony

Even though we have lived and worked in Asia for many years and we both have many friends from the other culture, we are constantly reminded of double glazing on a daily basis, both in and outside of work. Without doubt, we have noted that Asians and Westerners respect and acknowledge each other. However, they have not displayed the confidence in themselves or the desire to go the extra mile required. The comfort zone of their own community and culture draws them back. This is most evident between expatriates and locals, particularly in the workplace, where a superficial pseudo-community exists.

The expatriates' initial enthusiasm to break down the panes of glass is soon deterred by the realization that getting involved means not just throwing their lives into the arena but that of their families too. The interrelationship between work and family in Asian culture can be so powerful and overwhelming. The motivation starts to wane after 10 wedding invitations within a year, karaoke evenings every alternative weekend, and seemingly endless dim sum lunches and meals that involve all family members. The families (wives and children) find it hard to fit in and relate to the very different lives of their Asian counterparts. Conversations and activities become limiting and drawn out. Mahjong, premier league football, golf, and Xbox become the only common denominators. Moreover, private time for the family is seriously affected.

The initial euphoria therefore ends up with a tactical but polite withdrawal to a line much further back, but still ahead of the point of arrival. The expatriates move back into their cultural comfort zone of leading a Western lifestyle, appreciating their colleagues from other parts of the world, and demonstrating their own unique culture with more fervor than if they had been back in their home country. Even many of our "Asianised" and culturally sensitive friends recognize that they are operating in this zone. They acknowledge that the situation is not perfect, but have intuitively or by experience learned to live with it, and to accept it.

However, they will continue to pick and choose the elements of Asian culture that give them the most pleasure, such as the cuisine, the domestic helper at home, the level of service compared to back home, the exotic travel locations, the clubs (both recreational and golf), the spas, and other self-indulgences. They retain a polite co-existence with the locals but, in the majority of cases, hold back from full integration. An expatriate described it as follows:

"It is very natural for a human being to want to integrate into another culture, but neither side wants the integration to be complete. It is 'Respect my culture and I'll respect yours'. Both cultures enjoy the other without wanting it fully. A sort of no man's land is established, where both sides come to learn."

In essence, a gap will always exist, which everyone needs to be mindful of. The width of that gap is critical and needs to be minimized as much as possible so that the radar does pick up the essential signals.

What is frustrating, however, is when less sincere expatriates proclaim loudly how wonderful Asia is (which is true) and paint a positive, and at times somewhat exaggerated, picture of their relationships with the locals when senior business visitors, normally from the global head office, are in town. Do not be deceived by the backslapping, cocktail question-and-answer sessions when the double-glazed patio doors are briefly opened. This is a convenient demonstration of unity, solidarity, and purpose supported by both cultures to give external bosses a false sense of comfort and well-being.

Asians are similarly responsible for the double glazing they have put up. They too have their comfort zones, their set of networks and relationships, which maintain harmony among them. So, why change? After all, they have largely been brought up under the Confucian model to respect conformity and hierarchy. They know they have to work together, especially if they work for a multinational corporation (MNC). It takes time to develop a relationship and much more time to build trust. The constant changes, with expatriate bosses arriving and leaving on the corporate merry-go-round, and new vision statements, strategies, and business processes, cause high levels of anxiety and discomfort. It is easier to play the game of quiet acquiescence and loyalty than to rebel and complain. It is easier to participate in some of the Western communication exercises and not challenge or question. In some cultures, the vast differences in remuneration and benefits between expatriates and locals make the double glazing even sharper and more precarious. For example, when costs come under pressure among MNCs and foreign companies operating in countries such as Indonesia, Vietnam, Thailand, and China, some of the more uncomfortable discussions center around the vast disparity between local and expatriate compensation.

Many readers may feel that we are being too cynical and unfair with these broad, sweeping observations. Of course, there are many MNCs and people from both sides who do not fall into these categories. However, we do believe that our observations and views apply to many cases. Double glazing is a real issue which is often skirted because people do not like to discuss something that is deep down because it can create severe discomfort. As such, it is far better to retain harmony, friendliness, and polite respect. Indeed, it takes a very serious and significant event to trigger any action.

Perception and Reality

Take the case of racism, which exists in various forms and degrees in many societies. Yet few politicians or policymakers would want to admit or confront it. The British television show *Celebrity Big Brother* provides a startling revelation. In early 2007, two contestants in the show, Jade Goody and Danielle Lloyd, made provocative racist remarks against Bollywood Indian actress Shilpa Shetty, who was a housemate in the show. Shilpa cried and complained. Indians in India demonstrated and protested against the remarks, so did their newspapers. The Indian community in Britain also took issue with the treatment of Shilpa Shetty who is a very popular actress in India. In an attempt at reconciliation and to salvage their careers, both Jade Goody and Danielle Lloyd apologized. However, it came too late. A number of companies such as insurance company Bennetts and retailer The Perfume Shop ended their contracts with both of them. Other companies pulled out their TV advertisements.

We would like to make a number of significant observations and comments regarding this episode. First, while Shilpa Shetty cried and complained, she was also the first person to retract her comments about racism, which led to the apology from the other two contestants. Clearly, her retraction was an attempt to maintain harmony and was made perhaps out of polite respect for the show and her host country, Britain. More significantly, she appeared to be the most sensitive party as she made the first move toward reconciliation, although she was wronged by the other two contestants.

Second, various other newspaper editorials took up the subject. For example, the editorial of the *Independent* recounted that the sniping about Indian hygiene, housing, and culture in the show showed that "barely submerged xenophobia in Britain is a significant phenomenon in our society still," and further added that the show "holds a mirror to contemporary society." These editorials, to some extent, reflected the capability of Western society to comment on and criticize itself when necessary. On the other hand, they could also be written as subtle attempts to improve the sales of their papers. Whatever the motives, it showed the openness of a Western society.

Third, the issue was brought up in the British parliament by Labour Party lawmaker Keith Vaz, who is of Indian origin. Instead of capitalizing on the issue to gain popularity with the 72,000-strong Indian community in his constituency, he played it down as the view of a tiny minority, apparently trying to maintain harmony just like Shilpa Shetty. Clearly, despite growing up in Britain, Vaz demonstrated traits that reflected Asian values—the need to take a more holistic position and to consider the interests of the community at large rather than his personal or political agenda.

Fourth, there were calls to Channel 4 to withdraw the show. Obviously, these calls were made by parties and people who were concerned that Channel 4 might use the episode to further sensationalize the issue and improve its television ratings, thus incensing the feelings of Indians and Asians, including those living in Britain.

Fifth, instead of playing down the issue, Channel 4 chose to exploit the controversy. In fact, its audience figures jumped by over 60 percent as a result of the episode, from 3.5 million viewers to 5.7 million within a few days. Without doubt, Channel 4 saw the episode, despite its controversy, as a way to boost its television ratings. Commercial reasons were probably the main driving factor behind such a move. Nonetheless, it also showed the higher tolerance of a Western society toward open differences in views and positions, something that a typical Asian society would not be prepared to risk.

Finally, the episode sparked a national debate in Britain about the extent of racism and xenophobia within the country. When such an episode was played out in the world arena, it was something that the British government could not choose to ignore, more so when it is a major beacon and advocate of democracy and freedom.

By recounting the episode in such detail, we hope readers will notice the contrasting positions taken by the Asians Shilpa Shetty and Keith Vaz versus their Western counterparts. Clearly double glazing has been going on in Britain for a long time, but it took a show like *Celebrity Big Brother* to bring out the innate feelings that have been brewing within individuals from diverse cultures. This being the case, one can only imagine the extent of such a phenomenon in the corporate world. Of course, the tolerance level would be much higher, given the greater stakes of one's career and job if it were not handled carefully. Not surprisingly, the more acceptable option is not to surface the issue openly. Better still, everyone pretends that it does not exist at all.

What is important to note, as illustrated by the *Celebrity Big Brother* episode, is that when such differences erupt into the open, it may become more difficult to control the consequences and backlashes. As a result of globalization and the widespread influence of the media, the price to pay for such incidents may increase significantly. In other words, ignoring such issues and hoping that they will not surface openly may not be a good option at all. It is like sweeping dirt under the carpet. The dirt is still there, and, over time, it will accumulate. Better options must be developed to handle such issues.

The Way Forward

In Philippe Rosinski's book, *Coaching and Culture*, he argues that in reality we all belong to multiple groups of culture, not just geography, but also religion, organization, gender, and social life. Our identity, therefore, is a personal and dynamic synthesis of multiple cultures. So categorizing us as Asians and Westerners is a far too simplistic definition. More importantly, he adds, "Leveraging cultural differences is a proactive attitude. You look for gems in your own culture and mine for treasures in other cultures. Leveraging means achieving more output with a given input." However, this needs to be undertaken in such a way that cultural differences are accepted, adapted, integrated, and ultimately leveraged. That means a significant mindset shift, where a Westerner would give up the assumption that his own culture is central to all reality. The best place to start for Westerners is to accept, as Richard Nisbett describes, "the possibility that another valid approach to thinking about the world exists and that it can serve as a mirror with which to examine and critique (our) own beliefs and habits of mind."

Most people never reach this level in a complete, honest sense. We are not sure if we have ever got close to this point. We are open to consider other cultures, and even attempt to embrace and adopt parts of them. However, whether we have fundamentally changed our central mindset is another matter. Most people will give it a try, but generally the Asian fallback position is that of Confucius and for the Westerner, that of Aristotle.

However, if you are open and willing to acknowledge that we have a long journey ahead of us in order to bridge this fundamental gap, which exposes the differences between the East and the West, then half the battle is won. As the authors of *Doing Business Internationally: The guide to cross-cultural success,* acknowledge, cultural competence is about more than understanding traditions and rituals.

> *"It is about understanding how cultural value orientations drive assumptions and behaviors, ... then converting that knowledge into improved relationships ... it's a continuous process, which starts with an open attitude."*

Hopefully, reading this book will provoke you into changing some part of your philosophy of life.

Endnotes

1. In an ironic twist, one of Goldman Sach's top executives was prevented from occupying the chief executive officer (CEO) position of its joint-venture in China in June 2007. This was due to his inability to write the Chinese language well, as he failed the test that was set up by the Chinese authorities. What caught the attention of the international financial community was that this person was an overseas Chinese. Thus, it appears that as China continues to exert its economic prowess, anyone ascending to the top corporate positions in Chinese joint-venture companies in China may also hit glass ceilings although different kinds of barriers may be erected.

2. Readers are reminded that our definition of Asians, as mentioned in Chapter 1, includes the group of people who have been heavily influenced by Chinese culture, traditions, customs, habits, and thinking.
3. This applies to the Islamic faith too.
4. Readers who are interested in exploring how yin-yang can impact Chinese business decision-making can refer to Chapter 13, "Strategic Tradeoffs and Yin-Yang Contradictions: Seeking the Balance," by Wee, C.H. *Sun Zi Bingfa: Selected Insights and Applications*. Singapore: Prentice Hall, Pearson Education (Southeast Asia), 2005, pp. 309 to 340.
5. As of 2008, he is the Minister Mentor of Singapore.

不用乡导者，不能得地利。
bu yong xiang dao zhe   bu neng de di li

Those who do not use local guides will
not be able to gain the advantages of the
terrain.

(Sun Zi Bingfa, 孙子兵法, *Line 7.26 of*
Chapter 7 on Military Maneuvers,
军争 *(jun zheng)*
and Line 11.96 of Chapter 11 on Nine
Battlegrounds, 九地 *(jiu di))*

CHAPTER 4

Using the Messenger

Achieving What You Cannot Do

Breaking an Impasse

Years ago in Vietnam, one of us witnessed a very difficult joint-venture negotiation meeting in Ho Chi Minh City between a former employer and its Vietnamese partner.[1] Tensions were high, especially on the multinational corporation (MNC) side. This was because its representatives felt strongly that previous agreements were now being disputed by the other side. An emotional time-out was called for things to cool off.

In the middle of the emotional time-out, an aide from the Vietnamese partner came over to suggest that everyone stop negotiations for the day and take a trip to the beach instead! Two surreal hours later, the two teams were on the beach in Vung Tau, trousers rolled up, ice cream in hand, and everyone went paddling in the sea. The following day, everyone was back in the boardroom for the next round of negotiations, all with a considerably more positive mindset to reach a solution.

Clearly, the tactical time-out for some social interaction paid off in creating a more conducive atmosphere for both sides to continue and conclude the negotiations. More significantly, the time-out was called and initiated by the Vietnamese side, and the message was conveyed by an aide—he was the messenger who helped to break the impasse.

Dangers of Miscommunication

Many of you who have experience in Asia will fully realize the perils of any miscommunication between business partners, particularly between Western and Asian companies. Often, negative situations are created, and the causes could be many. To begin with, the Western partner may have chosen the wrong interpreter who can cause much confusion and misunderstanding. Second, the tone, mannerism, and body language may have given the other party the wrong signals and impressions. Third, the setting for negotiations may be inappropriate, giving the impression of one-upmanship over the other side. Fourth, the pace to rush through the negotiations may also create much misunderstanding, tension, and anxiety for both sides. Finally, noise and other distractions could also affect successful negotiations.[2,3] Not surprisingly, frustrations and dissatisfaction often set in, and they can easily affect the subsequent business relationship even if a deal has been struck.

Many times, we have attended meetings where one party felt that the meeting went well while the other party thought it was disastrous; where one party thought that agreement had been reached on all points while the other party was still struggling with the first point; where one party passed on a harsh reprimand and the other shrank away; or where one party intended to praise but the other felt dejected. The smiles, nods, and hospitality often deceive both parties into assuming that all is well, when things are clearly not.

In Asia, the following formula for negotiation is often very true:

$$Communication \; + \; Behavior \; = \; Trust^4$$

Asian partners need ample demonstration of both communication and behavior before they can feel comfortable with the relationship. In the West, this process is considerably shorter and more businesslike in approach. Often, in Asia, the Western company wants to quickly get past the getting-to-know-each-other stage and into the action mode when the Asian company is still deciding whether this is a partner it can trust. One communication tool that many Western companies do not consider or exploit in these early stages is the messenger.

Messengers throughout History

Throughout the history of mankind, messengers have played critical roles. Emissaries and ambassadors have been used regularly to deliver key messages. Intermediaries or facilitators, known to both parties, have been used to help resolve differences. In fact, they have played very effective roles without having to embarrass the parties involved. In Asian society, intermediaries were used even more extensively to resolve conflicts and mitigate severe differences.

Take the case of an intermediary who was used to resolve family disputes in the past.[5] In an Asian family, a newly wed daughter-in-law would usually live with her in-laws. Not surprisingly, occasional serious differences and misunderstandings would arise between the daughter-in-law and her mother-in-law. When this happened, the direct and confrontational approach was often avoided. This was because if no amicable solution was reached, the consequences could be very serious, and the relationship would be impossible to reconcile. Everyone would be caught in a no-win situation, including the husband/son and father-in-law. This was where the intermediary would come into the picture.

The typical family intermediary would be a senior relative of the family who was well-respected by both sides. As he/she did not live under the same roof, he/she would be more objective and in a better position to offer his/her views, suggestions, and advice by virtue of his/her seniority. By ferrying messages from one party to the other, the intermediary could also help to moderate the differences and, in the process, bridge the differences. More often than not, he/she would succeed in reconciling the differences and healing the relationship.

In the same way, business disputes between dissenting parties were resolved more by mediation through a third party than resorting to the courts. The intermediary in such instances would be a respected elder of the village or community. By virtue of his status and position, he was able to bring both parties to the negotiating table for an amicable discussion and to find an agreeable solution. At other times, when the dispute was very severe, he would act as the messenger for both parties. Like the person who helped to resolve family conflicts, this business mediator would act as the go-between and play peace-maker. Indeed, he was a powerful messenger, intermediary, and mediator who would dictate the positive outcome of any dispute.

The West Prefers Direct Communication

Today, in the West, the role of messengers or intermediaries in business negotiations has largely disappeared or diminished substantially. Instead, direct communication and straightforward, honest answers are encouraged and preferred. This explains why Western leaders prefer face-to-face communication. There are many reasons for this. To them, it is a faster and more efficient method. The participants can easily observe the responses of the other party, including their body language, tone, and mannerism. Concerns, questions, and doubts can be addressed immediately and directly with minimal loss of time. To the West, time is money, and the sooner one gets over the business at hand, the more efficient it is.

Tough and blunt talking is also welcome so long as the message is clearly communicated in unambiguous terms and the receiving party's "face" is not disrespected.[6] Playing hard ball in order to gain more is the rule of the game. To the typical Westerner, one must fight for his own rights and gains, and not leave them to the mercy of the other party. As such, if he were to lose, it can never be due to the lack of effort in trying.

In contrast, Asian leaders are generally not comfortable with direct communication. This is because if the message is not well received, the unintended reactions may cause embarrassment to both parties—the communicator and the receiver(s). Tough or blunt talking has never been the forte of Asians, who prefer the indirect and subtle way. This is where the messenger becomes very useful. As explained earlier, the use of the messenger as an intermediary and mediator has been part and parcel of Asian society for centuries.

What Messengers Can Do

The messenger plays many roles. Often, the messenger is sent literally to convey the message, thus sparing the leader the embarrassment or awkwardness of having to do so himself. At other times, the messenger is also used to sense the mood on the ground and determine the readiness of the receiver(s) before the leader brings up the subject, or he may even alter the content and/or approach of how he wants to convey the ultimate message. For example, if the content is sensitive, the leader will choose to approach the subject in an indirect way instead of choosing the head-on approach. For the shrewd listener(s) who is accustomed to such an approach, the message is clearly taken in.

Realizing the differences, the shrewd Westerner will use messengers to develop trust between his Asian partner and himself, and to ensure a smoother path to business success. The use of messengers is particularly useful for negotiation purposes. The following are some examples of what messengers can do.

Expectation-Setting

A good messenger can pre-communicate the points that a Westerner wants to put across and gauge the reactions. In this way, the Westerner will be in a better position to craft his words at the meeting and avoid any surprises. At other times, the messenger can also help to prepare the other party on the likely issues to be discussed by the Western party.

Thus, the Asian party would have more time to think about the appropriate response. This is particularly important as Asians are not accustomed to responding immediately nor are they good at handling "surprises." Often, they need to consult among themselves before making a response.

Deal-Making and Negotiation

A good messenger can pass on concerns or issues that the Asian partner is unwilling to express directly. This is because the typical Asian is very sensitive to embarrassing the other party, as he too does not want to be embarrassed. Likewise, the Western partner could use the messenger for the same role. The messenger can also propose time-outs in the negotiations either to allow both parties to "cool off" or to ensure that both parties are given more time by themselves to think through the issues again. In this way, sensitive matters and key points can be brought to a close effectively without embarrassing either side. In fact, the Vietnamese episode mentioned at the beginning of this chapter is an example of such a role played by the messenger.

Managing Personal Sensitivities

A good messenger can help pass on a message to the other side if one party has concerns about certain people in the other team whom he feels uncomfortable with. While this may seem a rather torturous route, it at least guarantees the Western or the Asian company the opportunity to have the right people chemistry in place at the beginning to ensure the success of the negotiations. It is better to resolve this early than to face it awkwardly later on.

Performance-Related Issues

A good messenger can express the concerns that a company may have about the other party regarding performance-related issues. These could include various performance indicators and milestone events that the other party must fulfill in order for the business deal to go through. Without doubt, such issues can, at times, be very sensitive and more time and effort will be needed to explain them.

Translation and Interpretation

In many instances of doing business in Asia, the messenger may also double up as the interpreter and translator. When this happens, his role becomes even more critical in ensuring the success of the negotiations. In fact, a good messenger in this instance can ensure a quicker resolution to the whole negotiation process. A skillful and shrewd messenger playing the role of an interpreter can also ensure that unnecessary friction, direct confrontation, and challenges be averted when a deal is turning sour. Let us illustrate with an example. One of us was privy to a negotiation in China.[7] As expected, the Western party was very tough and rough in the negotiation, at times resorting to raising their voices and condemning the quality of the Chinese products. Interestingly, throughout the high tension, the messenger chose not to translate everything that the Western party said. In particular, he deliberately left out all the nasty remarks made by the Western party. It was only after the Western team had left the room that the messenger told the truth to the Chinese side. Of course, the deal did not go through.

When and How to Use Messengers

As mentioned earlier, Asians in general do not always say things directly, especially if what they have to say is unpleasant. Sometimes direct feedback can offend, and indirect or nonverbal feedback can produce ambiguity or just the reverse. This is where messengers can fulfill very useful purposes. They provide a clear way of communicating something difficult through an indirect and trusted way. On the other hand, messengers can also be used at times to deceive or wrong-foot the other party. Of course, if both parties are all out to seek a long-term sustainable business relationship, such ploys must be discouraged. This is because, once discovered, the relationship can be soured. Let us consider a number of hypothetical scenarios,[8] which many of you will be able to relate to. Afterward consider whether the use of a messenger had been the right approach.

Scenario 1

A Western company wants to seal an investment joint-venture in Indonesia. It has pursued a particular Indonesian partner for the manufacture and distribution of a certain product, but it is concerned that the partner may not have the necessary government relations to protect the joint-venture investment or the required depth in management to handle distribution. Several other partners are therefore being considered and pursued. The managing director has decided to visit Indonesia to explain this to the Indonesian partner and also to meet other parties.

There are a number of critical points here, which will backfire, if not handled correctly.

1. The Indonesian partner will be greatly offended if other parties are being actively pursued. It is an enormous loss of "face."
2. The other parties will also feel uncomfortable and will likely question whether the Western company is one they can trust in the long term.
3. The Indonesian partner, in all likelihood, will consider his government relations to be excellent and his management team perfectly adequate to handle the distribution challenge. Therefore, he will be taken by surprise if told that this is his weak area.
4. There may already be a relationship between the Indonesian partner and the other parties, which the Western company is not aware of.

The Western managing director may see very little wrong with the approach he is taking. In fact, such an approach is commonly practiced in the West, that is, telling the potential partner his inadequacies while, at the same time, pursuing other potential partners and having direct discussions with them. However, taking this approach in Indonesia would be disastrous.

What the Western managing director should have done was to have tested out potential candidates through local trusted messengers even before making a clear proposal to the favored one. If there were shortcomings, then these could have been addressed earlier through messengers. For example, the message might have been as follows:

1. The Western company would really like to work with you. It feels you have most of the required skills, and it can trust you. It is considering other companies as well but you are the first choice.

2. The company has a couple of concerns, however, which I know the managing director will share with you when he arrives in two weeks to meet you.

3. The company is unsure whether you have the necessary government contacts should help ever be required, for example, to ensure a level competitive playing field against local competitors.

4. The company feels that some of your old managers may not be up to the job of setting up the distribution network required.

5. If you can address and prepare for these issues positively, then the chances of securing the deal are strong when the managing director comes to meet you.

The more likely outcome if a messenger is used is that when the Western managing director does make his visit, a dinner would have been arranged with the local governor and a 15-minute audience granted with a minister. The Indonesian partner might also acknowledge that some new managers need to be recruited to supplement the existing management. However, he will also emphasize to the Western managing director that he needs to respect the importance of customer relations and hence the old managers will be retained.

It may not be the perfect answer. However, the use of a messenger would greatly facilitate this meeting for both sides. Even if the decision is negative, that is, the Western company still decides to pursue other options, the messenger can also help to relay the bad news to the Indonesian partner.

Scenario 2

A Western company gets bogged down in difficult negotiations with a Chinese state-owned enterprise (SOE) over a joint-venture that it is trying to establish. After a positive first meeting where the two negotiating teams were introduced to each other and some basic principles were apparently agreed on, the second meeting reveals some unexpected hard-line positions taken by the Chinese party. This effectively disorientates the Western company. These positions include:

1. The Chinese party states that the original 50/50 joint-venture agreed upon will never be accepted by the Beijing government, and it would need a majority control for the deal to go through.
2. The proposed manufacturing site cannot be located in the province selected by the Western company but in a different city and province.
3. The Chinese contribution to the joint-venture will be in the form of land and old machinery. The Western counterpart suspects that these are offered at over-inflated values.

The frustrated managing director returns to his board in New York to explain the situation. There, he is instructed to pass on a very strong message that these are deal-breakers and, unless addressed positively by the Chinese SOE, the deal is off. Again, there are a few important issues here that anyone experienced in negotiation will appreciate, and where messengers can play a more constructive role. These include:

1. In direct negotiations, there are two teams on different sides of the table. The Western company may not know perhaps that the chief executive officer (CEO) on the Chinese side has to play to a more important audience than the Westerners, that is, to his own

team! He needs to prove that he is strong and tough on the foreign party so that this is reported positively within the state apparatus, even if he is actually reasonable and flexible.

2. There is a natural risk aversion to agreeing so readily to Western demands, without getting complete support from the system upward.

3. There are other political interests at stake, which are interfering with the choice of manufacturing location, probably a province that has been lobbying for preferred foreign direct investment (FDI).

The use of messengers from the outset would have helped the Western team to realize the following:

1. The Chinese would not raise too many objections in the first getting-to-know-each-other meeting out of fear of offending the Western party.

2. The decision-making authority does not lie with the Chinese SOE team that is doing the negotiations. It can only make carefully considered recommendations within the system that would not reflect badly on themselves.

3. The negotiating process cannot be rushed. Relationships need to be formed, individual motivations understood, and time-outs allowed for external factors that can disrupt the process.

Furthermore, the Western managing director could have more informal discussions with his Chinese counterpart, away from the wider audience, perhaps in a social setting over some drinks and dinner, where concerns could be shared more openly and solutions sought.

Scenario 3

A Western drinks company is dissatisfied with the performance of its distributor in Thailand, and in particular, with the leadership of the distribution manager, due to the following reasons:

1. Insufficient sales data.
2. Poor distribution coverage (20 percent below benchmark competitors).
3. High turnover of sales representatives.

The company has decided to issue an ultimatum to the distributor—either it removes the distribution manager in question or risks having the distribution agreement terminated due to failure to meet contractual targets.

To have reached such a situation in the first place suggests a real breakdown in communication between both parties. The use of a threat or an ultimatum is a virtual no-no in Asian culture and normally ends up making matters worse, not better.

There may have been strong grounds for getting rid of the distribution manager, but adopting a messenger system from the outset would probably have created a more positive solution. There is without doubt a bond of loyalty between the owners of the Thai distributor and the distribution manager, one which would make it difficult for them to remove him. However, consider the following:

1. Separate messengers from the Western company to the Thai distributor and its distribution manager would have helped to build a case for substantial improvement needed, a number of potential solutions, an action plan, and a timetable.

2. A messenger from the Thai distributor to its manager would have helped to prepare him for the worst, given the difficulties and embarrassment it might cause the owners.

3. A messenger from the Thai distributor to the Western company might have relayed some of the actions it was taking and also warned them to tone down their aggressive behavior.

Knowing What It Takes to Succeed

Maintaining a regular and casual exchange of information, asking trusted third-party groups to convey information, and anticipating problem areas are all ways to improve the giving and receiving of feedback. Unfortunately, Westerners who are not attuned to the nuances and subtleties of Asian culture miss out on the golden opportunity to use one of the most useful tools in improving their negotiation strategies and winning more business deals and contracts. What is more ironical is the person who removed the messenger is the Westerner himself.

We are not advocating the use of messengers to handle all kinds of communication. This is far from it. They need to be selectively used for critical issues only, especially when the Westerner is new to the Asian culture and environment. Once the Westerner is familiar with the Asian way of doing things, he must learn to engage the other party personally. Of course, this does not mean that he can resort to his blunt and direct methods. Rather, he should approach the other party by trying to understand his position, views, feelings, etc. At the end of the day, he still has to be very tactful and know that what works at home may not work in Asia.

Any overuse of messengers can lead to over-dependency. More dangerously, it can lead to a loss of control over the messengers themselves. This is particularly true if the Westerner does not understand the local language and has to rely on the messenger to do the necessary translation and interpretation. Messengers, in such instances, can overestimate their own power and abuse it to the detriment of the Western company. Often, they may end up closer to the other side and, in essence, may end up as double agents.

Some Westerners who are particularly gifted at handling communication themselves with Asians rely less on messengers. They have learned to become almost Asian themselves. This gives them the advantage of hearing first-hand what is going on. For example, in Asia, it is useful to consider nonverbal, implicit, and, therefore, more indirect feedback. It is common for Asians to criticize someone who is not present. However, through subtle hints, such criticism can also be targeted at someone else who is present.

This is exactly what is meant by the Chinese stratagem, "Pointing at the mulberry but scolding the locust tree, 指桑骂槐 (*zhi sang ma huai*)." It is a way of saying what needs to be said without provoking confrontation and causing any embarrassment to the target (listener). This stratagem can be very effective in a sensitive situation if employed tactfully. The message will get across to the Asians who are trained to understand these hints. To the foreigners who are more used to the direct way of communication, such hidden messages and signals often get lost. As such, Westerners who can learn and practice this art will gain a significant strategic advantage.

Willingness to Bridge the Gap

When a Westerner comes to Asia, he must acknowledge that there is indeed a cultural gap that needs to be bridged. As he is the one who decides to come to Asia, the onus will be on him to initiate the bridging process. This is similar to someone who decides to migrate to another country. Surely, the immigrant must make conscious attempts to integrate himself into his newly adopted country. In the case of business, the Westerner is in Asia to make money. How he is able to integrate himself into his operating environment will also determine his degree of success.

Bridging the gap between the West and Asia is usually more successful when people can combine personal values and behaviors that translate well between cultures. These people are considered global citizens with values that create seamless cooperation across organizational lines between nations, ethnic groups, customers, and corporate business units. However, at times, messengers will be good intermediaries to help facilitate and expedite the process.

Doing business in Asia is much more about knowing people, and knowing the right people well. As such, people skills are very important. So next time, when you find it difficult to get your points of view across to your potential partner in Asia, consider the messenger option. In the case of negotiations where there are major points or issues that may be sensitive, the messenger can play an even more significant role for you. He can save you a lot of unnecessary time, stress, and potential confusion. It is up to you to exploit and leverage such available resources to your advantage. In the process, you can accomplish your mission faster and more efficiently, leaving you with more time to enjoy the sights and sounds of Asia.

Endnotes

1. The second author.

2. This would include a wrong interpretation of the intention of the other party, etc.

3. This would include the insertion of too many unrelated items to the agenda.

4. Interestingly, the Chinese word for "trust" is written as 信 (*xin*). It actually consists of two other words or characters. The word on the left is *ren* (人), which means "a person." The character on the right is *yan* (言), which means "words." As such, "trust" (信 *xin*) means to believe in the words of the person, and the integrity of the person depends very much on what he says (his words).

5. To some extent, this is still practiced in some traditional and rural parts of Asia.

6. Of course, this is much harder to judge. In addition, the typical Westerner is less concerned about losing "face" than gaining the business. The concept of "face" is discussed in more detail in Chapter 11.

7. The first author.

8. Though they are hypothetical, they are based on the consulting and working experiences of the authors.

怒 而 挠 之， 卑 而 骄 之，
nu er nao zhi   bei er jiao zhi
佚 而 劳 之， 亲 而 离 之。
yi er lao zhi   qin er li zhi
攻 其 无 备， 出 其 不 意。
gong qi wu bei   chu qi bu yi

When the enemy is easily angered, seek ways to provoke and irritate him.

When the enemy has a low opinion of you, encourage his arrogance even more.

When the enemy is well rested, use methods to tire him.

When the enemy is in harmony and united, use schemes to divide him (and his troops). Attack the enemy where he is not prepared.

Move, appear, and strike at areas where the enemy least expects you.

(Sun Zi Bingfa, 孙子兵法, Lines 1.38 to 1.43 of Chapter 1 on Detailed Assessment and Planning, 计 (ji))

CHAPTER 5

Moving Goalposts

Concealing Intentions or Testing Your Patience?

Testing Your Patience

"They moved the bloody goalposts again!" This would become the familiar frustrated cry of the second author's boss as the multinational corporation (MNC) continued to remain in the mire of protracted and seemingly directionless negotiations with their elusive and quick-footed business partner to establish a new joint-venture in Vietnam. That was over 10 years ago, and, thankfully, the MNC has become a lot wiser and more experienced in negotiating with the Vietnamese today. The multinational in question now has an incredibly successful and profitable business in Vietnam.

On hindsight, there had been no company training and development to prepare the team for those negotiations. They got there eventually through a combination of perseverance, humility, learning from mistakes, flexible leadership, and, admittedly, elements of good luck. Indeed, along the way, they paid heavy tuition fees for such lessons.

Today, similar stories about the deep-rooted frustrations faced by international companies doing business in Asia are heard and told everywhere. It is interesting to note how few companies seem to place any significant investment in preparing their leadership teams for such eventualities. In difficult negotiations, the risks are that the strategy descends into a tactical dogfight, confrontation leads to loss of "face," resources are wasted, and competitors steal an advantage. No matter how these companies attempt to position themselves and articulate their situation, there is enormous weight and trust lying on the shoulders of the leader. It is a "sink or swim" dilemma. You had better pray you have the right leader and an experienced negotiating team. Otherwise, a catastrophe is just waiting to happen.

The Art of Concealment

One of the main weaknesses we often see in Western international companies operating in Asia is their failure to appreciate one ingrained trait in many Asian business negotiations: the long practiced and skilled art of indirectness and concealment, to the extent that it appears like deception to the uninitiated. The ability to mislead an adversary has always been practiced in war, as expounded by *Sun Zi Bingfa* (孙子兵法). However, it must be seen in the right context. In war, deception is commonly practiced by all armies and advocated by all military strategists—whether from the East or the West. In business, "deceptive practices" are used not so much as deliberate attempts to cheat the other side. Rather, they refer to attempts to mislead or throw the opponent off-guard so as to gain the upper hand and create advantages for oneself. More importantly, it is also used to conceal one's real intention. Of course, if the other side is misled, it is more a failure on their part to comprehend that Asians prefer to use the indirect approach than to be blunt and direct, and that they tend to conceal their real intention rather than make explicit their position. Such practices are viewed as tolerable and acceptable in light of the quest to gain advantages. In the context of relationship-building, such approaches are also viewed as acts of humility. In contrast, Westerners tend to view concealment of information, attempts to mislead the other side, and not being upfront and candid at the beginning more negatively. To them, these are considered to be unfair, almost unethical, practices, which are definitely not in the spirit of good business relationships.

As mentioned earlier, when it comes to warfare, both sides are in agreement that deception is a valid master craft, a decisive skill that has determined the outcome of most wars and battles. Alexander, Hannibal, Sun Zi, and Napoleon were all masters in the art of deception. However, when it comes to business, Western companies tend to frown upon deceptive practices. To Westerners, battles and wars are fought between adversaries, and winning at the expense of the opponent is the ultimate goal. In short, having zero-sum outcomes are to be expected. Business, however, is conducted among partners, customers, and suppliers, where win-win outcomes are sought and mutually beneficial relationships are pursued.

In many parts of Asia, business is regarded more as a battlefield. This tends to create a different mindset. First, Asians tend to think in terms of clear winners and losers, instead of seeking win-win outcomes. Second, when they view the other side as adversaries, they tend to suspect that they have hidden agendas against them, causing them to approach the matter with a highly suspicious stance. Third, and arising from the second point, they tend to have a higher tolerance for the use of "deceptive tactics" as means to fish out the real intention of the other side, and, if necessary, to throw the other side off-guard so as to gain the decisive advantage. When Asians see little difference between competition in the military and the business realm, it is not surprising that they end up embracing more military-like practices in the corporate boardroom, in negotiations, and in conducting their business deals. Here, it is useful to point out that many Asian leaders today have gone back to ancient knowledge gained from the examples of history to seek guidance and wisdom for their day-to day business and political affairs. It is something that Westerners must not be ignorant of.

Moving beyond tactics, stratagems, and strategies, it is interesting to note that the qualities required in a military commander to succeed in war and the qualities needed by an industrial leader to succeed in business are very similar. Both military and industrial leadership require the same characteristic qualities of wisdom, trust, sincerity, integrity, benevolence, courage, and strictness to carry out policies. This, of course, creates another confusing challenge to the Western corporate strategist.

How can Asians talk about trust, integrity, sincerity, and all the other admirable attributes of their leaders and yet seem to condone seemingly deceptive practices? Surely, they contradict all the traditional Asian values, especially the qualities of good leadership. How can these Asians live with such contradictions?

This is actually not an issue if you view such seemingly deceptive practices not as outright attempts to cheat, but rather as shrewd and calculated tactics to gain advantage and to conceal one's intentions as much as possible. While they may seem unacceptable or even unethical in the eyes of Westerners, they are not illegal to the extent of landing one in jail. To be fair, many Westerners also employ similar tactics to gain advantage. For example, one would dress very well to impress his/her date or to impress the interviewers at a job interview. One would even present accounts and numbers in ways to impress the bosses (remember the chapter on double glazing?). In marketing, the creative packaging of products, services, and ideas is designed to gain the added advantage, including getting a higher price. Do we view all these behaviors and actions as deception? Surely not!

Even in the noble realm of sports, which have universal rules, almost every player uses "deceptive" moves and tactics to throw his opponent off-guard. Thus, we have the deceptive pass in football and rugby; the deceptive spin behind the serve in tennis, badminton, and table tennis; the deceptive move in basketball and soccer; the deceptive leap by the front players in a volleyball game; the seemingly wrong move on the chessboard, etc. Are all these considered negatively to be cheating and deceptive, or are they favorably perceived as smart, tactical, and strategic actions to gain advantage?

At the end of the day, we suspect that there exists a moral chasm between the East and the West. While the East has been more fluid and flexible in the way it approaches the matter, the West is still stuck in its own backyard in trying to give a straight and direct interpretation of the subject.

Going Behind the Mask

In general, Asians tend to obscure their plans and intentions. In fact, few chief executive officers (CEOs) of typical Asian companies would share their plans with their managers. Westerners tend to be far more open and clear. Through his body language, a Westerner, untrained in controlling his outward manner, sends off signals of which he is not aware. This exposes more of his thinking than is prudent to the scrutiny of an observant Asian.

As Chin Ning Chu, author of *The Asian Mind Game*, argues eloquently, "If the Westerner does not make an attempt to understand something of the Asian mind, he will find it almost impossible to detect the web of complicated strategies that is woven about him by his Asian counterparts and will fall victim to them."

For example, if someone told you to visit the Củ Chi tunnels outside Ho Chi Minh City, prior to entering negotiations with Vietnamese partners, you may be better equipped to deal with the frustrating situations and difficulties that arise during any complex negotiations. When you visit this enormous labyrinth of underground tunnels and rooms, you will be spellbound by all of its ingenuity and technical design. You will appreciate rather soberly why the Americans could never have won the war, and why Vietnam has never really been defeated militarily. You will also appreciate how the Chinese, the French, and the Japanese lost their way in Vietnam too. More importantly, when you transfer the Củ Chi tunnels to a business context, you will realize how determined, patient, and skillful your Vietnamese partners can be when it comes to negotiating and working with foreign investors. Just as military hardware cannot overcome the commitment and passion of a people united in their struggle, international "expertise," deep investment pockets, and impressive Power-Point presentations cannot overcome the resourcefulness, resilience, and shrewdness of the Vietnamese business partner.

Many of us working in Asia suffer from so many "if only I had" regrets, which, in hindsight, could have accelerated and shortened negotiations with Asian partners: mistakes that were made, opportunities lost, messages misinterpreted, and emotions unleashed. All of these could have been avoided if a company had spent more time and effort in preparing their managers for "business battles."

Here are some suggestions for dealing with the art of "deception" in Asia:

1. Acknowledge first how Asians view the marketplace as a battlefield. They are in it to win. Your views of a win-win scenario may be too optimistic upfront as they tend to view the outcome as a win-lose situation. As such, they would prefer a "we win, you lose" scenario. Your job is to convince them that it is possible to have a win-win outcome.[1]

2. Get into the mind of your partners and management team. Understand the individual motivations and team interaction.

3. Invest time and resources in non-business activities: dinners, karaoke, golf, overseas trips, etc., with your partners. These are not only icebreaking activities, they also help to build bonds and relationships. Often, the best advice is received outside the negotiating room through the same individuals, but on their own turf and in a safe environment.

4. Do not overstate cultural differences as the cause of differences in a particular situation or for the lack of a breakthrough in a negotiation. You could have been over-sensitive and missed the opportunity to find the common meeting point.

5. Do not issue ultimatums. They seldom work on Asians as yielding to them would cause a severe loss of "face." Do not lose your temper and have a tantrum. It is totally unnecessary and gives away too much to your opponent.

6. Do not be overly open and trustworthy until you have won the other side over decisively. Too much candid information upfront can cause you to be vulnerable.

7. Persevere and enjoy the process. It would be a miracle for any Western company to seal a deal on the very first trip. Always prepare for the long haul. Do not give in easily. Negotiations can be a long, grinding process, and persistence and patience are absolutely essential. This is a battle of minds; both sides will come to appreciate and respect each other through the process.

8. Balance your management team with the right resources. For example, you need a determined but flexible leader, a quiet yet analytical No. 2, and an amiable and emotionally intelligent No. 3. Divide the responsibilities among yourselves and help each other to do the checks and balances. Most importantly, never change the team during the negotiation of a contract or business deal.[2]

9. Take time to check and verify subtly. Do not take in everything mentioned by the other side. You need to know if the facts are indeed true and verifiable. This is where the messenger (*see* Chapter 4) can be used effectively.

10. Walk away if necessary. If all efforts have been made to seal the relationship but to no avail, it is only prudent to walk away from it and look for a new partner in due course. It is better to suffer the immediate loss than to carry on with persistent pains and heartaches in managing the relationship.[3]

There is a very interesting Chinese saying on business partnership that captures the kind of relationship that you want to avoid in Asia. This saying, which was also cited by Chin Ning Chu in her book, goes as follows:

同 床 异 梦
tong chuang yi meng

Sharing the same bed but having different dreams.

Thus, you can be partners in bed but, in reality, have different agendas and motives. Such a relationship will inevitably end in divorce. Regretfully, many Western companies find out that they are in bed with the wrong partners too late in the game, and have to incur severe costs and inconveniences in breaking up the partnership.

Same Lens, Different Pictures

As mentioned earlier, it is interesting to know the difference in which "deception" is perceived by Westerners and Asians. This difference can be attributed to the various influences at work. For example, other than the philosophy of Sun Zi, which has wielded great influence on the mindset of the Chinese strategist, there are other Chinese classics that exert much influence too. For example, another Chinese classic, called the "36 Stratagems (三十六计 *san shi liu ji*),"[4] also contains many military tactics that focus on the use of indirect approaches, concealment of motives and intentions, and deception.[5] While the 36 Stratagems are about military tactics, they have been commonly applied to the world of business by Asians. Again, they have gained acceptance largely because they allow the Asian strategist to develop tactics and strategies that generate advantages to him.

We can dissect the art of deception into three components:

1. Security. Ensure that your competitor does not know too much about your organization, especially your strategies and future plans. Without doubt, there is a need to protect key information and secrets from being leaked to your competitors. Security is needed to ensure that the company is not vulnerable to exploitation by the competitors.

2. Intelligence. Find out as much as possible about your competitor(s) through whatever means possible, so long as they are legally and morally acceptable. Of course, there are always the occasional culprits who breach the legal and moral markers when attempting to collect information on their competitors.

3. Misinformation. This is done to proactively spread false leads and inaccurate stories to confuse and disorientate the competitor(s) and, at times, the market. This is where market rumors and gossip come in.

Note that all three components of deception are also practiced by Westerners, although in various degrees and intensity. In particular, the misinformation component may be frowned upon much more by the West.

A common deceptive practice used by Asians is weakening the resources of the other party. We know of several companies that have fallen victim to this. One MNC wanted to break into the Chinese market by proposing a multimillion dollar manufacturing joint-venture investment. Given the sensitivity of the industry, government approval was required at the highest level in Beijing. The company made one major mistake from the outset by using an intermediary as the consultant/agent between the Chinese government and themselves. In this case, it was the bad use of a messenger. By appointing a go-between with unclear accountability, the MNC had immediately placed itself at the mercy and discretion of the consultant.

Not surprisingly, the consultant insisted that all communication between the multinational and the Chinese government pass solely through him to preserve secrecy and avoid mixed messages. This was immediately agreed to. However, some of the senior Chinese managers working for the MNC started picking up signals within their own networks that all was not well. When they started to raise eyebrows internally about how the project was being managed by the consultant, the consultant reacted immediately. Stories were created about the trustworthiness and integrity of these senior Chinese managers. It was suggested that the joint-venture process was being delayed because the Chinese government partners felt uncomfortable with the Chinese senior managers in the MNC. As the joint-venture was viewed as a highly prized and desired investment, the MNC fell into the trap without doing any investigations into the accusations and concerns raised. It removed the experienced Chinese managers from its team, one by one. All that remained was a non-Chinese speaking group of Caucasian managers, who became even more dependant on the information given by the consultant. The attempted joint-venture never happened. The project became impossible because of the limited face-to-face communication between both parties and the impatience of the MNC. Relations with the Chinese government were severely dented, and will take many years to recover. The multinational also lost some of its best Chinese managers in the process. The consultant lost nothing. Instead, he earned exorbitant fees.

The strategy used by the Chinese consultant can be explained using a combination of the following stratagems/ tactics from the 36 Stratagems:

1. A dagger sheathed in a smile (笑里藏刀 *xiao li cang dao*): Clearly, the consultant must have won over the MNC at the beginning by convincing it that his services were much needed. Behind that "smile" was actually his own personal agenda—going for the big consulting fee.

2. Remove the ladder after the enemy has ascended to the roof (上屋抽梯 *shang wu chou ti*): Once the MNC was lured by the consultant into thinking that he was the best person to complete the task, the ladder was effectively removed, and there was no way for the MNC to come down from the roof.

3. Creating something out of nothing (无中生有 *wu zhong sheng you*): When the Chinese senior managers became suspicious, the consultant plotted to get rid of them. He did this by creating unfounded stories that were damaging to the Chinese senior managers of the MNC—that the Chinese government partners were not comfortable with their presence.

4. Killing with a borrowed knife (借刀杀人 *jie dao sha ren*): On his own, the consultant could never get rid of the Chinese senior managers of the MNC. So he had to do it through someone else. He used the Chinese government partners as the "borrowed knife," or pretext to pressurize the MNC into eliminating its own key Chinese senior managers. The MNC fell for the ploy. In turn, it became the borrowed knife used by the consultant to remove its own crucial employees.

5. Pulling out the firewood from beneath the cauldron (釜底抽薪 *fu di chou xin*): When the Chinese

senior managers were removed from the MNC, the consultant had effectively pulled out the "firewood" (crucial managers) from beneath the "cauldron" (MNC), hence denying it the necessary support to see through his ploy.

6. Deceiving the heavens to cross the sea (瞒天过海 *man tian guo hai*): With the Chinese senior managers gone from the MNC, it was literally crippled, and had to rely 100 percent on the consultant and believe everything he said/interpreted, etc. There was no way to tell the real from the fake, the substance from the froth …

7. Looting a house on fire (趁火打劫 *chen huo da jie*): At the end, being the only person left who was capable of handling the negotiations regardless of its outcome, the consultant was able to charge exorbitant fees, which was tantamount to looting the MNC in that helpless (on fire) situation.

From the above episode and explanation, we hope precious lessons can be learned. In Asia, you are dealing with a civilization of people whose cultures, traditions, and norms date back a few thousand years. Their minds and approaches to doing things are often more sophisticated than you can imagine.

Different Approaches Needed

Achieving business deals in Asia requires a different approach than in other parts of the world. It is important that the Westerner understands a few key pointers, which will better prepare him. The following are some useful rules that can be of help:

Rule 1: Spend time on the "who and how" upfront with your prospective business partner. Think carefully about who should be on your team to match their members, not only in terms of background and experience, but also credentials and job titles.

Westerners often like to "get down to business," supplying a list of negotiating items. They like to go through the agenda in a clinical and logical way. To them, time is money, hence the faster the deal is wrapped up, the better it is. Westerners normally build transactions, and, if they are successful, a relationship will ensue. Asian cultures depend on the establishment of a trusting relationship to prepare the mutual framework for a partnership. If successful, commercial transactions will follow. This difference underlies many misunderstandings that arise from business negotiations. Virtually all successful transactions in Asia result from the careful cultivation of Asian partners by the foreign investor, until a relationship of trust evolves. They like to spend time getting to know you, and socializing will form a big part of this process, which unfortunately will take more time and effort.

Westerners focus on action items and the content of the contract at hand. Asians focus on who is involved and the manner in which they will work together. They like to size up your seriousness about the relationship by studying who you have placed in the team and whether they are people who are easy to get along with. When you send junior and inexperienced members, they feel insulted and think that you look down on them.

Rule 2: Don't disclose your timetable and more than necessary information.

It is also important not to express too much urgency. Patience and control of time are critical. Many Westerners have a strong sense of urgency while Asians are less hurried, seeing today as merely a brief moment in a history that goes back thousands of years. A friend reported a comment from a senior Chinese official in response to why it was taking so long for a particular project to be approved. He replied, "It has taken a thousand years for China to catch up again with Western civilization, so what's the hurry? We can be patient!"

One critical mistake Westerners may make is to reveal their own company's negotiation deadline. Western business visitors are often deadline-driven and unwilling to adjust to the Asian pace when discussing business. It is an easy error to make, especially as most Western companies are impatient, and their senior leaders have internal expectations to manage. Those involved in negotiations know how long they can drag on when the Asian side is consulting internally or has other reasons for delay. Often, an imminent visit by the company's chairman or CEO is used to secure an accelerated plan of action, but this more than often backfires as it plays into the hands of the Asian company. Asians realize that foreigners who have traveled all the way to Asia will be reluctant to travel home empty-handed. They have learned that exerting pressure on foreigners just before they fly home can often create useful benefits for them. They will agree to all the easy issues, leaving the most difficult one to the end, pressurizing the Western company to concede rather than let its chairman or CEO return empty-handed to his headquarters. Asian negotiators use time more consciously than their Western counterparts. They are also shrewd and use a wide variety of bargaining tactics. The message is to build in plenty of time and remain quiet about internal operating deadlines.

Rule 3: Appoint a clear leader and decision-maker in your team. Establish ground rules on confidentiality.

Often, Western companies have more democratic and open cultures, which leave them vulnerable when negotiating in Asia. Asians are more hierarchical in orientation and therefore maintain an inherent discipline that gives them an advantage. The main requirement in maintaining discipline is to speak with one voice, never revealing disagreements among team members. You can always resolve such differences in private. It is easier for Asians to identify disagreements among members in the Western negotiating team or its superiors. This becomes even more dangerous for the Western team when they "let down their guard" in social situations with their Asian counterparts, particularly over drinks or dinner in the evening. They can easily be blindsided when talks turn once again to the day's business discussion. This creates the risk of disclosing additional information or, even worse, giving away important concessions.

Rule 4: Prepare well for negotiations. Show willingness for flexibility on certain points while being firm on critical areas. Never walk away or show impatience and temper.

Often, Asians will circumvent authority without defying it. Rules will be bent or adapted to ensure they are not being broken. Westerners often find out the hard way that Asians will take the same attitude toward contracts and agreements.

As far as negotiating in China is concerned, in order to protect against ongoing pressure to make concessions, it is critical to know the bottom-line position for each element of the deal before negotiation starts. Often a Western negotiating team will first decide its best-case position, determine a walk-away position, and then structure a set of concessions that lies between the two. However, this will often backfire in China because the Chinese team will see the first price as meaningless. A more useful approach is to view patterns of events as circular instead of linear, be flexible in all areas of negotiation, and avoid wrangling solely over price. Deflecting the request for a price concession makes it clear that price is not negotiable, but other components of the deal may be. In other words, it is important to maintain a flexible negotiating position, which has clear boundaries on certain points but can be shifted to concede on other points. For example, if the deal concerns the sale of certain expensive machinery, it may be easier to offer concessions on installation and maintenance costs or even credit terms as a way to deflect hard-nosed price negotiations.

Asian negotiators are patient and can stretch out discussions almost forever in order to wear their interlocutors down and extract concessions. Even excessive hospitality in the evenings can be a means of achieving these, so be on your guard. Remember to never lose your cool despite protracted and difficult negotiations. To the Asians, this may be interpreted as arrogance and a loss of respect for them. Despite the Confucian aversion to displays of anger, the Asian group may also put on a display of calculated anger to put pressure on the foreign party, who may be afraid of losing the deal. Try not to be intimidated by this nor react with anger. If necessary, have cooling-off periods or pre-planned time-outs throughout the negotiations.

If you walk away from the deal, you may not get another one, including those from their business associates. It is always better to let them be the initiator to walk away the deal. This is because "face" is very important to them.

Rule 5: Prepare yourself and your senior management for post-contract negotiations. View this as an opportunity to establish closer relations with your partner and not as a destabilizing threat.

Finally, Westerners must be prepared for post-contract surprises, including additional requests and renegotiation. In the West, we assume that once a contract is signed, the ink dried, and hands shaken, it is a clear and binding agreement. To a Westerner, it all seems straightforward: we start with a standard contract, change it to fit the different circumstances of the negotiations, and sign the final version. Law and logic are entrenched in our thinking. This is not the case with Asians. As Ernest Gundling, author of *Working GlobeSmart*, says, "For the Chinese, the contract is thus secondary in importance to relationships...this means that when unexpected problems arise after the contract is signed, as they inevitably will, the Chinese naturally look to the flexibility of the new relationship they have established to solve them." Obligations come from relationships, not pieces of paper. For Asians, a signed piece of paper is purely a sign of progress or evidence that both parties are beginning to trust each other. A contract may even be signed simply to appease Western needs, to make the foreigners feel better. However, it is just a moment in time; nothing is permanent. As a friend described it, a contract for Asians is just a snapshot of a set of agreements that took place sometime. Asians will reopen closed issues. Flexibility is required as in any relationship, hence concessions on the agreement are often requested.

This can be a very difficult prospect for Westerners to accept, partly because they have already pre-sold the deal to their superiors. They may have already shaved their margins down to the bone. Any change will not only upset their senior management, but also create a double take. They suddenly wonder if this is a partner they can trust, especially when the agreement seems to be up for renegotiation shortly after it has been concluded. It is very easy to become exasperated: refusals with no apparent reason, contradictory statements, illogical counterproposals, and impossible conclusions. It creates an extremely difficult, confusing, and uncomfortable situation for a Westerner. Asians, however, feel that they are not acting in bad faith. Rather, sealing the contract is part of an evolutionary process to build a better partnership and relationship for more things to come.

Rule 6: Learn to play the "Asian" game yourself to your own advantage.

The smarter Western companies will be very well-prepared for negotiations and will have foreseen most eventualities and situations as outlined above. However, they can also learn to use Asian tactics against the Asian negotiators. Here are some key points to consider.

Make sure that you have one member in your team who understands in absolute detail the key elements of the business deal. If necessary, demonstrate this understanding and attention to detail by making long, mundane speeches and presentations without giving much away. Talk over the entire contract with the Asian side. Be sure that your interpretations are consistent and that everyone understands his duties and obligations. This has a number of benefits. First, it shows you have a clear grasp of the details of the business deal. It is not rushed. Second, it allows you to play the game of attrition on them. Last, it removes the vulnerable risk of you being perceived to be under time pressure.

Take as much time as you want. Be patient. Be willing to cut your losses and go home if the going gets too tough, and the deal becomes extremely unattractive. It is all right to let them know that failure to reach a suitable agreement is an acceptable alternative to reaching a bad deal. This is honest and establishes trust no matter the outcome.

Finally, it is not always bad not to have all the details finalized in the agreement. It also creates greater flexibility for the Westerner. By having an "Asian" contract, it also allows the Westerner to go back and renegotiate elements of the business deal at a later stage. Because Asians accept emotion, trust, and obligation as part of business, they can also be manipulated.

Wider Lens, Bigger Pictures

All of this can be uncomfortable, but, with time and experience, it can become more normal. It is simply that we have been trained since birth to look through a pair of glasses prescribed by Western logic. When it comes to Asia, you need your optician to expand the periphery vision of your glasses to enable you to look beyond the immediate to identify the events happening behind the scene or out of sight.

For example, the first reaction of any foreigner starting work in Indonesia will be that the place is in chaos and that the country is almost ungovernable, given its size and scale. The more experienced will tell you, however, that this is not quite the case. In fact, behind the façade of chaos,

Indonesia is actually a fairly well-organized country. What you witness is similar to shadow puppetry, or *wayang kulit* in the local language. The actions that drive what you see actually happen behind the screen, not in front. The Westerner typically makes this mistake by seeing only the front, and does not go deeper to find out what goes on behind. Hence, he is often deluded into complacency.

Often, appearances in business in Asia do not resemble reality. Many of the real relationships are invisible to the outsider. One of the hardest challenges faced by any Western company not only in China, but also in much of Southeast Asia, is learning how to navigate through the complex web of relationships to get a deal concluded. Not only is the actual approval system very opaque, it is also frequently interfered with and distorted by invisible parties, ultimately leaving the Western company disorientated and extremely frustrated. We often hear Western business leaders commenting that they no longer know who or what to believe to the point that delays in getting the deal have irreparably damaged their personal credibility within the companies they work for.

The hierarchical and feudalistic social systems still dominate China and many developing Southeast Asian countries. *Guanxi* (关系) creates power and knowledge.[6] Most people have learned the art to survive and be successful in this complex web of relationships and power play. What you see in public is far from what is reality in private. The back-patting, smiles, and jokes at a public business event are intended to show the other party and the rest of the audience that the relationship is warm and close. The reality could be very different. The true relationships may or may not be demonstrated in public. Even if you manage to establish that there is a relationship from what you see, you still may not be able to figure out the extent, intensity, and intimacy of that relationship. All of these are typically managed behind closed doors.

This is similar to the society of medieval Europe, as outlined by Italian political commentator Francesco Guicciardini in 1532.

> *"Nobody knows his servants as badly as their master; nobody knows his subjects as badly as their ruler, because they do not show themselves as they do to others; they always strive to disguise themselves and to seem different from what they truly are. Deceit is the more fruitful and successful the more you enjoy the reputation of an honest and truthful man: you are more easily believed."*

The naïve Western investor is often deluded into feeling that he already enjoys a privileged relationship. He can be easily led on and become overconfident, even to the point of arrogance. He starts to assume that his Asian partners are weak, and it will only be a matter of time before the relationship moves more to his advantage. This is the biggest danger sign for any foreign investor.

How then should a Western company, or even an Asian company, weave its way through this labyrinth of appearances and hidden truths? There are no easy answers. However, we shall explore this subject in greater detail in Chapter 12 on *guanxi* (关系).

Endnotes

1. To be fair, many Asian businessmen are beginning to realize that it is possible to have a win-win outcome in business dealings. However, they need to be convinced by actions, not just sweet talk.

2. In extenuating circumstances, you may change one or two members of the team. However, try to avoid this as much as possible as it can work against you. The other side may use this as an excuse to stall or revisit terms already agreed on.

3. This is like the Chinese saying, 长痛不如短痛 (*chang tong bu ru duan tong*), which means that it is better to feel the pain in the short term than to suffer in the long term.

4. It is important to point out that some scholars and writers have used the word "stratagems" instead of "strategies." While it is true that the 36 Stratagems are a collection of military tactics (the only exception is Stratagem 35, "A Series of Interconnected Ploys" (连环计 *lian huan ji*)), they are not intended to be used individually. In fact, no strategist would use each one of them singly. Instead, each tactic is always combined with several others to form a strategy.

5. Readers who are interested in exploring more on this subject can refer to Wee, C.H. and L.L. Lan, *The 36 Strategies of the Chinese: Adapting Ancient Chinese Wisdom to the Business World*. Singapore: Addison-Wesley Longman, 1998.

6. This subject will be discussed in detail in Chapter 12. A general but not complete translation of this would be contacts and relationships that are personal to the holder.

将 不 可 以 愠 而 致 战；

jiang bu ke yi yun er zhi zhan

合 于 利 而 动，不 合 于 利 而 止。

he yu li er dong bu he yu li er zhi

A general must not go into battle out of rage. Move when there are advantages to be gained. Cease when there are no advantages to be benefited.

> (Sun Zi Bingfa, 孙子兵法, *Lines 12.35 to 12.37 of Chapter 12 on Attacking with Fire, 火攻 (huo gong)*)

怒 可 以 复 喜，愠 可 以 复 悦；

nu ke yi fu xi yun ke yi fu yue

Anger can return to happiness again. Rage can return to joy again.

> (Sun Zi Bingfa, 孙子兵法, *Lines 12.38 and 12.39 of Chapter 12 on Attacking with Fire, 火攻 (huo gong)*)

亡 国 不 可 以 复 存，

wang guo bu ke yi fu cun

死 者 不 可 以 复 生。

si zhe bu ke yi fu sheng

A destroyed nation cannot be reinstated. A dead person cannot be resurrected.

> (Sun Zi Bingfa, 孙子兵法, *Lines 12.40 and 12.41 of Chapter 12 on Attacking with Fire, 火攻 (huo gong)*)

CHAPTER 6

Forgiven But Not Forgotten

Less Scope for Mistakes

Mistakes Can Be Expensive

It is astounding how much bad history or a bitter experience with Westerners restricts progress for Asian companies and, equally, how easily bad manners or arrogance on the part of Western companies can destroy Asian relationships. There are many real-life examples of such situations, where Asian companies harbor resentment toward their Western counterparts for mistakes made. At times, such resentment can linger on for many years. At other times, it can lead to a boycott of foreign investments and products. In severe cases, diplomatic ties could even be severed. Such bad past experiences mean that Western companies doing business in Asia have to make that extra effort in order to win over the Asians.

Some of the basic mistakes made by these Western companies could be attributed to certain individuals who clearly did not understand the impact of their behavior on their Asian counterparts. They had, by their bad behavior and attitudes, unwittingly condemned themselves and, by association, their companies to a superficial and mediocre business relationship with their Asian counterparts. More seriously, when such mistakes are repeated time and again, it also reflects poorly on the companies that sent them. Obviously, they have either picked the wrong candidates or have not done enough to prepare them for such overseas postings.

Different Perspectives on Mistakes and Forgiveness

It is interesting to note that the East (Asian) and the West have very different perspectives on mistakes and forgiveness. It is precisely because of such different positions that much misunderstanding and adverse reactions often arise as outlined earlier.

The Western Perspective

In Western society, the concept of forgiveness is modeled on Protestant ethics and values. Two stories in the Bible—the prodigal son and the lost sheep—illustrate the Western perspective on forgiveness very well.[1,2] The assumption is that human nature is prone to make mistakes. Instead of condemning the person, one should be quick to forgive and give him a second or third chance. This is because he can be reformed, and should be given a new and fresh start. More importantly, the focus is on that individual— that lost son or sheep—and not on the whole group.

Building on such beliefs, it also means that mistakes and failures are viewed differently. They allow you to learn from the experience, and you will emerge stronger and wiser. Hence, forgiveness becomes crucial and critical for the reformation process to begin and for the person to develop himself. If the person who fails is condemned and not forgiven, he will never be able to learn from his experience and be a better person.

Not surprisingly, when it comes to doing business, failures in the typical Western society are never held against the person. They are viewed positively. In fact, banks are more willing to lend money to entrepreneurs who have failed before and are willing to try again. The view is that after each failure, the chances for his success in the next venture have to be higher and not lower. If anything, his reliability has increased, not decreased. After all, no one would like to fail every time. On the other hand, everyone would like to be a success, to make it big, and make as much money as possible. In sum, the typical stance is one of forgiveness, magnanimity, and encouragement to the one who has failed.

The Asian Perspective

It may come as a surprise to many Westerners as to how the typical Asian views failures and mistakes. To begin with, one can attempt to present the case of the prodigal son to an Asian businessman to ask for his response as to what he would have done. "I will disown him forever" is the answer that you will likely get. Ask him again on what he would do with regard to the one lost sheep among the 100. "I will forgo it and concentrate on the 99" will be the typical answer. Now, is the Asian response too harsh and unforgiving, or is there something more behind those answers?

In Asia, the concept of forgiveness tends to be less generous, particularly with regard to serious mistakes. Once a major mistake has been made, it is difficult to go back. Failure is generally viewed as incompetence and, at times, as a betrayal of trust as well. There is seldom a second chance. As the trust has been broken, the relationship is severely damaged too.

Take the case of the prodigal son. He was given his due inheritance, half of his father's wealth. The father trusted him to make good with the inheritance, and he had all the opportunities. Instead of investing and using the money in meaningful ways, he squandered it away. How could he then be forgiven so easily, especially when he must have hurt the feelings of his father deeply? Even if his father chose to forgive him, others around him might not have been as forgiving.

To the typical Asian, the prodigal son has had his bite, and it was a very big share of the pie. As such, the others should be given a chance too. In fact, in that biblical story, he had a good brother who stayed and toiled for their father throughout. In addition, there is the question of "face" (discussed in Chapter 11) if the father was an Asian. He has already lost much "face" in having to part with half of his wealth, and he lost even more "face" with a failing son. It reflected his poor judgment of his own son. Not surprisingly, as the trust was broken, the viable option to salvage some of the lost "face" would be to disown the son and sever the relationship.

In the case of the lost sheep, as a result of not following the orders of the shepherd and the behavior of the group, a lot of resources would have to be expended to find it. Even when the lost sheep is found, there is no guarantee that it will not stray from the group again. It makes more sense for the shepherd to focus his attention and resources on the 99 obedient sheep rather than the wayward one. Moreover, while the shepherd goes in search of the one lost sheep, the remaining 99 are left unattended and could be subjected to attacks by wild animals. The shepherd's life may be in jeopardy too when he ventures too far out to search for the lost sheep.

In the handling of serious failures and mistakes, the Asian is more concerned about the interests of the majority than the individual. He takes a holistic approach in finding solutions, and is also concerned about the feelings of others. This creates a more conservative and prudent approach to problem solving. To him, it is always better to cut losses and bet on the certain returns of what one already has than to take a risk on something that may not enjoy any returns. This explains the inherent risk aversion of Asian culture. It is an easier choice not to take any initiative, not to challenge the status quo, and not to stick your neck out because the consequences of their backfiring can be quite traumatic. Unfortunately, such an attitude can result in paralysis of actions and apathy. The following Chinese saying captures such a stance very well:

多做多错，
duo zuo duo cuo

少做少错，
shao zuo shao cuo

不做不错。
bu zuo bu cuo

When you do more, you make more mistakes.
When you do less, you maker fewer mistakes.
When you do nothing, you can make no mistakes.[3]

The Long Memory Curse: Get It Right from the Start

Not only are Asians less forgiving when compared to Westerners, they have longer memories too—they do not forget easily. This is particularly the case with the Chinese. They are knowledgeable about their history. They remember their past well, especially events in which they were severely handicapped, embarrassed, or humiliated by outsiders.[4] To some extent, the long memory syndrome of the Chinese may be attributed to its 5,000-year history, which trains them to dig hard into the past. More interestingly, it is significant to note that Chinese characters (words) are written in pictorial form and in relational format. Not surprisingly, they help the Chinese to think and remember things better.[5]

The ability to remember events better means that even if your Chinese business partner chooses to forgive you, it does not mean that he has forgotten about the mistakes or misdeeds done to him. Of course, the situation becomes worse if he chooses not to forgive you. What this means is that it is important to get it right at the early stage and avoid making mistakes when you do business in Asia, especially China. Your credibility and reputation need to be established early in the game.

What then needs to be done? Well, in the first place, any Western company serious about doing business in the region needs to ensure that it selects the right manager who has the right experience and emotional intelligence to be a leader in Asia. This Western leader must be trained and needs to understand the cultural impact his words or actions may create on his local partners, officials, employees, customers, etc. If offence has been caused, then words of apology or regret should follow quickly. In Asia, it is considered very virtuous to be the first to apologize in order to smooth over some unpleasantness.

More importantly, the Western manager must establish a strong rapport with everyone he comes into contact with. For example, when dealing with his Asian partners, government officials, customers, and employees, he must encourage them to provide feedback and comments to the Western company as quickly and as honestly as possible. They should not brood in silence. They must also be "educated" to accept and deal with the constant changes in leadership within Western companies and accept that, sometimes, some individuals can make mistakes. However, such mistakes should not be taken against the whole company.

The Silent Response Can Kill

It is never easy to draw out the relatively silent and reserved Asian. As mentioned earlier, to avoid making mistakes, the typical Asian would prefer to remain silent than to risk making his views public. The silent response is dangerous because it can be used to mask many things. For example, when a person chooses to remain silent, does he really have no views? Is he afraid to express them for fear that they may appear stupid or may offend his boss or others around him? Does he choose to remain silent so as not to show his real talents and let others steal his ideas? Is he upset by what he has heard and, therefore, chooses to remain quiet? The list of speculative possibilities goes on.

Indeed, it is the silent response that can "kill" the impatient Western manager, and causes him to lose his cool and inadvertently utter some strong words that he may live to regret. At other times, the Westerner may be unaware of how his behavior or words have offended his Asian partner, and a silent response does not allow him to realize what has happened. The only way to discover the Asian's real motive, intention, and answer is to make him speak up. And when he does, it is equally important to find out if he is telling the truth.

How should the Western manager go about breaking the ice? To begin with, most Asians believe in cause-and-effect, that is, events and consequences happen for certain reasons. Therefore, it is important to get to the root of the cause. For example, when an employee chooses to remain silent, is it really a cultural inhibition on his part or because of a bad experience in the past?[6] Asking him directly will not help. In Asia, it is always good to work through informal networks, that is, to probe in a discreet and informal manner through other people within the organization. If you are unable or uncomfortable to do so, use messengers or intermediaries as discussed in Chapter 4.

Socializing is another way to get to know the employees and other people better. By this, we mean joining the locals in activities and events that they are most comfortable with. These may include karaoke sessions, dining out, drinking sessions, etc. The expatriate boss will be pleasantly surprised to know that when Asians feel relaxed in a social setting, the walls of inhibitions come down very quickly, and they begin to talk.

Cultivating Good Business Behavior

Recognizing that Asians are less forgiving of mistakes, and also have good and long memories, it is always a sensible practice to cultivate good business behavior. There are basic manners that the Westerner needs to respect as part of his day-to-day behavior toward Asians. Some of these are courtesies that existed 20 or 30 years ago in the West. Regretfully, owing to changing social values, the pressure of time, and the attempts to seek politically correct responses, these practices have largely vanished. Let us revisit some of these basic manners, which are so important in Asia.

1. Do Not Show Aggression or Displeasure Easily

The typical Western leader is often keen to show his assertiveness and self-confidence. This is particularly true of American leaders. They like to demonstrate the one-upmanship as early and clearly as possible. In Asia, exhibiting such traits can result in severe backlash. Instead, one should not be too pushy about the agenda, nor display aggression to get things done quickly when doing business in Asia, especially during negotiations. Despite your displeasure, public confrontation should be avoided at all costs. Threats and ultimatums should never be used. Asians are not accustomed to such rough tactics. They have high respect for their "guests" and visitors, and they expect to be accorded the same respect and treatment. You should at all times maintain a high level of politeness and courtesy.

2. Show Appreciation

Asians will go far more out of their way to attend to your needs than most Westerners. Often, they will personally meet you at the airport, ensure that your hotel room is comfortable, help you with any cultural issues you do not understand, and take you back to the airport at the end of the visit. Often, their hospitality will overwhelm you. Do not take all of these kind acts for granted. Instead, when you are treated well, you must reciprocate accordingly. Interestingly, when you try to reciprocate, they may put up a front to turn you down.[7]

Such a reaction is largely due to their display of humility. On your part, you must not take it literally. Instead, show your sincerity and earnestness in wanting to reciprocate. At the end of the day, they will be more than pleased with what you have done. This is also the best way to build relationships, or *guanxi*.[8]

3. Be Patient and Flexible

In dealing with Asians, one needs to be patient and understanding. For example, itineraries, meetings, and dinners can be changed frequently with new guests and invitees. The typical Westerner will be very unused to this. However, the host often does this as a way of showing respect to you by inviting local dignitaries, government officials, and important business associates. This is his way of showing you his connections, network, and standing within the local community. It also strengthens his "face" in the local community. Signs of impatience or intolerance will only work against you. You need to go with the flow and smile as much as possible.

Similarly, in securing deals, do not expect contracts to be signed at the first negotiation. As you move along the negotiation, there will be requests for changes to the terms of the contract, although it already has been vetted by both sides. Even after the contract is signed, do not be surprised that there will be additional requests to change the terms again.

4. Do Not Take Advantage

As mentioned earlier, the typical Asian is not as assertive, articulate, and demanding as the Westerner. Never take advantage of the other side just because he has a quiet nature, appears to be very compliant, and has a poor command of the English language. Asians are very perceptive, and they can read your tone, mannerisms, and body language easily. They are already skeptical about your intention in coming to Asia. In other words, they implicitly think that you are in Asia to take advantage of the situation. Hence, any negative moves on your part can only reinforce such a perception. In addition, Asians, like the Chinese, have a long memory. They will not forget your good deeds, neither will they forget your bad deeds.

The following Chinese saying about the conduct of business is very telling:

商 场 如 战 场

shang chang ru zhan chang

The business world is like a battleground.

In war, the outcome tends to that of a zero-sum gain. Any gains on your part have to come at the expense of the other side. The challenge, therefore, is to create win-win outcomes and to assure your Asian partner that he stands to win in the partnership too.

5. Show Concern Beyond Business Matters

The impersonal Westerner likes to zoom in on business matters, and stay focused on them throughout. On the other hand, socializing and relationship-building is very much an integral part of doing business in Asia. As such, other than caring for the business itself, you should also show interest in and concern about the person with whom you are doing business. This includes knowing his likes and dislikes, his hobbies, etc.[9] Often, this also extends to knowing his family members, relatives, and friends. When meeting them, be polite and courteous, and also show interest in what they do. It is important to leave them with a good impression. This is because when you leave the gathering, they will typically talk about you and your behavior.

6. *Handling Business Cards*

Good business conduct at any meeting typically begins with the exchange of business cards. It is a simple act, but one that can be embedded with much symbolism and meaning in Asia. It is good practice to present your business card with two hands. It shows respect to the person. When a card is presented to you, accept it with both hands and take a few moments to read it. This applies to all levels of appointments, from the chairman to the assistant manager. You may even want to ask a question about the person's title or the company itself. It demonstrates consideration and respect on your part. Moreover, it helps you to clarify the level of importance of that job title, and its level of influence within the company. At times, it also serves as a natural icebreaker and can go a long way in building a rapport with everyone.

In some countries like China, it is important to have your name and job title translated into the local language. In addition, if the person has other responsibilities, it is important to list them down. This will allow the local host to accord you the appropriate protocol. When in doubt, it is always better to list more than fewer titles.

7. *Gift-giving*

Despite its potential abuses in the business world, gift-giving is a common practice in Asia. It is the custom of Asians to bring something for the host when meeting someone for the first time, visiting the home of a friend, etc. In fact, Asians will find every conceivable occasion to present gifts to one another.

When presenting a gift, it is important to bear a few points in mind. First, consider what the receiver likes, and not what is convenient for you to buy. It is better if you have spent some time choosing an appropriate gift for the person you are giving it to.[10] It demonstrates that your knowledge of the person extends beyond the business itself, and that you acknowledge his interests, hobbies, or indulgences. In fact, it is not uncommon for a person in Asia to spend a considerable amount of time and effort in gift hunting.

Second, put some effort in wrapping the gift. The final touches show your attention to detail and how much you treasure the relationship. A very well-wrapped gift also catches the eyes of the other people present, and the quality and intricacies of the wrapping can also demonstrate the value of the gift. More importantly, the receiver typically does not unwrap the gift in public, doing so only in the privacy of his room after the guests leave. Some even keep a record of the gifts received, and yes, including the names of the givers. Such records become important to him when he has to reciprocate the giving one day.

Third, the value of a gift must maintain some relationship to the value of the business relationship. It is important to get the balance right. While it is true that the focus should be on the intention rather than the value, the gift also symbolizes the importance that you attach to that relationship. At times, it is also an indirect way of saying thank you for all the support that you have received from that person. Good examples can be found during festive occasions. Companies will spare no effort in thanking their important customers with high-value gift hampers.

Finally, gifts and presents that are received, especially at the personal level, must be reciprocated accordingly. This is part-and-parcel of relationship-building and the bonding between parties. One should never take any relationship for granted.

Leveraging Local Partners to Avoid Mistakes

Other than cultivating and maintaining good business etiquette, another important way to ensure that one does not make serious mistakes (and risk not being forgiven) when doing business in Asia is to select the right local partner. Selecting the right partner is probably the most essential ingredient in ensuring a long-lasting relationship that can weather difficult storms and build competitive advantage. However, it can often start with seemingly polar opposites.

In 2005, when Philip Morris International, the world's largest cigarette manufacturer, acquired PT HM Sampoerna Tbk, the third largest *kretek* manufacturer in Indonesia, for US$5.2 billion, it was the largest ever foreign direct investment (FDI) in the country. All the critics, cynics, and skeptics were out in full force. To them, it was an impossible business marriage that was destined to fail. Arising from this episode, the expression "Big Mac vs Nasi Goreng" was coined to depict how outsiders viewed the extreme cultural integration challenges the new company would face in Indonesia. In reality, the new company surpassed everyone's expectations and has grown in market share and profitability since the acquisition. The reason—the local partner was the right choice for Philip Morris International. It ensured the success of the acquisition from day one.

Of course, everyone wishes that every merger and acquisition will have the same success story to tell as Philip Morris. Unfortunately, more often than not, a poor choice of partner or ally leads to clear failure. What then are some of the steps that one can take to ensure that one chooses the right partner?

Proprietary Interest in the Business

It is clearly an advantage if your local partners have proprietary interest in the business venture. By having some equity stake, not only do they have the necessary business clout and local networking, they will also want to demonstrate success to the local community. If they are listed companies, this is even better as they are also answerable to their shareholders. Regardless of what shareholding they may have in the business, it is important to treat them as equals in the long-term relationship. Do not abuse your dominant shareholding or management control to undermine the relationship you have. Without proper consultation and advice from your partners, it is easy to make business or relationship mistakes. Such mistakes will come back to haunt you. Not only will damage be created externally, it will more often than not embarrass your partners. They will lose "face" in front of the local community. This can cause irreparable problems in the relationship.

Support Equal Partnership Openly

Even when the local partner is the minority shareholder, it is important to treat him as an equal in all business dealings and public occasions. By this, we mean according him the respect as if he is an equal partner of the company. By publicly supporting an equal relationship, you are acknowledging that you want to work closely with him. When he knows that he is being respected, he will be grateful to you for the protocol accorded. In all probability, he will work even harder to ensure the success of the partnership.

With a good start, chemistry will be built over time whereby each partner learns to recognize his respective strengths and skill sets. When a partnership is respected as sacred, then there should be no breakdowns. If breakdowns occur, then both parties are to be blamed, because it is the responsibility of one party to convince the other in a diplomatic way that the other is ruining the relationship.

Of course, it takes two to tango. The building of a relationship cannot be delegated or subcontracted. It cannot rely on subordinates. It has to be undertaken by the two key people. There is no way to shorten the "courting process" or bypass it. Time will be needed to cultivate it, and it will be tested through different experiences. Personal ties and relationships cannot be replaced entirely by systems and procedures. They cannot replace the warmth of handshakes and smiles, and the feelings and emotions that are accumulated through close interaction and socializing.[11]

Duo-Leadership and Symbiotic Relationship

Internal and External Leaders

Another way to avoid making mistakes and having to ask for forgiveness is to consider using duo-leadership, especially one that can create a symbiotic relationship between the partners. There are many good examples of situations where companies actually have two heads in charge, one a local head (often the partner) for external day-to-day management and one a foreign head for internal management. This creates two faces—one external, one internal. Japanese companies often use this approach. The Japanese director will manage the activities behind the scenes: financial and management reporting, head office politics in Tokyo, and business strategy and supply chain management. The local director will manage the government, local competitors, corporate affairs, and execution of the strategy. The positive aspect of this is that the local employees and customers feel comfortable with a local leader who understands their needs, while the Japanese company feels that it has the management control to ensure good governance, and hence minimize risk.

In appointing two heads, it is very important to ensure that their duties and functions are clearly divided as do Japanese companies. This is to avoid any conflicts and power play between them, and also to avoid putting the loyalty of the rank and file to the test. This complementary, or symbiotic, relationship also ensures that both leaders can contribute clearly to the area that each is best in.[12]

Having a Strong Local Number Two

Some multinationals not only employ an expatriate managing director, but also a local deputy managing director who has long service and experience in the local company. The advantage of this is that, even with frequent changes in the expatriate managing director, there is one constant for the local management and employees—the local deputy managing director. He is the linking pin to any changes at the highest level.

The deputy managing director can also advise the expatriate managing director and act as a temperature gauge of what is happening inside the organization. Furthermore, he can greatly assist in the external corporate affairs with the local government, business groups, suppliers, and customers, all of whom struggle to deal with the change of the managing director every three years. This will ensure that the business relationships that have been painfully built up over the years will not be lost as a result of leadership change.

The often felt resentment in a foreign-owned company is that the foreigners are making too many decisions. This can be avoided through the intervention of the deputy managing director by actively involving local managers in the process. Of course, the·chemistry between the managing director and the deputy managing director is absolutely critical. However, this arrangement generally works as both have to manage different audiences, one internal, the other external. This can be a dream solution for developing markets in Asia.

Minimize the Use of Lawyers

Another point to note is to minimize the use of lawyers, especially in the early stage of business negotiations with local partners, who are naturally suspicious of lawyers. As stated earlier, a written contract among Asians does not have the sanctity that it has in Western business. Among themselves, Asians prefer a vague agreement because it leaves plenty of room for adjustment later if things do not work out well. Although they realize that dealing with a Western lawyer is unavoidable at the final stage of any business deal, they dislike the Western process of laboriously going through the contract line by line. It removes the warmth and spirit of the relationship, the sincerity of the partnership, and converts it into a cold, lifeless piece of paper.

If legal proceedings are not carefully handled, the contract may turn out to be the obituary rather than the birth announcement. There is one thing that is absolutely critical throughout—it must be spelled out clearly to your Asian colleagues that you are in charge, and not the lawyers. Otherwise your role in the relationship with them may become confused and distorted. This is because the Asian way of doing business tends to start with relationships (feelings and emotions), followed by logic (reasoning), and finally legality (contracts). To Asians, the legality route should be avoided to the extent possible. In contrast, the Western approach begins with legality, followed by logic, before relationships come in.[13] Hence, when you bring along very assertive and pushy lawyers, they can ruin the relationship without you even realizing it. You will then end up being the one who is not forgiven nor forgotten by the other side.

Integrating Both Cultures for Success

The ideal way of doing business in Asia is when a company is able to integrate the best of cultures from both sides. In this way, not only will you be welcome, you will also avoid making mistakes. An excellent example of this is the Astra Group, which is the leading automaker in Indonesia in cooperation with Toyota. From the very outset, the company incorporated both Indonesian and Japanese cultural influences by having duo-leadership. As far back as 1975, the original founder, William Soeryadjaya, helped to define the corporate culture, which is based on four principles:

1. To be an asset to the nation
2. To provide the best service to our customers
3. To respect the individual and develop teamwork
4. To continually strive for excellence

The first principle shows the order of importance that both partners felt toward Indonesia. There is no mention of shareholders, being part of a global company, or growing profitability. It recognizes the importance of relationships with the government, the contribution to the local society, and the desire to be a source of national pride and admiration—to be an asset to Indonesia.

Note that this is followed by the second principle, which focuses on the customers. Again, the shareholders and management do not come into the picture. Instead, it is about serving the constituents as the customers are the ones who actually ensure the survivability of the company. To put it blatantly, they are the ones who pay the salaries and bonuses of Astra's employees, and ensure that the shareholders get their returns of investment.

The third principle highlights the focus on the employees of the company and reflects the family values of Japanese culture. At the end of the day, the company is as good as its employees in helping to market its products and ensure that it remains competitive. Note that the focus is on respecting the individual as a fellow human being and recognizes teamwork is essential for success.

While ownership of the Astra Group has changed hands many times since 1975, the corporate culture has remained largely the same. This has arguably been the biggest contributing factor to the company's success. The Japanese learned much earlier than the Americans and Europeans that "emotional ownership" of the business by locals is absolutely important for success.

Endnotes

1. In the story of the prodigal son, he went to his father to ask for his half of the inheritance (he had a brother). After

squandering away all his inheritance, and realizing his mistake, he decided to return home to ask for his father's forgiveness. On reaching home, not only did his father forgive him, he also threw a big party to celebrate his son's return. The father's magnanimity was indeed remarkable and laudable.

2. In the story of the lost sheep, a shepherd had 100 sheep. When he discovered that he had lost one sheep, he went tirelessly to find it. When he found the lost sheep, he carried it over his shoulder and rejoiced over the other 99 sheep. The shepherd's determination to go after one lost sheep over the 99 reflected his selfless nature and readiness to embrace and forgive the lost one.

3. A variant of this saying is, "When you say more, you make more mistakes. When you say less, you make fewer mistakes. When you say nothing, you can never make mistakes," (多说多错，少说少错，不说不错 *duo shuo duo cuo, shao shuo shao cuo, bu shuo bu cuo*). This also explains why many Chinese choose to remain silent in meetings, especially when their bosses are present.

4. For example, the Chinese never forget how they were humiliated by foreign powers in the 19th and 20th centuries. Against Japan, they have never forgotten the Nanking massacre, and are still demanding that the Japanese apologize for their war crimes.

5. Remember the common expression that a picture is worth a thousand words!

6. For example, when he tried to speak up on a previous occasion, he was "gunned down" by the previous expatriate boss.

7. A good example is the tipping of drivers in places like China. The driver will typically say, "No need, no need," and will try to push the money away. You should never take it back as this is how he is expected to behave.

8. Please read Chapter 12 for a more in-depth treatment of this subject.

9. This is also one sure way to demonstrate that you want him to be your partner for a long time. Otherwise, you would

not bother to spend time and effort getting to know him better.

10. This is very unlike the practice in the United States. Let us cite an interesting episode. When the first author was a PhD student in North America, he was very excited when his thesis supervisor invited him and his family for dinner at his home. He went through considerable time and effort asking all the other professors what he should buy for his supervisor, only to be told, "Just get him a bottle of wine." He then wanted to know what kind of wine to buy for his supervisor as this was very important to him—to get something that his supervisor liked. This time around, he was told, "Oh, just get the bottle that you would like to drink." "Why?" he asked. "Well, he is going to open it to drink, and it is always better to take a bottle that you like to drink because we don't know what he likes to drink anyway." The first author was totally stunned by such a response. He then recalled, with great embarrassment, what happened when he first invited all of his professors for dinner at his house. Each of them brought a bottle of wine, unwrapped, and in a brown paper bag. Instead of opening each of the bottles given, he carefully kept them in his basement, and even recalled which professor had given which bottle of wine.

11. Please read Chapter 12 where more details on this subject will be discussed.

12. This was not the experience of foreign companies investing in China in the 1980s and early 1990s. Many joint-ventures then had joint appointees for each position. Unfortunately, as the roles were poorly defined, there was much conflict and misunderstanding. Since then, these joint-ventures have come a long way in redefining job titles and responsibilities.

13. These concepts will be explained in greater detail in Chapter 12.

上下同欲者胜；

shang xia tong yu zhe sheng

He who is able to unite himself with his officers and men as one mind, spirit, and purpose will win.

(Sun Zi Bingfa, 孙子兵法, Line 3.47 of Chapter 3 on Strategic Attacks, 谋攻 (mou gong))

CHAPTER 7

The Expatriate Phenomenon

How Valuable Are They to Building Businesses?

The Ever-Changing Expatriate

From our various consulting and training experiences, the most consistent and vociferous complaint we hear regarding Western companies is the constant changing of the senior and middle management. It really frustrates Asians. This is one area where they are courageous enough to give regular feedback, but see little action taken in response. The Western-oriented organizations do generally acknowledge the issue but counter with the rationale that to build a portfolio of global managers, they need to develop them in different parts of the world, hence the need for change. The trouble is that this creates a number of dangerous side issues for these organizations operating in Asia.[1]

In Asia, many people and organizations will not take you seriously until you have shown your intention to stick around. You need to project an image of stability, reliability, loyalty, and a long-term approach. Business in Asia is built to a large degree on personal relationships.[2] Once relationships have been cultivated and established, they are far too valuable to throw away.

Labeling of Foreigners

Different terms are used by the Chinese in Asia to address foreigners. For example, in China, all foreigners, whether they are Americans, Europeans, or Asians, are labeled as *lao wai* (老外). This literally means "old outsider." However, it means more than that. *Lao wai* (老外) also refers to someone who is a *wai hang* (外行). This means someone who has no experience or knowledge on the subject matter or knows nothing about how to go about completing the task at hand. Such a labeling implies that to the Chinese in China, a foreigner, and that includes overseas Chinese, can never be one of them nor be able to understand the Chinese completely. For those who know the Chinese language well, the term *lao wai* is thus not very complimentary. However, many others have accepted it as a neutral and casual reference to all foreigners.

The Chinese also use other fascinating terms to describe foreigners, especially those from the West. At a polite level, they will refer to all Westerners as *xi yang ren* (西洋人),[3] which means "foreigners from overseas." This label is now shortened to *yang ren* (洋人). Early in the 20th century, a different term for Western foreigners, *yang gui zi* (洋鬼子), was used. This literally means "Western or foreign devils." Such a derogatory term was used because during that period, quite a few Western countries invaded China. Obviously, these Western invaders were hated by the Chinese who did not hesitate to call their invaders devils. Today, this label is rarely used in public anymore as the Chinese recognize that it can be racist and inappropriate.

In Hong Kong, the Cantonese-speaking population call Caucasian and Western men *guailo* (鬼佬) and women *guaimui* (鬼妹).[4,5] For those who find such labels offensive, it is useful to know the background of how these terms came about. When the early Hong Kong people first encountered Westerners, they were frightened by their pale or white complexions and features (including blond hair). To them, these Westerners look like ghosts.[6] Hence, the label that expressed their fears has stuck till today.

While some Westerners today may find labels such as *lao wai* (老外), *yang ren* (洋人), *guailo* (鬼佬), and *guaimui* (鬼妹) somewhat unacceptable and negative, there are many Westerners who are equally neutral about such terms, with some even enjoying being called such. In fact, with the advancement made by Western and foreign countries, terms like *lao wai* (老外) and *yang ren* (洋人) are now sometimes used in a complimentary manner by the Chinese. They can also be used creatively by the Western expatriates as means to put their Asian counterparts at ease or to make them feel more relaxed. For example, phrases like "Look, you know how different we *guailos* are!" or "Beware the *yang ren*" can actually help to make your partners or employees laugh at the occasional cultural disparity, and help to reduce tensions in negotiations.

What is important to note from all these labels placed on foreigners or outsiders is that to understand the locals, much work, time, and effort will have to be put in. It is not something that can be done overnight. Imagine, how can humans and devils (鬼佬 *guailo*) communicate and under-stand each other so quickly? How can a *lao wai* (老外) be like a Chinese overnight? How can someone from overseas

(洋人 *yang ren*), who has just arrived, know the system, culture, and local taboos in China so soon? More seriously, if the *lao wai* corporate leader is changed frequently, the problems can only be compounded. This is indeed food for thought—behind those labels are implicit meanings and undertones that need to be fully understood by the uninitiated foreign businessman who thinks he can make a quick buck and exit from a country like China.

Friendship First, Business Will Then Follow

One of the biggest surprises Asians face when meeting Westerners for the first time is how quickly the Westerner wants to get started with the business at hand. In contrast, Asians, especially the Chinese and Japanese, first want to get to know the person(s) that they will be dealing with. This is because the typical Asian businessman treats business as a long-term relationship, and not an ad hoc exercise. As such, he wants to make sure he is dealing with the right partner even before he gets to the first transaction. He views the first transaction as the beginning of a long-term partnership.[7] To him, having partners that can be trusted and relied upon is very important to any sustainable business relationship. The focus is on the person he is dealing with, and, in most cases, this is more important than the products and/or services that are being transacted. Not surprisingly, socializing becomes an important process to get to know the potential business partner. It is a case of friendship first, and then business will come later.

The Western businessman, however, is able to treat each business deal as an exercise by itself. He believes that so long as he provides the most competitive terms and the other party needs his products/services, a deal can be struck, and it should be struck as soon as possible before his competitors come into the picture. Moreover, coming from a much more capitalistic society, where time is money, he simply does not think that engaging in "small talk" is productive to the business deal at hand.

The contrasting approaches to handling business between a Westerner and an Asian can be likened to running. The Westerner approaches the business as if he were running a 100-meter sprint. He wants to start and finish the race as fast as possible. The Asian, on the other hand, views the business as if he were running a marathon. He wants to start slowly, settle into a rhythm, pace, and position himself competitively for the whole race. The Westerner holds a more short-term view on achieving results while the Asian's is more long-term, and he is also more patient about getting there. The Western mentality is more "Let's start some business together and we will get to see whether we like each other along the way." In contrast, the Asian mentality is "Let's spend some time together, perhaps even a long time, getting to know and trust each other, and then start one or several business opportunities."

This is why it is absolutely critical for the Westerner to invest more in the small things at the beginning, even if it takes, by his standards, a lot more time, effort, and patience. He will find that in the long term, it will pay dividends, and often, very handsomely. This, in fact, is one of the most important reasons why it is not advisable to change leaders or senior executives during this process of relationship-building. It is not a long relay race to be run by a team of runners. Doing business in Asia is like a marathon to be run by a single person. If the Western company takes this analogy and simply uses sprinters, who pass on the baton to each other as in a relay race, then more often than not, the company is destined to fail. If, however, the company carefully selects the right leader with the appropriate cultural skills, matches him with a good business partner, and leaves them both to develop the business for a longer period (a minimum of five years), then the business has a far greater chance of success.

As will be explained in greater detail in Chapter 12, the Chinese way of doing business, which applies to many other Asian countries as well, is a process that focuses more on feelings and emotions,[8] followed by logic and reasoning, and finally by legality and rules. In contrast, the Western approach focuses more on rules and legality,[9] followed by reasoning and logic, and finally by feelings and emotions.

Recognizing the differences, it is important for Westerners to appeal to the feelings of their Asian counterparts. This means that the early part of the courtship may require more attention to little kindnesses, small courtesies, and words of appreciation. Getting to know and understand each other's families is equally important in building rapport. As Asians are being-oriented, rather than doing-oriented, they believe that it is important to build and maintain solid relationships. The process of building and developing relationships often therefore leads to reciprocal obligations, which will be an extra bonus for your business, as new opportunities may be presented, which were never visible before.

To face up to such challenges, the Westerner will have to recognize that he has to go beyond his office hours if he wants to get to know his local counterparts better. This also requires him to be humble to learn, and to realize that his own skill set may be limited.[10] As such, and when necessary, he must be prepared to involve more of his local staff in his "education" process, and even learn from them how to win the hearts and minds of other local business partners, officials, customers, etc., that he has to come into contact with.

When indeed a change of senior leadership is required in a Western company operating in Asia, the transition will be much easier for the successor if the relationship foundations are already firmly established by the incumbent. However, the newcomer must never take things for granted. The outgoing person can do the introductions, but it is up to the newcomer to build on those ties, and never assume that they operate on an autopilot basis. Indeed, the newcomer will have to demonstrate the same level of emotional engagement as his predecessor to earn the trust of the Asian partner or the Asian employees. He can do better or worse—it all depends on him. He cannot depend on "inherited" ties to tide him through. If anything, he will find that he will be tested very early on in his leadership role by the local subordinates, business associates, government officials, etc.

Expatriate Freakonomics

A fascinating book to read is *Freakonomics: A Rogue Economist Explores the Hidden Side of Everything* by Steven Levitt. It is an unorthodox business book, which "has to do with thinking sensibly about how people behave in the real world." It requires a novel way of looking, discerning, and measuring. Levitt explores a wide range of subjects from schoolteachers to sumo wrestlers, from the Klu Klux Klan to estate agents, from drug dealers to perfect parents, and not surprisingly he turns out some unconventional and interesting facts.

The book made us wonder what if Levitt had taken a similar "freakonomics" approach to observing, monitoring, and measuring the effectiveness of expatriates operating in various Asian countries. After all, hiring expatriates represents an incredibly high investment, not purely in financial terms, but also in opportunity terms for any company. If you get it right, the return on investment can be extraordinarily high. If you get it wrong, and there are many shades of this, not only are resources wasted, there can also be negative long-term side effects. Unfortunately, the data is probably not that easily accessible or available. After all, most organizations want to "spin" and present the positive aspects of the expatriate phenomenon, namely enhanced multiculturalism, international diversity, and a global workforce. Few are prepared to face the hard facts, that is, hiring expatriates entails high costs, the results are not guaranteed, and success/failure cases have rarely been quantified.

Frighteningly, we suspect that, in general terms, the expatriate success rate is very low, perhaps in the range of one in four. In other words, we believe that roughly 25 percent of expatriates deliver more value to the overall business than the costs of hiring them.[11] By value, we are not referring to pure dollar returns on business development or marketing investment alone. The financial payoffs are certainly very important. What we believe is of greater value and return to the organization is the ability of the expatriate chief executive officer (CEO) to harness people investment and development. By this, we mean his willingness and devotion to train a strong local team, including grooming his potential local successors. In doing so, he is truly able to help his company to harness greater returns and to ensure the continuity of senior management.

Types of Expatriates in Asia

In a discussion with Nihal Kaviratne, a friend and former chairman of Unilever in Indonesia, we agreed that there are basically three broad categories of expatriates. Let us start with the best one.

The Legacy Builder

This is the genuine business developer. He has got the potential to reach a senior management position, including being the CEO of the company in the country that he is posted to. He wants to leave a strong track record of business success in every country he works in. He comes to the country because he wants to, because he feels challenged by the opportunities, and because he is open-minded and prepared to listen to the ideas of local employees and partners. He is not constrained by corporate ways, rules, and regulations. Instead, he is prepared to be flexible so as to meet local needs. At times, such behavior may incur the displeasure of his bosses at the headquarters. However, his talents and dedication will typically win his bosses over.

More importantly, he is a visionary who sees the need to develop local talent. This is because he believes that the business would be best managed by the locals eventually, and he is there to ensure that this happens. As such, he spares no effort to locate potential local successors who can replace him in three to five years' time. Even if he fails, his efforts in developing a strong local team will ensure that a leader will eventually emerge among them. He wants to leave behind a strong legacy, and move on to the next assignment. Such an individual is able to accomplish much because he also has a supportive family who shares the same vision and goal.

Obviously, corporate headquarters of multinationals should seek to identify, recruit, and develop legacy builders and send them to head and lead the respective Asian operations. Unfortunately, legacy builders are few in number and difficult to find. They are like precious corporate gems and should be highly valued.

The Colonial Missionary

This is the type who comes to the country with prejudiced baggage. He believes he is superior to the local managers and employees. After all, he thinks he is better educated, has multicountry experience and a "God-given" task to reform people. If only the locals could follow his way of working, the business could be transformed. He fails to listen to local advice and does not genuinely engage the local team. Not surprisingly, he alienates himself from the rank and file and is never part of the team from day one. The locals, sensing his superiority complex, also choose to distance themselves from him and avoid giving him any feedback.

Typically, after about two years of high commitment and extraordinary missionary zeal, such a person becomes bitter and frustrated and begins to encounter increasing roadblocks and obstacles in moving things forward. This is because he has not bothered to gain the support of his subordinates. More seriously, as he has failed to develop the local talent, the better ones have also opted to join the competitors or other companies. As more frustration sets in, he starts to hate the place, acts miserable, and constantly complains about how his performance is affected because he has no good people to work with. He feels there is a better country to go to that will truly appreciate his skills and added value.

Not surprisingly, he puts in repeated requests for another transfer.

The Hibernator

This is the worst type among the three. This is because the colonial missionary makes some attempt to add value to the business, and he tries very hard at every new posting. The hibernator, on the other hand, never wants to come to the country where he is posted. His spouse and family members are also not willing to relocate. He is only there because he has to be. Otherwise he would be back in the head office, facing mortgage payments, school fees, and taxes, etc.

Such a person will not do anything to improve the welfare of his local employees. He is predominantly lazy, disinterested, and self-indulging. He will keep his head down and avoid all possible challenges. After all, to him, the country where he is located will not change, so why should he bother? He does not want any scars. He just wants to survive until the next posting comes up. As such, he puts in minimal effort, and, if anything goes wrong, he will blame his predecessor, the system, and/or corporate policies.

In sum, he has no interest in the country nor the posting. However, he can survive in the system and cover up his shortfalls and/or nonperformance because he is a master of corporate diplomacy. He knows how to please his bosses and is an expert in the art of pretence.

Other Types of Expatriates

Many of you who may have worked for large multinationals can easily recognize the above categories. There are other categories, which are adaptations of these, such as:

The Corporate Boy: He is non-risk-taking, obedient, and a loyal follower who will only take action after due consultation with the corporate headquarters. To a large extent, he is a much trusted corporate lieutenant. While lacking in drive and initiative, he is unlikely to place the company in any serious trouble.

The Rebel: He is the direct opposite of the corporate boy. He is very independent and impulsive, and rarely takes counsel or advice from the head office. Such an individual can sometimes put the company in embarrassing situations. However, recognizing his shortcoming, the corporate headquarters will also generally give him enough rope to hang himself, and he eventually does.

Assessing Expatriates' Performances

It is interesting to note that at annual career development and talent review meetings when decisions on expatriates' performances and succession plans have to be made, these somehow get buried among many other human resources (HR) issues and statistics. If we rely on purely sales and financial objectives as targets for expatriate leadership incentive schemes and base expatriate career decisions on conventional HR statistics, ignoring the basic "rights" of a receiving country, then the phenomenon of expatriate "freakonomics" will continue. There will be far too few legacy builders and too many colonial missionaries and hibernators.

As of today, there are no well-established and reliable yardsticks to measure expatriates' performances. At the expense of provoking more debate, we would recommend adding the following measures for assessing the genuine contribution of an expatriate in a particular country.

A Legacy Statement

The expatriate should write down in his first week what he plans to leave behind after his posting to that country. Among others, he should include how he would like the business to grow during his tenure, how strong his team will be, and when his local successor will be fully trained and available. This document can then be reviewed on an annual basis and at the end of his posting.

360-Degree Evaluation

Allow a full 360-degree annual evaluation by local managers, employees, and partners on how much value the expatriate has given to the business and the country. If all of them cannot be surveyed, then the views from a cross section of these people should at least be solicited. Issues to be probed include asking how committed and supportive the local team is toward the expatriate leader, how he assimilates into the local culture, his involvement in developing local talent, his dealings with local customers, his relationship with local government officials, and his involvement in the local community.

Commitment to Posting

This is a very basic measure, and it seems absurd to mention it. Many organizations are faced with an accelerated pace of change, intense competition, and pressure to expose more executives to international experience. In the process, short overseas stints have become a quantitative norm rather than a qualitative effort to develop an experienced pool of global managers. As such, in posting a senior staff member overseas, it is very useful to ascertain his level and intensity of commitment to that country.

To begin with, is he keen on the posting, or is he choosy about where he wants to go? Is he committed to serve the minimum posting period, and even be prepared to stay on longer when needed? Of course, this measure can easily be verified when the company also conducts the 360-degree evaluation as mentioned earlier.

Dangers of Playing Frequent Musical Chairs

In overseas postings, the first year is very much a learning experience. The expatriate, including his family members, will spend a lot of time trying to understand and assimilate into the local culture and system. It is only in his second year that he can play a more contributing role and exhibit productivity. As such, we are of the view that the minimum posting for each location should be at least three years, and ideally up to five years. For some places such as Asia, a posting duration of up to 10 years can even be considered.

Yet, it does not take a shrewd observer to notice how many expatriates are churned through various overseas postings faster than they can actually cope with and contribute to their respective outfits. Before the expatriate can get his hands dirtied, he is moved out, and the next one comes in. It is like playing musical chairs to a very fast tempo. Before the person can warm up the seat, he is asked to move again.

Indeed, an ever-changing expatriate leadership can create incredible, lasting damage in many countries. First, it creates a culture that lacks accountability for results. This is because when a stint is so short, it is difficult to attribute corporate performances to any particular individual. What is even worse is that the expatriate can become very short-sighted and pursue policies and actions that will make his short-term performance look good but at the expense of long-term results. After all, he will not be around by then.

Second, as the time is short, minimal attention will be paid to succession planning and to train the local people. This is because all the effort and resources that he puts in may end up being dismantled by his successor. Moreover, he is also not around to see the benefits—so, why bother?

Third, when posting periods are short, the incumbent will probably be thinking more about where his next exciting assignment will be. This literally means energy that should be directed at running the business may be diluted in the process. The concerns become greater if he has children who go to school and a wife who also needs a job.

Fourth, and this normally happens in Asia, frequent changes of senior expatriates also create opportunities for the locals, especially the business partners and associates, to test the new leadership by revisiting old issues, bringing up new issues, attempting to renegotiate the existing agreement, etc. This can be particularly challenging for the newcomer, who is unfamiliar with the local situation and culture, to be confronted by a bunch of seasoned and shrewd locals.

Finally, and this is the reverse impact of the fourth point, having to adjust to the different management styles of changing bosses can be a nightmare for the locals, especially for those reporting directly to them, and the local employees. At times, this can also extend to the local business partners. Deep frustration and even resentment can arise when the new boss starts to make decisions and take action that threaten well-established working relationships. This will be further aggravated if there is no detailed and careful handover between the incumbent and the newcomer. Even if there is, it is impossible to cover all bases.

In sum, unnecessary rotation of senior expatriate staff should be avoided. It is very unsettling for Asian businessmen to have to deal with a new representative every other year. In our view, this would be the worst legacy as it causes a complete loss of corporate knowledge about the business at the local level. This, in turn, creates an even greater temptation for higher-level meddling, and serial mistakes will continue to be perpetuated by the corporate headquarters.

Playing the Victim

The following observation may prove too controversial for most people's liking, but we have found elements of it to a certain degree across Asia. We often sense Asians playing the victim. And if you play the victim, you will always be the victim.

Given that there are expatriates who, instead of adding value to the organization, actually end up devaluing the business by damaging internal and external relationships and fail to deliver proper succession development, resulting in a very high cost for the company, we are very surprised and even disappointed that Asians do not speak up to voice their disapproval of such expatriates. Clearly, part of this is cultural—the fear of offending or upsetting the system—nevertheless, there is a strong need for Asians to voice their dissatisfaction if they are not getting the right level of motivation and emotional support. We are not just talking about the employees; we are also referring to business partners. Sometimes it is amazing what surfaces after a particular expatriate has moved on to another country—suddenly the doors open and the views once held back burst through: how he ruined the relationship with certain major customers, why so-and-so left, how the budget was wastefully spent, how nobody respected his leadership, how he spent no time developing his local successor, etc. In fact, if one bothers to plug into the informal grapevine, such talk, although to a much lesser degree, can also be heard. The only thing that does not happen is that it is not brought up to the formal and proper channels that are actually available.

➤While we can sympathize greatly with Asian employees and business partners who have been landed with senior Western leaders and managers with poor cross-cultural skills, low emotional intelligence, and arrogant attitudes, we also sense that these Asians should be more forthright and speak up to provide truthful feedback. Western companies are well aware that they are dominant in Asian society, and the majority of them want to maintain the status quo. If they perceive that Asians are submissive and will accept whichever expatriates they put into an organization, then they will continue to perpetuate such behavior.

Asians have to be more assertive and take control of the decision-making process regarding expatriates wherever possible. Asians have an obligation to think about their own prospects by dropping the old colonial victim mindset and moving on. In his book, *Can Asians Think?*, Kishore Mahbubani states, "The most painful thing that happened to Asia was not the physical but the mental colonization. Many Asians began to believe that Asians were inferior beings to the Europeans. This mental colonization has not been completely eradicated in Asia, and many Asian societies are still struggling to break free."

In *Breaking the Bamboo Curtain*, Jane Hyun argues strongly that Asians really need to take responsibility for their own personal brand. People's behavior is often misinterpreted by other cultures because they are influenced by what they see, and not the underlying feelings, intentions, aspirations, or thought processes.

As Jane Hyun reassures, "Your Asian-ness doesn't have to work against you however. Your Asian background is integral to your identity. It's unrealistic to expect that your managers will automatically want and know how to unearth the true you. Training in selling, presenting, negotiating, and assertiveness can tap and channel your knowledge to enhance your presence and capabilities."

Surely, the time has come, given the recent resurgence of Asia, for Asians to exert themselves and make their views and opinions count. In particular, they need to speak up on things and issues that they do not agree with or like. Providing truthful feedback on expatriates' performances through the appropriate channels would be a good start.

Localization

There can be fewer less emotional issues than the issue of localization, that is, how to train up the local talent to run the business, and how fast the pace can be. It is a multidimensional issue, which largely depends on:

- **The nature of the business.** Some businesses are more complex than others and require much more time to train local talent.
- **The maturity of the country.** Obviously, for a less developed country, the pool of talented and qualified local executives will be much smaller in number. Their education level may be low, and the ability to assume management positions may not be there.

- **Competitiveness of the market.** Even when there is available local talent, a highly competitive market also affects localization programs.
- **The future of the business.** If the growth of the business is expected to continue for some time, it is definitely worthwhile to train and groom local talent. However, if it is a turnkey project, the incentives may not be high.
- **The attitude of the expatriate leadership.** Whether the expatriate leaders sent to manage the local business are legacy builders, colonial missionaries, or hibernators will affect the success or failure of any localization effort.
- **Past experiences.** The lessons learned from the multinational corporations's (MNC) worldwide experiences in developing local management will also affect the willingness and speed of localization.
- **Corporate headquarter's policy.** Some MNCs, like US companies, have more enlightened policies in grooming and developing local management talent than others. Obviously, if an MNC has enough holding power, it may be more willing to accept the high cost of deploying expatriates.
- **Availability of resources.** Without doubt, localization programs require time, effort, and money. Unless adequate resources are committed, the development program may still not succeed.

Finding the right balance among all these dimensions is going to be very challenging for many organizations. The majority of them get it wrong because, as the saying goes, "A chain is only as strong as its weakest link." It only takes one weak element in the dimensions above to bring the whole localization plan crashing down.

Grooming and developing local talent is never an easy task. It is like the following Chinese saying, which is often used as an analogy to illustrate that it will take a long time and much effort to cultivate a person:

十 年 树 木， 百 年 树 人 。
shi nian shu mu   bai nian shu ren

> It takes ten years to grow a forest, but it takes a century to nurture a majestic tree.

We have seen companies that have tried to localize too slowly and others that have tried too quickly. For those that have done it too slowly, it can be very demotivating for current and future employees. Asians are extremely perceptive. They can sense where there is genuine sincerity in Western organizations to train them to take up middle and senior management roles. In developing markets in particular, they will be very attracted to the organizations that offer them the fastest development and promotion opportunities. If they feel that the Western organization is not clearly focused on localization, they will simply not stay with it.

However, for those that do it too quickly, it can lead to locals being promoted too early and the organization being stretched. Often there is a shortage of coaching resources to manage the remaining local future managers. More importantly, if not managed carefully, this situation can lead to a simple lack of experience to keep the business on track. In the developing markets, it can also lead to local Asian managers resorting back to Asian-style leadership traits (more autocratic, less open and tolerant) rather than the Western-style leadership traits that they have been trained in. The short-term benefits of major cost-savings can be easily eroded. Once an aggressive localization plan has been executed, it can be extremely difficult to reverse without major upheaval. Inevitably the re-arrival of new expatriates is a major loss of "face" to those locals who have been promoted and will often lead to many resignations.

Another common issue faced by many companies is identifying, developing, and appointing local country heads/general managers and regional heads. For sure, very few multinationals have Asians heading regional outfits or occupying senior regional positions. While the situation has been improving in recent years, especially in the appointment of country heads and general managers, many senior regional positions are still occupied by expatriates.

To be fair, there is certainly a strong desire among Western MNCs to pursue localization. For example, Asian talent is given mid- to long-term career development assignments across the globe in preparation for general manager and senior regional leadership appointments. However, when they get to a position of fairly high authority, say, as a senior head of a functional role, many Western MNCs seem unable to provide the next step for these Asian talents to progress further. Something holds them back. We can only conclude that within these Western-oriented organizations, there is still a deep-rooted fear or discomfort about having a local Asian as the local country or regional head. We venture the following as plausible reasons for this reluctance:

1. Appointing an Asian as the country or regional head changes the dynamics of the business relationship with the regional/corporate head office. Western MNCs prefer the convenience of a Westerner as it is safe and easier to speak more directly with him because they share the same values and interests.

2. Appointing more Asians as country or regional heads threatens to change the "club-like" atmosphere of Western organizations, where the real camaraderie exists not in meetings or boardrooms, but in the bar, after the meetings. Given that some Asians have different after-work lifestyles—dining, karaoke, perhaps even gambling—this also changes the dynamics and a "Them and Us" situation is created.

3. Appointing an Asian as the country/regional head might create challenges that an expatriate general manager might not face—more requests for help or assistance from the local community, as he is "one of them," or risk potential exposure to corruption.

The Way Forward

Ignoring and/or delaying localization, in our view, borders on discrimination and racism. Every MNC appears to be committed to diversity in the deployment of talent, but only, when truly tested, up to a certain level. It is really unfortunate that many Western companies still feel that one of their own must be present in Asian countries to look after their interests. To us, given the large pool of talent in Asia, it is time that this issue of deploying expatriates rather than locals as country/regional heads be seriously revisited. There are good reasons for our view.

First, it is clearly a very high cost to the companies concerned when senior expatriates are used. This is clearly evidenced by the fact that many Western companies are cutting back on expatriates' perks today. Second, Asians can do as well, or better, if they are aligned with the company's goals and values in running the business. Third, appointing locals/Asians gives a huge morale boost to the local organizations. It gives a very strong signal that the company is 100 percent committed to diversity and strengthens the recruitment drive. Fourth, appointing locals/Asians creates a group of role models for other Asian managers to follow. Finally, appointing locals/Asians means that there is a proper two-way dialogue on business in Asia at the regional and global levels. The right conversations and exchanges of ideas are taking place.

With the passage of time and with the center of gravity moving toward Asia, the smart companies will be accelerating the development and appointment of local/Asian country/regional heads. Those who do not do so will risk losing their competitive advantages.

Endnotes

1. Such issues relating to persistent leadership changes may not necessarily create the same level of frustration in other parts of the world.
2. *See* Chapter 12.
3. The word *yang* (洋) actually means "seas and oceans." In the early years, Westerners arrived in China via ships from the seas and oceans. Hence, the term *xi yang ren* (西洋人) was used to describe such people who came from the West.
4. In Cantonese, this literally means "ghost men."
5. This literally means "ghost ladies."
6. Even till today, the Chinese perceive dead people as having a pale complexion.
7. *See also* Chapter 12.
8. This is reflected by the strength of the friendship and relationship between the two potential business partners.

9. This will normally be enshrined in a contract.
10. To begin with, language is always the biggest hurdle.
11. Such costs are not limited to salaries. Often placing a senior expatriate in an Asian country entails many other hidden costs and perks such as educational allowances for children, fully paid home leave and holiday for the entire family (this could be up to twice a year), golf and/or country club memberships, medical and dental coverage for the entire family, extra posting allowances, chauffeur-driven car, etc.

孙子曰：

Sun　Zi　yue

凡用兵之法，将受命于君，

fan　yong　bing　zhi　fa　　jiang　shou　ming　yu　　jun

合军聚众，交和而舍

he　jun　ju　zhong　　jiao　he　er　she

Sun Zi said: In any military campaign, the general will first receive his orders from his ruler. He then assembles the troops and mobilizes the citizens (people). He must harmonize (the interests of) these diverse groups, and build their relationships and comradeships by encamping them together.

(Sun Zi Bingfa, 孙子兵法*, Lines 7.1 to 7.3 of Chapter 7 on Military Maneuvers,* 军争 *(jun zheng))*

CHAPTER 8

Handling Nocturnal Activities

From Drinking Binges, Karaoke to Making Speeches

Socialization in the Business World

Every society has its own ways of socializing. However, not all of them are intended to be settings in which business deals are negotiated. It is important to note that they can be very different, hence it is essential for someone working and living in that society to know where and how friendships and relationships are built, and where favors can be exchanged or traded.

In France, business matters are often discussed over long lunches that include a wide selection of fine wines. It can be a challenging experience for someone who is not a good drinker to hold himself while trying to talk business. In some Mediterranean countries, such as Turkey, dinners can be very long drawn affairs. However, it is in such an environment that relationships are established and business deals discussed. While on a consulting assignment in Finland, one of us was quite intrigued to discover that taking saunas with business associates is one of the best ways to discuss business matters.[1] To the Finnish businessmen, the sauna provides a relaxed and conducive atmosphere for discussion. It reduces one's tension, and there is also minimal interruption. To them, it provides an ideal environment in which even difficult issues can be resolved.

In Britain and the United States, it is very common to see office employees socializing over drinks at pubs every Friday evening. For them, it is an occasion to unwind and relax, gossip, and chat. At times, they will also watch football or some other sport during the drinking session.

In Asia, socializing in the business world can be a chore and a torture if you are not well informed and prepared. In this chapter, we will highlight some of the common activities that you could be involved in, and which you may not know how to handle.

Drinking Binges

Drinking is indeed a social pastime in many societies. In particular, after a long, hard day at work or a whole week of sweat and toil, having a drink or two at the local bar or lounge is a very common way to unwind and relax. This is what many business executives do in many Western countries. However, drinking in Asia can take on a very different perspective. One of the biggest challenges of working in Asia, particularly in China, Japan, Korea, Taiwan and in developing non-Muslim parts of Southeast Asia, is to avoid destroying your liver! If you are one of those people who are able to sustain serious nights of alcohol bingeing and pick yourself up the next day with little aftereffect, then this section is not targeted at you—although you might want to get another annual check-up with your doctor, just in case! If you are not a good drinker, then some advice on this matter may help you to be on your toes, and be more attentive to how you should handle yourself before you get overly intoxicated.

Beyond Drunkenness

In both Western and Asian societies, drinking is a common practice to celebrate birthdays, anniversaries, weddings, festivities, and so on. In Asia, however, these seemingly happy and joyful acts can turn into serious drinking binges. This is particularly so in the business world where drinking binges can become an integral part of celebrating annual sales conventions, major company achievements, the visits of very important persons (VIPs), the signing of major contracts, etc. We have witnessed and attended events all over Asia (China, Vietnam, Cambodia, Thailand, the Philippines, Myanmar, Singapore, and Taiwan) in various roles, where, generally, senior and middle managers have been expected to join in and get riotously drunk with all their business associates. They have drunk almost everything from the normal red wine, cognac, and whiskey selection to the hard liquor of China and unusual vodka/lobster blood cocktails of Vietnam. Of course, they have also woken up the next day with the worst possible hangovers.

Beyond drunkenness, drinking in many Asian societies also serves another important purpose—to size up the character of the other person. As a Korean proverb says, "If you wish to know a man's true nature, watch him play Go, gamble, or drink." The Chinese believe drinking will enable a person to tell the truth. The Japanese also hold similar beliefs. Indeed, in the normal office setting, the typical office executive puts on a mask. So do his bosses, customers, and other business associates. However, after several rounds of drinks, in a non-threatening atmosphere such as a karaoke lounge, the real feelings and emotions begin to spill out. For example, some people, under the influence of alcohol, start to crack colorful jokes, talk nonsense, or engage in harmless small talk. Others may begin to leak the personal secrets of senior management staff, their colleagues, customers, etc. Worse still, they may even leak corporate secrets.

This is where the true character of a person can be easily exposed. If a person, after a few drinks, can spill the beans and "play out" the other people whom they have come into contact with, then they can easily do the same thing to you. Such a person can never be trusted as a business partner or associate. Further character traits can also be detected during drinking sessions. Some people can become more aggressive, others remain composed, and yet others get more excitable and less reserved. These are behaviors that can provide useful cues as to how such people should be handled in future.

Handling Drinking Binges

As mentioned earlier, drinking sessions are used as platforms to size up the personality and character of a person. Not surprisingly, if you do not drink, your local host or business associate will find it difficult to get to know you better. To him, your mask is still on, and it will take him a much longer time and through other means of socializing (for example, karaoke sessions) to get to know you better. In fact, some expatriates have attempted to use their inability to drink as an excuse to avoid getting drunk.[2] However, if you use such a ploy, ensure that you stick rigidly to it throughout each of your social outings and that none of your own colleagues betrays you. This is because when your Asian counterpart discovers that you can actually drink, they can be quite offended by your insincerity, and the business relationship may be affected. Thus, when you are able to drink, it is better not to avoid it. Rather, it is more important to handle such drinking binges skillfully. The following are some pointers that may be worth considering:

1. Prepare for the drinking session by eating beforehand or when the first couple of dishes are served. Food in the stomach helps to mitigate the effects of alcohol. This is because when the drinking and toasting get into momentum, the food is hardly touched at the dinner.[3]

2. Start slowly and carefully during the calm before the storm. This is not a game to demonstrate bravery or gung-ho behavior.

3. Balance out the drinking responsibilities amongst colleagues. This is a sensible precaution when there is a two-team dinner (Asian side and a Western side), as the very senior people tend to get targeted more. A protection strategy can be formulated, similar to blocking in American football, to defend the quarterback.

4. Minimize "drinking" opportunities by choosing carefully the events that really need your presence, using the 80/20 rule. Depending on your seniority, a lot can be delegated.

5. Stick to the same alcoholic beverage, whatever poison it might be. If you are in China, avoid *maotai* (茅台) or its equivalent Chinese white liquor. It typically has over 50 percent alcohol content.

6. Avoid or restrict the 50 or 100 percent bottoms up swigs to just a few senior people. A good excuse would be to say that you are not a strong drinker.
7. Know when to go home. If all the speeches have been given and most glasses toasted, then an escape plan is essential. If you happen to work for a multinational corporation (MNC), the pretext of having to take a conference or telephone call from your corporate headquarters in Europe or the United States would be a very acceptable reason. Another excuse is to say that you have to attend another important event, although this may not go down as well at times.

Fortunately, over the years, Asian business partners have become more prosperous and health conscious, and are more aware of the harms of excessive drinking on their health. In China, austerity measures enforced by its government have also helped to curtail excessive drinking. More importantly, as Asian business-men begin to interact more with the Western world, they have also learned to improve their drinking habits instead of indulging in drinking binges. For example, Chinese officials and businessmen used to down almost a full glass of wine at one go repeatedly. Today, they have learned to sip elegantly and, at most, only toast in small glasses that are barely a quarterfull. This helps the guests too, as the chances of getting drunk indiscriminately will be greatly reduced.

Karaoke Blues

Imagine that it is two o'clock in the morning. You are sitting in a dark karaoke club somewhere in a city in Asia. Your colleague is making a tired but brave attempt at singing "Bridge over Troubled Waters." Your local partner and host for the evening has just fallen asleep again while one of the hostesses pours you another glass of whiskey and enquires whether you are happy. Your eyes circle the dingy room, wondering how you could get out of this rabbit warren if a fire broke out. You shiver at the thought of it, smile and nod to the lady, and turn back to another girl beside you, who cannot speak a word of English.

Noting that your colleague may be overdoing it and may need to be dragged away from the microphone, you start thumbing through the song list for your piece, the one you have rehearsed and sung across Asia in many a karaoke lounge. You are dreaming of the crisp clean sheets of the bed back at the hotel and a decent night's sleep, before taking the morning flight home where family duties await. But no, you are still here, and, all this time, your head is screaming out questions like "Why did I end up here? Why did I agree to join them? Must I be here? Frankly, I really do not need this!"

We are sure many of you who work in Asia have been in this situation at one time or another. While singing and socializing with your Asian partners can be a lot of fun, at times, the night can seem very long and tough. In particular, when you have been repeatedly told that it would be rude to "walk out" on your Asian partner during such sessions, you wonder how to end the evening outing, more so when he could already be drunk and fast asleep in the lounge itself!

We often reflect on the rich cultural differences that create these situations and wonder whether our Asian partners also share similar views as us, that sometimes these can be pleasurable experiences and sometimes a real drag! In reality, both sides are simply too polite to each other and are reluctant to be open about their true feelings for fear of offending the other party. Yet, there must be better ways of getting out of such awkward situations, especially when one does not enjoy the proceedings anymore.

Understanding Karaoke

As you may have guessed, Kara-Oke is a Japanese word, and the practice began in Japan. It means "empty bathtub," where one literally sings in the comfort of the bathroom. Over time, it has become extremely common and popular across Asia. For example, many social functions in Asia will include karaoke as part of the entertainment for the evening. Many restaurants and clubs provide karaoke rooms for their clients. Many homes also have their own karaoke sound systems, with some even having dedicated karaoke rooms. Unsurprisingly, karaoke lounges can be found in many Asian cities.

The camaraderie of people singing songs together has always been popular in traditional Western folklore—whether in an Irish pub, in people's homes, or round a fire. Karaoke is simply a high-tech version of this. The karaoke system provides the music and lyrics of the songs, and people take turns singing. Amazingly, a very wide range and selection of songs is available, ranging from patriotic to sad and romantic songs. One can also choose the songs in various languages, including Western songs.

Typically, the singing session will begin with someone who is more outgoing and more familiar with the songs available. However, once the momentum is built up, there will be no shortage of people queuing up to sing their favorite songs, with some even going for a second and third song, and so on.

Participating in Karaoke

There are several points worth noting about karaoke sessions. First, it is all about participation and having fun together. When such sessions are held in a karaoke lounge, they are often accompanied by snacks, drinks, and, if requested, lounge hostesses who are well trained in singing along with their guests. As such, one should not be afraid if one does not sing well. It is perfectly fine to croak like you do when you sing in the shower or bathtub! No one will jeer at you. If anything, they will applaud you for your bold attempt. In fact, it is also not uncommon to ask your "audience" to clap for you, something that they will be most willing to do.

Second, when you are invited to sing, you should not refuse even if you think you cannot sing well. By refusing, you will be deemed a spoilsport, more so when you have joined them for the session. Your host may also feel that you are not giving him "face." Remember that the purpose of karaoke is to relax and have fun. When you are not part of it, he finds it more difficult to figure you out. More seriously, he may think that you have something to hide, which is not positive. This is where learning and practicing a few songs can come in very handy. You will never be embarrassed, and your host will be too glad to see you "on stage."

Third, during the singing, it is always good to encourage participation. This would be in the form of inviting your audience to clap or sing along, or even requesting for singing partners. This would certainly liven up the atmosphere and demonstrate your sincerity in trying to engage your local hosts. The key is to show them that you are not afraid to let your hair down, and that you are very much a social being as anyone of them.

Finally, you do not need to initiate or volunteer to sing. Even if you are a great singer, do not be too eager to show your talent. Let the locals have their chances first. You will certainly be invited to sing. This is not only out of respect for them, it is also a good way to demonstrate your humility.

Shedding Inhibitions and Cementing Relationships

The whole purpose of drinking and karaoke is to shed inhibitions with business partners, colleagues, and friends. It is a good icebreaker, providing one with the opportunity to truly relax and enjoy oneself. With potential business partners and clients, such sessions also offer the best platform to size up the personalities and characters of the people you want to do business with. The uninhibited singing sessions show that everyone is as human as the next person, and that everyone has inadequacies, whether it is an inability to consume high levels of alcohol or an appalling singing voice. Socializing in a relaxed and uninhibited environment provides a much more comfortable platform for everyone to get to know each other better, and, over time, business relationships are cemented and trust built up. In essence, it is an unobtrusive way of building unity among all partners.

In some societies, particularly Japan and Korea, the only way to find out how people really feel about the business is by going out and getting drunk with them in the evening. They may be quiet, polite, and reserved in the office, but in the karaoke bar, their real emotions and feelings will surface. Many Westerners who have gone drinking with their Japanese and Korean counterparts can easily experience how emotional these evenings can turn out to be, especially when individuals openly discuss their concerns with them. At times, the Westerner may even have to face the challenge of counseling them while keeping up with the drinking. Yet, this is where bonding begins, and personal relationships are built. In turn, they will lead to smoother business negotiations and bigger and longer business contracts.

The need to know the other party better through socializing before serious business deals can be struck is something that many foreign businessmen and executives fail to grasp. It is generally true that in the West, one can conduct business without even knowing the other party. This, however, is not the case in Asia. Let us illustrate with another example. There was an American chief executive officer (CEO) who made business trips in and out of China for more than a year in the mid-1990s. Each time, his trip was more of a "hi and bye" visit that lasted no longer than two days. No attempt was made to get to know his Chinese business associates, including his own senior Chinese management team.

While listening to a talk on the topic "Doing business in China and building *guanxi*,"[4,5] this particular CEO was so struck by what he heard that he quietly asked that his stay be extended by a couple of days. That same evening, in an unprecedented move, he decided to join the local team and their business associates for dinner. He was so overwhelmed by the experience—everyone was queuing up to take a photograph with him and to drink with him. He never felt so great and welcome in his whole life! Amazingly, he even joined the local hosts for karaoke after dinner. After that episode, many walls came down, and the relationship between this American CEO and his Chinese team and Chinese business associates was never the same again.

Some Cautionary Advice

While it is important and necessary to recognize that business relationships are established in different ways in Asia, one must also not be misled into doing unnecessary, and at times, regrettable things. The following are just two examples of what an unknowing foreigner should watch out for.

Other Extracurricular Activities

After a drinking or karaoke session, your local host(s) may invite you to join them for other extracurricular activities.[6] It is part of their way of showing you hospitality. Such extracurricular activities may include very healthy ones such as going for a foot or body massage, or the more wild and exotic variety. This is where you can decide whether or not to join them. Unlike the pressures of drinking or singing, this situation is very different. It is very much discretionary, and they will respect your decision. There will be no negative impact on the business relationship even if you opt not to participate. No judgment will be passed on you regardless of which action you take.

Do Not Gloat about What Happened the Night Before

In the West, it is common to find people talking and discussing about the good fun they had the night before. They may even enjoy dissecting and analyzing the various events and activities that happened, including who got drunk, who was sick, etc. This is done in good humor and spirit, and often talked about publicly and loudly too.

Typically, nobody is too sensitive about such "day after" gossip, and people generally get over it and look forward to the next night out.

Now, this is something that you must never do in Asia. Whatever happened the night before should never be discussed the day after. It should strictly remain private and is not intended for public discussion and gossip. At the very most, if one of the members was drunk the night before, one only needs to show concern the next day by asking if he/she is fine. Never ever raise or talk about issues such as the conduct and behavior of members, which exotic places they went to, and what they did. These are highly sensitive, explosive and damaging matters that will definitely ruin whatever good relationships were cultivated the night before.

This "as if nothing happened the night before" stance is a cardinal rule that is to be respected and strictly adhered to. Indeed, this is one of those very rare incidents where many Asians make a clear demarcation between what can or cannot be divulged about their social activities, especially those that occur at night. They are to be treated as highly private and confidential, and not as the subject of office gossip. Any betrayal of this implicit trust and prohibition will not be easily forgotten or forgiven. It is a taboo not to be broken.

It is important to remember that the relationship has been built, and both parties are to move on. It is implicit, and one does not even have to ask if the relationship is now better. You can tell by the smiles and the positive atmosphere that the business relationship has taken another step forward. The business discussions are more open, amicable, and conducive to agreeing on what the next step is. The last thing you want to do is to torpedo the good efforts and "investment" that you have painstakingly built up.

Making Impromptu Speeches

It is almost impossible to work and travel in Asia as a senior manager without being asked to make speeches, whether they are prepared or impromptu. They could come in the form of a simple toast and thank you speech to the host at a dinner or a full keynote speech in front of several hundred people. This is where you should be aware of the social and cultural settings and your audience to ensure that you do not get frustrated or feel disappointed. Owing to the wide array of diversity in Asia, you may get different receptions to your speech. In the developed parts, especially Singapore and Hong Kong, you will be listened to with reasonable silence and respect.[7] In the developing countries, however, you may end up competing with a lot of noise, especially at dinners, where eating and drinking may be considered more important than listening to what you are saying.

A few years ago, one of the former bosses of the second author was the guest-of-honor at a large dinner banquet in Cambodia. He was invited to make a speech before hundreds of noisy Cambodian VIPs such as local businessmen and government officials. Despite being the guest-of-honor, nobody paid any attention to what he said during his entire speech, which was also translated into Khmer (the local language). They simply continued to eat, drink, and chat noisily. Even the second author, who was among the audience, could hardly hear a word through the din. This was the boss's first visit to Cambodia, and the experience was truly educational. His speech had been prepared in advance for the audience, but nobody seemed to care. When the boss read out from his speech that this dinner banquet "had to be one of the highlights of [his] long career," it was hard to suppress a laugh such was the comic irony of the situation. Absolutely nobody was listening, yet at the end of the speech, he was greeted with long and loud applause.

The second author can also recall making speeches in Indonesia when he worked there. On several occasions, he encountered situations where an important and serious speech, related to the restructuring of a business, was greeted with laughter. Another colleague of his recounted a similar experience and had wondered whether there were some serious mistakes in the Bahasa translation as he was very shocked by the reaction of the audience. Only later did it emerge that this is not uncommon in Indonesia—it is a form of ironic laughter in response to bad news. Nevertheless, it can be very unsettling for the person making the speech.

At other times, one can also be caught completely off-guard by the sudden request to make an impromptu speech at a banquet or in response to the speech made by the host. This is where, like attending karaoke sessions, it is always wise to go prepared with some thoughts in mind, regardless of whether you are asked to speak or not. Like the Chinese saying, "It is always good to be prepared for the occasion" (有备而来 *you bei er lai*) than be embarrassed publicly by not knowing what to say.

The real lesson to bear in mind is that you never know exactly what to expect in Asia when it comes to delivering speeches. The request to do so may come suddenly, and the responses of the audiences can be so different. However, it is definitely to be expected, and, whatever the reaction may be from the audience, you should just simply smile. This will keep everyone happy. Of course, you should always bear in mind the "KISS" principle—keep it simple and short. Never embarrass yourself with long speeches.

Remember the Source

There is a powerful Chinese saying, 饮水思源 (*yin shui si yuan*), which means "when you drink your water, remember its source." It is used to invoke a sense of obligation and gratitude to those who have helped you along the way. We have often found that Asian friends and partners will always be very grateful when we help them with their businesses or other things in life, and will seek ways to reciprocate our kind deeds. Often their sense of wanting to reciprocate may even seem exaggerated, unnecessary, and embarrassing to you, especially when weighed against the help that you might have rendered. Yet, it is such a strong desire to reciprocate that it makes you feel very good that a deeper relationship has developed with those you have helped, and that the bonding and gratitude are much more real and alive than the more superficial relationships you may have experienced elsewhere in the world.

Asian cultures stress the importance of never forgetting those to whom you owe your success and those who lent a helping hand when you were in need. If such a debt cannot be paid back in one's own lifetime, it becomes the obligation of one's children and grandchildren to repay the debt. If anyone receives a great favor but is unwilling to repay the obligation, he and his family are badly disgraced. In Asia, friendship is a two-edged sword. Friendship carries with it an additional set of obligations that are not common in the West. It is more than the simple "you scratch my back, and I'll scratch yours" of Western civilization. It is deeper, more emotional, and can be a source of great discomfort and shame if the obligation cannot be fulfilled. This is the root cause of the over-hospitality and excessive generosity that Westerners often face.

The smart Westerner will take advantage of the obligations held by his Asian partners to further his business, but he must do it carefully, as there is one major catch. Once an obligation has been fully repaid, it means everything is quits and, unless the relationship has been carefully cultivated over time, the Westerner may find himself out in the cold very quickly, wondering where this wonderful friendship has disappeared!

Asian entertainment is more than just obligations. It is a way of life, a way of conducting business, a way of getting to know each other in a more relaxed environment, and it is used to show gratitude as well. Many Westerners are trapped by the "9 to 5" work model while many Asians work to the "Beyond 5" model. This is the time when true feelings are expressed, when people's characters are genuinely assessed, and when deals are struck.

Therefore, when you and your Asian partner are next back in the karaoke lounge at two in the morning, crooning out old favorites such as "My Way" and "Wonderful Tonight," you should be able to appreciate each other a lot better. Despite feeling exhausted and having had one whiskey too many, you can both feel you are in this relationship for the long haul, whether it is for pleasure or out of obligation. But, whatever you are drinking, remember its source!

Endnotes

1. The first author.
2. For example, citing medical reasons.
3. Even so, when there are opportunities in between the drinking and toasting sessions, try to quickly eat whatever food is served.
4. In this case, the speaker was the first author of this book.
5. *See* Chapter 12.
6. In fact, during the drinking or karaoke session, your local host would have typically invited some ladies to join in the drinking and singing.
7. Even so, at times, the audience can be quite noisy too, especially if it is an evening function.

将 能 而 君 不。御 者 胜。

jiang neng er jun bu yu zhe sheng

He (the general) who is capable and not interfered with by the ruler will win.

(Sun Zi Bingfa, 孙子兵法, *Line 3.49 of Chapter 3 on Strategic Attacks*, 谋攻 *(mou gong))*

CHAPTER 9

The Industrious and Adaptable Asian

Going the Extra Mile and More

Purposeful Sacrifice

One of the most remarkable traits of Asians, particularly those of Chinese descent, is their pure industriousness and willingness to make sacrifices for long-term benefits.[1] Much of this can be traced back to Confucian values and ethics. To some extent, this is similar to the Protestant work ethic of the West, except that over the years, much of the Protestant work ethics have been greatly eroded. In contrast, Chinese Asians do not seem to lose their determination to work hard, their resourcefulness to achieve more, and their willingness to make sacrifices.

Take the case of education. We are constantly amazed and impressed, for example, by how far Asians will stretch themselves to educate their children. They will sacrifice themselves financially to give their children the best start in life. Of course, Westerners do the same for their children, but Asians seem to be willing to go that extra mile to operate at a different level of selflessness. This is because many of them missed out on educational opportunities themselves and want their children to do better than they did. As such, they are willing to forgo luxuries such as holidays, new clothes, a new car, or a new home so that they can channel all their savings into their children's education. In many cases, they will downgrade their living standards, borrow heavily, or even mortgage their homes to allow the next generation to study in the United States, Australia, or the United Kingdom.

It is true that in the more developed and richer parts of Asia such as Hong Kong, Singapore, and Taiwan, the more privileged children may not quite have the same zeal. However, they are constantly reminded by their parents of the importance of academic excellence and the need to work hard in life. In fact, this accumulated wealth has enabled these richer parents to engage private home tutors for their children as well as expose them to other kinds of training, including music, dancing, painting, etc., all aimed at getting their children ahead in life.[2]

What is significant to note is that such a trend is being repeated among the rich in China, Indonesia, and Malaysia today. Many successful businessmen even go a step further by sending their children, many of them no older than 10 years old, to boarding schools in Singapore, Australia, the United Kingdom, and the United States. The aim is to ensure a better future for their children. In the process, sacrifices are made by both sides. The parents will have to work harder and miss their children while they are studying overseas. The children, in turn, also miss their parents and, at the same time, will have to work extra hard as a way of repaying the investment made by their parents. All these efforts and sacrifices are all focused on achieving long-term results.

Insatiable Appetite for Hard Work

This willingness to make sacrifices for a purpose translates into working even harder to earn more money. In Vietnam, you see mothers working as hotel cleaners six days a week and studying English or computer-related subjects every evening while still managing to get their children to and from school. The same phenomena are repeated all over China. The hunger to move ahead is overwhelming and is not confined to married people. Young people behave likewise. They are like sponges, wanting to soak up whatever knowledge available as quickly as possible. For example, in China, bookstores are always filled with youngsters. As they often cannot afford to buy the books, they can be seen eagerly reading in the stores themselves.

Young Asians are also very keen to work for foreign companies. The reason—not only do they pay more, they also provide better training and exposure. Gaining working experience in foreign companies is a definite way to move ahead in the corporate world. Indeed, there is absolutely no shortage of diligence and ambition.

We often sense that the hard work and commitment shown by Asians are not necessarily nor fully recognized by Westerners. For them, it is a 24-hour, 7-day week, 365-days-a-year business. In contrast, the many years of affluence, social reforms, and strong union powers among Western societies have reduced working hours tremendously. Today, it is more of a 8-hour, 5-day week, 230-days-a-year business, with some Western countries, like France, working even fewer hours. This anomaly of work ethics has made it more difficult for Westerners to understand their Asian counterparts, causing some lobby groups to even accuse Asian companies of exploiting their workers. The truth is, Asian workers do not seem to mind at all.

The hard work ethics also spill over to the management of businesses. For example, the typical Asian retail store owner will never turn away customers if they show up when he is about to close the store for the day. To him, it is natural and sensible to keep the store open for a while more so as to clinch more sales. The same seldom happens in the Western world.[3] The retail operator is more than likely to tell you to come back the next day. The same is also true of larger companies. The big Asian bosses have no hesitation about working overtime, over the weekends, and even during public holidays. His working style and behavior can become very infectious too in that his senior management team ends up doing likewise.[4]

Beyond Official Duties and Office Hours

Other than working beyond office hours, Asians are superb at going the extra mile outside office hours and official duties in order to get things done. A friend recounted this story. One day, while on his way to Singapore's Changi Airport in a taxi to catch an international flight, he took a call from a client who needed him to travel to Vietnam on some urgent business the following week. The trouble was, he needed a visa to enter Vietnam, and he would be out of Singapore for the rest of the week. His second passport was at home, and he was carrying the only spare passport photos in his briefcase. Fortunately for him, the taxi driver, Halid, whom he soon came to respect and admire, overheard his predicament and swiftly offered to take his passport photos from him, collect the other passport and visa form from his home, and drop them all off at the Vietnamese embassy.

Owing to this out-of-the-way gesture by the taxi driver, this friend was able to make the visit to Vietnam the following week. Needless to say, he was incredibly impressed with the whole experience. In a very courteous matter-of-fact way, the taxi driver, Halid, had transformed himself from a humble taxi driver into our friend's travel agent, personal assistant, and savior, all in one. More importantly, he had demonstrated a unique kind of entrepreneurial spirit and hospitality. Halid is certainly not the only example that one will experience in Asia. There are many such Halids in Asia, and this is what makes Asia extra special.[5] Indeed, that many Asians are known to go the extra mile to get things done, and to ensure that the other party feels welcome and treasured, is something that can give them the competitive edge in this modern and fast-changing business world.

Socializing and Relationship-Building

Another very strong attribute of the typical Asian businessman and executive is his ability to cultivate business ties and relationships, which is done largely outside and beyond office hours. As this subject will be dealt with in much greater detail in Chapter 12, we only wish to raise several points here.

First, socializing and relationship-building are very personal issues; one must be prepared to go the extra mile and put in the time and effort in order to be successful. Second, having done so, more time and effort are needed to sustain, maintain, and improve the personal relationship that has been established. It must be done individually; it cannot be delegated or outsourced to someone else. Third, the returns, including that in the business realm, are often not immediate and unpredictable. One cannot insist on or include business deals as part of the relationship. Finally, and as mentioned earlier, there are no official working hours for the building of personal ties and relationships. It is a 24-hour, 365-days-a-year job.

In sum, one must believe that there are more benefits to be gained from having strong and sustainable personal relationships with one's business partners and associates, and that this goes beyond offering the best products and services. In other words, having strong business relationships that are anchored on personal ties can even help to smooth over some inadequacies in the product and service offering, as well as the terms in any business contract. In fact, it is a very powerful approach to doing business in Asia.

The Ambidextrous Organization

One of the latest management jargons in the West is "the ambidextrous organization." Uncertainty in today's business environment and intense business competition make adaptability a strategic issue for many companies. Successful companies must not only be adaptive, innovative, and proactive, they must also be good at running efficient operations, rolling out new products, and meeting the fast-changing needs of consumers. In other words, these companies have to be ambidextrous to excel. They must have the ability to respond to threats quickly, be adaptive to new opportunities, and, at the same time, be able to align their businesses and activities around their core competencies.

At first sight, all of this seems incredibly sensible until you sit back and reflect on what holds back most of today's organizations from being ambidextrous. Most Western organizations today are enslaved to processes and engorged with initiative overload. Overstressed managers struggling with an ever-increasing portfolio of tasks simply have no time to pause and think. Everyone is expected to be a leader, a great coach, to display drive and initiative, to be socially responsible, to challenge the status quo, to be a clear and convincing communicator/influencer, to multi-task, to innovate, to run projects efficiently, and to deliver results to keep the boss and shareholders happy. The modern-day manager, quite simply, has become so bloated with responsibilities that when threats and/or opportunities arise, his flexibility to respond is painfully slow.

The Ambidextrous Asian

Interestingly, the concept of an ambidextrous organization actually fits nicely with Asian culture, particularly those of Chinese descent. The Chinese hate to be constrained by Western work models, unless they have been brainwashed by a zealous multinational or by a conformist regime. They appreciate the need for discipline and a clear strategy, but they desire the freedom to be adaptive and opportunistic, and to be risk takers. In fact, this is very much reflective of the teaching of the great Chinese military strategist Sun Zi, who argued that when it comes to matters of war, there is a need for strong discipline, clear communication, and ruthless determination. However, he also emphasized the need to be flexible and adaptive to the changing environment and battle situations. This can be clearly demonstrated by the following saying:

水 因 地 而 制 流， 兵 因 敌 而 制 胜。
shui yin di er zhi liu   bing yin di er zhi sheng

Just as water controls its flow according to the characteristics of the terrain, an army should create its victory according to the situation of the enemy.

~ *Sun Zi Bingfa*, 孙子兵法,
Line 6.61 of Chapter 6 on Weaknesses and Strengths,
虚实 (*xu shi*)

More importantly, Sun Zi also implied that to be able to exercise flexibility and adaptability, there are times when one may have to go against the strict processes, procedures, orders, and discipline that military orders entail in order to gain that decisive advantage in war. Thus, he said:

军 命 有 所 不 受。
jun ming you suo bu shou

There are some military orders that need not be obeyed.

~ *Sun Zi Bingfa*, 孙子兵法,
Line 8.12 of Chapter 8 on Variations and Adaptability,
九变 (*jiu bian*)

What this means is that while rules and conventions are important, there are times when one must be prepared to act and behave differently. In fact, Chinese entrepreneurs and businessmen are not only known to seize opportunities when they arise (见机行事 *jian ji xing shi*), they are also known for their ability to adapt and adjust their strategies and tactics according to the opportunities that have arisen (随机应变 *sui ji ying bian*). Of course, such actions are possible as they are premised on the assumption that the person closest to the ground knows best, and he needs to be empowered to make those decisions. Not surprisingly, Sun Zi advocated this empowerment principle by the following quotes:

故 战 道 必 胜 ，　 主 曰： 无 战 ，　 必 战 可 也；
gu zhan dao bi sheng　zhu yue　wu zhan　　bi zhan ke　ye

战 道 不 胜 ，　 主 曰： 必 战 ，　 无 战 可 也。
zhan dao bu sheng　zhu yue　bi zhan　　wu zhan ke　ye

If the assessment of the battle situation is one of definite victory, the general must engage in battle even though the ruler has issued orders not to do so. If an assessment of the battle situation is one of definite defeat, the general must not engage in battle, though the ruler has issued orders to do so.

~ *Sun Zi Bingfa*, 孙子兵法,
Lines 10.40 and 10.41 of Chapter 10 on Terrain,
地形 (*di xing*)

In sum, in dealing with Asian, especially Chinese, entrepreneurs, businessmen, and companies, one can easily witness the ambidextrous spirit at work. Surprisingly, when it comes to Asian managers working for Western multinational corporations (MNCs), the ambidextrous Asian spirit seems to disappear into thin air. What has happened? Let us venture some possible explanations for this anomaly.

The concept of the ambidextrous organization, as originated in the West, is clearly a move in the right direction. However, the problem lies in its implementation. Western companies operating in Asia tend to load their Asian managers and executives with overwhelming rules, processes, and procedures that have been built up over the years to run a highly structured and controlled organization. We are certain many of you have encountered this before. When you first joined one of these MNCs, you were very impressed but also overwhelmed by the volumes of manuals that you had to read and follow. Even annual budgeting and planning can turn into a "fill-in-the-blanks" exercise that is strictly enforced.

To release the ambidextrous spirit that is inherent in Asian managers, these Western companies need to radically trim back the workload clutter and the follow-the-rules mentality. This is necessary in order to create the needed space to allow Asian managers to be proactive, adaptive, and innovative. The smart ones will also consider some of the best attributes of Asians today: the service culture, the entrepreneurial spirit, and the hunger to improve oneself. Of course, a certain degree of business discipline and trans-parency is still required, but the more successful Western companies in Asia will strive for the right balance between control and flexibility. Not only will this attract, motivate, and retain the best Asian talent, it will also deliver success faster in the marketplace.

Beware of Job Destruction

It seems that in the West, senior leaders, especially the human resources (HR) departments, are absolutely focused on defining, measuring, and benchmarking what employees do, how they perform, and how they compare to the standard criteria of a global company. This is indeed laudable, but often the whole purpose of the process is lost as it becomes overcomplicated and, with the rise in information technology, increasingly depersonalized.

Let us start with the job description or job profile, as some companies define it. This is a classic case of logic gone demented, a titanic clash between Aristotle and Confucius, which Asians in the large part dislike. The objective of a job description is to capture in two pages what exactly every manager or employee actually does. This makes it easier to advertise the position and also, more arguably, to determine the value of that job, and how it should be rewarded. This is pure Western logic, which Aristotle would have been proud of, but it does not take into account the potential growth opportunities, which Asians like. The job description becomes job destruction.

Asians in general do not like to be constrained by their job titles or descriptions. In fact, they work far harder and broader than these documents might suggest. They do recognize the importance of order and hierarchy, how the approval process works, and who is the boss. However, at the same time, they want the freedom to operate beyond the normal definitions of their position. Often, their tremendous networking or business relationships can lead to other commercial benefits for the company they are working for. Unfortunately, if this falls outside their box of responsibility, as defined by the company, they may not act upon it.

The same applies to the objective setting and appraisal system most Western companies employ. Limiting the operating environment to, on average, five to six business objectives, restricts the enthusiasm and ambitions of the Asian mind. Asians recognize the impact of other events on how any business will operate. They also know that change is inevitable. Therefore, the long drawn out affair of negotiating business objectives and targets becomes a rather pointless and futile process and exercise to them. It is only done to keep the Western companies and their bosses happy. Asians, we suspect, would far rather be told, "Look, you did a great job last year. I just need you to grow the business this year with the same positive attitude. Let us overcome any obstacle along the way, and I will be fair in evaluating

your performance as a whole, whether it is good or bad."
End of story. This can then be accompanied by a series of
coffee meetings throughout the year to see how they keep
themselves motivated and on track.

To reiterate, job specifications, descriptions, and performance appraisals that are used on Asians are tools
used to appease Western HR requirements rather than
to define their responsibilities and goals. As an Asian
colleague said to one of us in his previous role, "Boss, tell
me your expectations, keep Head Office off my back, and
I will always deliver." This, he did, year after year. How
much more enriching and empowering our business could
be if we just put an end to the never-ending corporate
pipeline of rules, policies, and initiatives and created more
time and space for the ambidextrous Asian to blossom
in his job.

Evaluating Asian Managers

Another area of potential difficulty is in the criteria used
by many global companies to assess Asian managers. Too
often, we have seen extremely good and effective Asian
managers lose out to their Western peers because the criteria
used are Western created. In general, Asians tend to lose
out in areas such as communication and influencing skills.
This is because their Western peers are more articulate,
accomplished, and experienced in making presentations.
They also talk louder and more confidently. In contrast,
the Asian peers tend to talk less and remain silent during
heated debates. What is often overlooked is that these same
Asian managers are working hard behind the scenes with
their networking to get deals done and relationships sorted
out. They are actually extremely good at influencing and

communicating, but only to their clients and not before their bosses. Moreover, these activities usually take place late into the night and even over the weekend, largely out of sight of their bosses.

By keeping things simple but, at the same time, remaining straightforward, fair, and honest, Western companies will get a lot more out of their Asian managers and employees. They would save themselves an incredible amount of time and bureaucracy by downplaying the Western HR models. Overreliance on them not only creates bias against the Asian managers, it can also strangle the potential energy and lateral thinking of their Asian talent. Asians, like most human beings, respond well to the personal touch.

The Middle Way

It is often the case in Asia, particularly when it comes to undertaking business deals in China, Vietnam, Thailand, Indonesia, and other parts of Southeast Asia, that a Western business will come up against unexpected obstacles that were not foreseen in the business plan. At other times, it may well be after the deal is concluded that surprises appear, normally business practices, contracts, or relationships that were unknown at the time of acquisition or partnership. This can be extraordinarily frustrating and stressful for the Western investor if he is not prepared for such eventualities. Such unconventional difficulties require unconventional managers, who have lateral thinking, a street-smart attitude, and wheeler-dealing skills to come up with the solutions and implement them. Often, it is not a question of black or white but shades of gray, and learning to deal with ambiguity is something many companies have to get used to if they are to survive.

This can often be referred to as the "middle way," the route of compromise and quid pro quos, where outright conflicts or breakdowns in the business relationship can be avoided. To work your way through this requires a high degree of open-mindedness and flexibility on the part of the Western company, and a willingness and trust to allow one or two of its unconventional managers to do the problem solving.

These days, there appears to be an overemphasis on leadership in Western organizations, in other words, trying to make everyone a leader in their own right. Leadership is extremely important, but let us be real. We also need a lot of managers who can execute the strategies and do the fire fighting when required. At the end of the day, any organization needs both types of people. Yes, we do need some visionary leaders to come up with the big and bold ideas, concepts, and plans; to inspire the rank and file; and to point the company in the right direction. However, we also need many more mid-level managers who are able to solve the day-to-day problems, have the initiative to take the right course of action for the benefit of the company, and go the extra mile to bring in additional business for the company.

In Asia, where opportunities come very quickly and disappear equally fast, and where threats abound, you do need plenty of outstanding officers and soldiers in your team. You only have to play the enlightened general. For the most part, these officers and men will operate as a well-disciplined and organized army, but occasionally you will need them to act as guerrillas in order to take on a less orthodox approach to business. The unconventional "middle way" can become the critical path to sustain business success.

Understanding Asian Leadership

Western corporate leaders operating in Asia would do much better if they bothered to study and understand more about Asian leadership. Many of these attributes can be found in the works of philosophers like Confucius, Lao Zi, and Sun Zi. They have much to contribute to what makes an excellent leader. In particular, they share the view that a great leader is someone who is felt, not seen. In other words, he gets his work done without being over-bearing and over-interfering. The following quotation from Lao Zi's *Dao De Jing* (老子: 道德经) probably sums up this aspect extremely well:

太上，不知有之；其次，亲而誉之；
tai shang   bu zhi you zhi   qi ci   qin er yu zhi

其次，畏之；其次，侮之。
qi ci   wei zhi   qi ci   ru zhi

信不足焉，有不足焉。
xin bu zu yan   you bu zu yan

悠兮其贵言。功成事遂，
you xi qi gui yan   gong cheng shi sui

百姓皆谓："我自然"。
bai xin jie wei   wo zi ran

The best leader governs without being known and felt by his subjects. The next best is a leader who is loved and praised. Next is a leader who is feared. The worst kind of leader is one who is despised. Such a leader does not trust his people, and they, in turn, are unfaithful to him. When the best ruler's orders are accomplished successfully, his subjects will feel as though they have done so by themselves.

~ Chapter 17 of Lao Zi's *Dao De Jing*
老子道德经第十七章

According to Lao Zi, the greatest leader is someone who does not need to make his presence felt. After giving out his orders, he has a high level of trust and confidence that they will be carried out successfully. This can only be done if he has selected the right people to join him, trained them well, and empowered them to complete the assigned tasks. He refrains from intervention and interference, and uses empowerment to achieve his goals. As such, when the tasks are completed, the subjects have a great sense of fulfillment as they feel that they have done so all by themselves. In this way, the great leader gains the trust and loyalty of his subjects. This element of reciprocal trust builds unity to the extent that the leader and his subjects are in perfect harmony with one another. This is what effective governance is all about. It starts with an enlightened leader who brings out the inherent entrepreneurial and ambidextrous spirit within each of the people he leads.

Every leader in a Western organization likes to profess how important people are and how well he delegates. Yet, the reality will be self-deluding if he tries to enforce strict adherence to organizational processes and procedures. It will be even worse if he is also too controlling and smothering, and cannot stop interfering or feeling that he knows better. It will be very difficult to implement Lao Zi's style of Asian leadership in these Western organizations. This is because a major mental and paradigm shift is needed, and Western leaders have to be trained and sensitized to recognize such differences. However, companies and leaders who are prepared to understand what makes effective leadership in Asia will be amazed at how far they can go in managing their Asian subordinates and businesses.

Becoming a More Effective Leader in Asia

How can one then become a more effective corporate leader operating in Asia? Here are some key points that may be worth considering. First, it is extremely important to be open-minded. The wise leader does not impose a personal agenda on his management team. It is critical to be open to whatever may happen. Events cannot always be controlled or predicted. Therefore, the business needs to respond to challenges and opportunities as there are plenty of these in Asia.

Second, the leader must learn to let go. This is very much advocated by the philosophy of Lao Zi, as cited earlier. Once a new business or project has started, try to stand back as much as possible and learn to let go and let the managers take over. Avoid the temptation to interfere or spoil the process. Try not to be overly helpful. If you let people feel trusted and empowered, they will find the right solution. By trusting the process, you are also inspiring them to become leaders. Of course, it takes a lot of courage and trust to empower people. However, if you have trained your people well, and have selected the right person for the job, you must have the confidence, trust, and faith that he will complete the job successfully. In fact, we will argue that this is an effective test of your leadership— have you been successful in grooming and training your people? If he fails and/or if you have to intervene, it reflects poorly on your leadership qualities.

Third, the leader must learn to free his mind from worry and from being clogged up with opinions, bias, judgments, etc. He needs to unclutter his thinking and focus on the more important macro and long-term issues of the company. Leave the short-term operational matters to the managers and the rank and file. We only have a limited number of hours a day, and if we spend most of them majoring on the minor issues, then we will have limited time to major on the major issues. This is such a simple rule in managing time. When you spend less and less time worrying about whether your Asian managers and employees can perform, you will have more time to think about long-term strategies for the company. The quality of your thinking will also improve. You will then see how positively this will impact your people and your business if you do not let the mundane issues worry you and occupy your thoughts.

Fourth, the leader must learn when to be soft and when to be strong. This seemingly contradictory approach is yet another powerful way to manage people and business issues. In fact, it is known as the yin-yang (阴阳) approach in Chinese, and it involves balancing seemingly contradictory and opposing positions. This is very different from the typical trade-off approach that is commonly used in the West.[6,7] In Asia, a corporate leader must learn that being soft does not mean that one is weak. Rather softness can also be used to create strength when used appropriately. The metaphor of water has been used extensively by Chinese philosophers such as Sun Zi, Confucius, and Lao Zi. Water, by nature is soft, fluid, and adaptive. Yet, it can be very exploitative, damaging, and powerful as it can push boulders, cut valleys, and destroy properties when it turns into tsunamis. In essence, its characteristics depend very much on the environment that it is in.

Fifth, and this also contradicts very much the limelight-seeking approach of Western leadership, the leader in Asia should learn to be humble and be part of the larger community in which he is. Many Asian cultures advocate humility as a virtue. It is a way to build and maintain harmony with those around you. One is judged more by his deeds and actions, and not by what he can promise. Even when one has achieved a lot, one should avoid glorifying oneself.

Go Beyond and Beneath What You See

In the fast-paced Western corporate life, face-to-face communication between senior and middle managers is often restricted to sporadic meetings, where people are largely judged by their appearance, communication skills, ability to influence—both commercially and politically— and, ultimately, delivery of results. Westerners, in general, tend to do far better in the first three criteria than their Asian counterparts, who often end up in the shadows. This is due to the fact that Westerners have more experience in manipulating and influencing audiences with their carefully choreographed presentations and written documents.

As senior management remains largely Western, Western managers are typically on the right side of the double glazing.[8] This is because Western managers are more likely to argue their points aggressively and do not hold back in confrontations. Consequently, their Asian counterparts can end up being easily misjudged, even when they are actually better at delivering business results. There are many examples of situations where, if not careful, a Western chief executive officer (CEO) operating in Asia may end up misjudging an Asian employee and, as a consequence, condemn him to a mediocre career.

Job interviews provide another interesting example. Asians tend to be humble about their achievements and, rather than trumpeting them out loud, would prefer that you discover these for yourself during the interview. It is therefore critical that the Western CEO or senior manager who is doing the interview is able to dig deeper into the curriculum vitae of the Asian candidate. You need to ask and probe more in order to get the best candidate.

Another method used by Western companies that may be biased against Asians is that of assessment centers. These tend to be frequently used by Western companies at the recruitment stage or, increasingly, at middle management level to determine the right candidates for immediate employment or for promotion to senior management positions. In the latter case, the company will put, say, 10 to 12 middle managers from all over the globe through three or four days of various projects and activities, which are observed by a group of senior managers.

Again, the more modest and humble Asians will generally lose out because they will be out-shouted and out-gunned by their Western peers. The percentage of Asian participants who voice their opinions publicly tends to be very low, and, consequently, they risk looking uncompetitive and even disinterested. As one senior Western manager admitted, "I judge silence as acquiescence rather than as a means to signal disagreement whilst maintaining harmony." If assessment centers are to be successful, assessments should be conducted with only Asian candidates in an Asian setting, with a mixture of Western and Asian senior management operating as observers.

Another area to watch out for is that of making presentations. Sadly, the PowerPoint presentation has become one of the most critical deciders in an executive's career. People literally live or die by them. It has also become one of the most abused communication tools. With careful statistics presented in beautiful graphs, and accompanied by outstanding photos and a video, an underperforming business unit can be made to look fantastic. While we have seen some Asians do an excellent job in their presentations, there are many who do not. Some, unlike their Western counterparts, do not spend enough time preparing, drafting, and rehearsing the presentation. Some do not like to either be vocal about their successes or, on the contrary, their failures. In most cases, they simply do not play the "game of charades" that is going on. Rather than judge Asians by their presentations, it is better to have a one-on-one business discussion with them to gauge how things are going. This is far more engaging for them and will elicit a more positive response.

Judge Actions and Results, Not Words

Ultimately, most Asians prefer to be judged by their results and not by the verbal and visual diarrhea that can take place in corporate life. They prefer to just get on with the job, work very hard at it, and for as long as possible in order to achieve results that can surpass expectations. They are not very skillful in formal corporate politics nor are they articulate enough to impress their Western bosses. However, when they do deliver, like everyone else, they expect to receive the well-deserved rewards and recognition. When this comes about, it can become a very powerful motivator for the next level of achievements. Thus, the Western leader's ability to distinguish the substance from the froth among his mixture of Western and Asian employees will determine whether he can keep the best Asian talent within his company—something so essential if he wants his company to excel even more.

Endnotes

1. Without doubt, there are some Asian races that do not share such an industrious drive for work.

2. Indeed, private tuition is a very big industry in Taiwan, Hong Kong, and Singapore. Those parents who are unable to engage home tutors resort to sending their children to tuition centers.

3. The exception would be a store run by an immigrant Asian. Even then, he would have to abide by the local laws governing retail store opening hours.

4. Indeed, the big bosses and senior management team of two of the companies in which the first author is on the board of directors are known to behave exactly as has been described.

5. In another episode, the spouse of the first author was shopping in downtown Kuala Lumpur in November 2007. She was trying to get to another place but could not get a taxi. Through sheer hospitality, a female shopper, who was a total stranger to her, gave her a ride, with absolutely no strings attached.

6. Readers who are keen to pursue and understand more about the yin-yang approach may wish to refer to Chapter 13, "Strategic Tradeoffs and Yin-Yang Contradictions: Seeking the Balance," by Wee C.H. *Sun Zi Bingfa: Selected Insights and Applications*. Singapore: Prentice Hall, Pearson Education (Southeast Asia), 2005.

7. In the trade-off approach, you only opt for one. In other words, you either choose the soft or the strong approach.

8. *See* Chapter 3.

辞卑而益备者， 进也；
ci　bei　er　yi　bei　zhe　　　jin　ye

辞强而进驱者， 退也；
ci　qiang　er　jin　qu　zhe　　　tui　ye

无约而请和者， 谋也；
wu　yue　er　qing　he　zhe　　　mou　ye

When the envoy (of the enemy) speaks very humbly and lowly while preparations are being intensified, the enemy is planning to attack.

When the envoy (of the enemy) speaks arrogantly and aggressively with threats to attack, the enemy is actually preparing to withdraw.

When the envoy (of the enemy) asks for a truce when there is no prior agreement nor understanding, the enemy is scheming.

(Sun Zi Bingfa, 孙子兵法, *Lines 9.45 to 9.47 of Chapter 9 on Movement and Deployment of Troops,* 行军 *(xing jun))*

CHAPTER 10

Deciphering the True Message

The Key to Removing Misunderstanding

Deciphering the Truth

One of the greatest challenges a Westerner faces when he works in Asia for the first time is trying to get a straight answer or understand what the local is trying to tell him. Westerners will find that the cultures and political systems in Asia have a built-in bias against confrontation and disagreement. This makes it hard to get people to express their opinions or give straight answers to questions, especially to bosses who are Westerners. Most Asians are uncomfortable with giving a direct response for fear of offending or upsetting the other party. To be polite and to avoid conflict, Asians will put a message across in a more indirect way. As such, it takes the listener much skill and experience to figure out the truth. This includes understanding the body language, facial expressions, the context in which the message is given, and the kinds of qualifiers being used. Indeed, the real challenge for Westerners is to differentiate what is truly a "yes" from a "no" answer. This is because the outright "no" is often "packaged" in a polite "yes" response that can easily confuse and mislead the listener.

Watch Out for the Subtlety of Responses

The ability to read the correct message is crucial to business decisions and actions in Asia. Take the case of a business meeting to address important and critical issues that are confronted by a company. In the West, such a forum is often used as the "be all and end all" process for determining the correct course of strategic action to take. Participants can even whip themselves up into a frenzy, proposing various solutions and courses of action to take. Fierce arguments and debates will be the order of the day. No one will give in if he thinks his view is the best. At the end of the process, a solution will be found even if not everyone agrees to it.

If such a process is to be repeated in Asia, the Western bosses will be in for a big surprise. It will be worse if these senior management teams think they are seemingly blessed with the gift of local expertise. At such a meeting, they may still whip up the same frenzy and propose all kinds of action and solutions. Then the pivotal moment arrives as they ask their Asian counterparts, who have remained rather silent throughout the meeting, if such actions and solutions can be executed. In many instances, the Asian counterparts are likely to give a qualified "yes" rather than an outright "no," even if the proposed courses of action and solutions may be largely improbable or impractical in the Asian context.

The irony is that many Western senior management teams will take the qualified "yes" as a definite "yes," and fail to understand all the qualifiers, observe the body language, and read all the other subtle facial expressions, mannerisms and tone of voice when their Asian counterparts give their answers. Typically, these senior Western management teams will leave such meetings feeling highly satisfied. They may even feel that their presence has brought much added value to the meeting and that they have now decisively moved things forward. They then enjoy their flight home and happily report to their superiors that they have now "fixed" whatever issues were bothering everyone in that Asian country.

The shock will come some months later, when hardly any progress has been made and the problems remain largely unresolved. The reason—the views and opinions of the Asian counterparts have been grossly misinterpreted. Put another way, many of these Western bosses have assumed things that were not there and have misjudged the messages that were conveyed to them. Such incidents are by no means uncommon. In fact, they often happen and can cause much misunderstanding, unnecessary tension, and friction, even within the same company.

A Case Example

Without doubt, one must be extremely careful when it comes to the comprehension of messages in Asia. You really need to supercharge the antennae to sense what your Asian partner, customer, or employee is telling you. For example, in Sri Lanka, the body signal denoting agreement is mainly through waggling one's head. However, there are actually three subtle but distinct waggles, which only the experienced expatriate can detect. It ranges from the confident and clear "yes" waggle, meaning "you are absolutely right," to the rather hesitant "yes" waggle, meaning "I am not entirely sure you are correct," to the most difficult "yes" waggle, meaning "I have never heard such a stupid idea!" Indeed, after working in Sri Lanka for three years, the second author would often find himself waggling his head in business meetings without realizing that he was doing it.

Understanding Chinese Expressions and Behavior

In view of the increasing importance of China as an economic power, it is perhaps relevant for us to discuss more about Chinese expressions and behavior. To begin with, like many Asians and unlike in the West, the typical Chinese tends to be rather humble in the way he speaks and behaves, at times to the extent of being apologetic. Take the case of a Chinese banquet. The typical Chinese host, despite preparing a sumptuous 8- to 10-course dinner with unlimited wines and liquor, will always say that the food is plain and simple, and hopes that his guests will enjoy it. Few Chinese hosts will brag about the food and drinks that he is offering, despite the fact that they could be the finest dishes prepared by the best chefs in the country. They are very indirect and humble, and expect the guests to show their appreciation once they have witnessed and tasted what has been served.

In contrast, when such an elaborate meal is offered in the West, the host will take advantage of the occasion to talk about how much detail has gone into the preparation of the food, the wines, etc., and will also not hesitate to introduce the chef to his guests. This is the Western way of telling his guests how important they are, and how much effort has been put into the occasion. They are very direct and clear so that the guests know the importance that has been attached to their presence.

Trying to decipher what lies beneath the expressions and behavior is probably one of the most common forms of misunderstanding between Westerners and Asians. Yes, it is a paradox faced by any senior management from a Western company. Yet, if one bothers to spend time understanding the Chinese culture and expressions, it will not be that difficult to figure out the subtlety. Let us explain.

Indirect and Vague Expressions

As mentioned earlier, in the West, direct expressions and clarity are often preferred. People tend to say what they mean and mean what they say. Transparency and directness are keys to avoid any misunderstanding and misinterpretation of the message. However, such an approach is perceived as rude and offensive by the Chinese. To avoid the embarrassing and hurting the other party, the Chinese prefer to speak in euphemisms and to use the indirect and subtle way.[1] For example, 声东击西 (*sheng dong ji xi*) literally means "making a feint to the East but hitting out in the West." It is often used to highlight that the intention is not the one that is being expressed. Similarly, 指桑骂槐 (*zhi sang ma huai*) literally means "pointing at the mulberry but scolding the locust tree." It is often used to point out someone's shortcomings and mistakes without mentioning the name directly. It is also an effective way of indicating one's hidden desire or intention, which is expressed indirectly.[2] The following are more examples of indirect expressions:

1. 发福了 (*fa fu le*): This literally means that "(you) have prospered." However, it actually means that you have put on weight. It is a very nice way of expressing something that may not be very complimentary.

2. 哪里哪里 (*na li na li*): It literally means "where." However, it is used in a humble way to indicate that it is not really the case. For example, when someone says that you are very intelligent, it is only polite to respond with "哪里 哪里 (*na li na li*)" rather than to say something like, "I am glad you noticed."

3. 不错 (*bu cuo*): This literally means "not bad." However, it will take some skill and knowledge to decipher what exactly "not bad" means. For example, when you ask a Chinese businessman how his business is doing, he will typically respond with "not bad." However, this can imply that he is driving a Mercedes S class and living in a bungalow, or it could also mean that he has made very modest achievements. The same applies when you ask a Chinese executive, "How are things going?" and you get the same "not bad" response. You really need to observe, discover, and, at times, probe to find out what exactly "not bad" means.

4. 还好 (*hai hao*) or 还行 (*hai xing*): These two sets of words are typically used to mean "it's still OK" or "still good." Like 不错 (*bu cuo*), you will have to decipher what exactly the person means when he uses such expressions. They can mean different things to different people. This is because they could be used to conceal some underlying problems, which the person does not wish to disclose, or they could be a humble way to avoid overstating the achievements. In reality, he is conveying a message that can easily be misunderstood by a listener who is not astute enough to know the difference.

As a further illustration of how easily a misunderstanding can come in the way of figuring out Chinese expressions, the first author had the amusing experience of encountering one such episode when he first visited China in the early 1980s. He was supposed to meet one of his clients for dinner at a fine restaurant in Beijing. Upon calling his client, the Chinese counterpart responded by saying 我马上就到 (*wo ma shang jiu dao*), which means "I will come immediately." Thinking that this should not take more than 15 minutes, he waited outside the entrance to the restaurant. The client did not show up for two hours! Of course, the client, on arrival, apologized saying that it took him longer than expected because of a traffic jam. It was too awkward to ask the client why he had used the phrase "马上就到 (*ma shang jiu dao*)," which gave the impression that he was going to arrive very soon.

Interestingly, several similar episodes happened to the first author, each time his Chinese counterpart arriving at least an hour late, and commonly closer to two hours. Each time, out of respect and courtesy, he refrained from asking them directly. It was some time later during a social conversation that he finally understood the real meaning of "马上就到 (*ma shang jiu dao*)." When a Chinese person uses this term, he means he is leaving immediately from where he is, and not that he will arrive straightaway! Thus, it is very important when one hears such a phrase to immediately ask where the person is and the estimated time of his arrival at the meeting site.

Rarely Lie, But May Not Tell the Truth

The ambiguous and vague approaches adopted by the Chinese have resulted in a rather misunderstood phenomenon faced by their Western counterparts. Let us put it this way—the typical Chinese rarely lies but may not tell the truth as well.

This means that he/she will not deliberately distort the truth but, more often than not, is unwilling and reluctant to disclose the full truth either. This is because the Chinese find it difficult to say "no" and would prefer, to the extent possible, to avoid any possible confrontation or embarrassment to either party. Thus, vague phrases such as "In principle, it is ok" or "I will do my best" are used to avoid using the difficult word "no."

How can one then overcome this "rarely lie but may not tell the truth" approach? How can one distinguish the "yes" from the "no"? First, to know the real answer or the truth, the listener must learn to ask the right questions, and continue to probe appropriately. This is particularly true in dealing with Chinese subordinates. To them, the simple assumption is that the boss should always know more, so there is no need to tell him more unless he asks. Interestingly, the Chinese have a very interesting saying that states "When you say more, you make more mistakes. When you say less, you make fewer mistakes. When you say nothing, you can never make mistakes (多说多错，少说少错，不说不错 *duo shuo duo cuo, shao shuo shao cuo, bu shuo bu cuo*)." Not surprisingly, the more logical strategy is to talk less than more, and to disclose less than more.

Second, to figure out the actual answer, one needs to observe body language and other nonverbal cues. This means that one has to be very sensitive and observant, and should not take what one hears for granted. Third, and as mentioned earlier, understanding the subtlety of the language helps. Fourth, the use of the messenger, as discussed in Chapter 4, will help to ease any discomfort of any possible direct confrontation or embarrassment. The use of messengers is particularly useful in negotiations with

Chinese partners and when one needs to have a better grasp of the situation. It also allows any rejection of a proposal or any suggestion or criticism to be made indirectly.

Finally, we recommend that it is always better to have a private conversation. This is an excellent way of communication that leads to both learning and "face-saving." By meeting the individual privately, you show your respect for him. When you communicate in this way, he will be more focused on digesting what you say and giving suitable feedback rather than worrying about what others may think of him. If you are unsure of the answer that has been given, probe the opposite point. If that elicits a different sort of "yes"—with affirmative nonverbal indicators—the first "yes" probably meant "no." Silence can also play an important role. In Asia, silence is active, not passive. It designates thought, not disengagement. By remaining silent to a "yes" or a "no" and not rushing ahead, it allows time for the respondent to qualify his point and potentially save face.

Understating Capabilities, Promises, and Accomplishments

Another important point to note is that the typical Chinese tends to understate his capabilities, promises, achievements, accomplishments, knowledge, etc.[3] The Chinese do not usually like to brag about what they can do but would rather let the other party discover the truth. For example, if a Chinese says he does not feel qualified for a particular responsibility, one must learn to decipher this statement more. What he actually means is that he is qualified but is very humbled by the responsibilities and challenges ahead. It is for the listener to perceive the virtue in his humility and then to convince him of his worthiness. To accept his protestations at face value might mean losing the perfect candidate for the job and, in the process, create a very dissatisfied employee.

This unassuming characteristic can perhaps be found in the teachings and influence of Confucius (孔子 *Kong Zi*). When Zi-gong (子贡), his disciple, asked him what constituted a gentleman (君子 *jun zi*[4]), Confucius responded by saying:

先 行 其 言 而 后 从 之 。
xian xing qi yan er hou cong zhi

Actions take precedence over words and then one can speak of his actions.

~ *The Analects of Confucius*, Chapter 2, verse 13,
论语第二篇：为政第十三节

Thus, the focus is on actions, not words. Moreover, if one overpromises but fails to deliver, it can lead to shame:

古 者 言 之 不 出 ， 耻 躬 之 不 逮 也 。
gu zhe yan zhi bu chu chi gong zhi bu dai ye

In ancient times, men hesitated to speak up liberally. This is because it would be very disgraceful if they cannot fulfill what they said.

~ *The Analects of Confucius*, Chapter 4, verse 22,
论语第四篇：里仁第二十二节

Beyond the Chinese

Trying to decipher the truth and distinguishing the "yes" from the "no" are not confined to the Chinese. A Western chief executive officer (CEO), experienced in Asia, once told one of us, "As a Westerner in Asia, it is such a fundamental and difficult thing to understand when 'yes' means 'no'. The communication through silence is a really tricky one where a European (like him) judges silence as acquiescence rather than as a means to signal disagreement whilst maintaining harmony. After too many years in Asia, I eventually found that witnessing conversations and understanding the true meaning of 'yes' was a good training ground. Being able to be part of a conversation and understanding the true meaning of 'yes' poses another level of difficulty. What helped me most was the admission of my inability to read 'yes' to a helpful Asian colleague who replayed meetings with me to see if I had understood the meaning of conversations correctly."

Don't Rock the Boat

Westerners need to appreciate fairly quickly that what they hear should not be taken literally. This is because Asians avoid saying unpleasant or negative things directly. This is especially so when it comes to dealing with issues that may entail serious consequences or affect the well-being of other colleagues. In such a situation, they would prefer to say nothing than risk rocking the boat. Even when they disagree with their superiors, they are unlikely to oppose their views openly as it would be seen as disrespectful. There is an inherent desire to please the boss rather than the desire to oppose him. Thus, when asked directly for their views, they may say what they think the boss would like to hear, making it very easy to assume that all is well when indeed it is the opposite.

When an urgent course of action is required, the inability to decipher what exactly the true message is can cost the Western bosses dearly. This is because in the quest for speedier communication and execution, tunnel vision can be formed regarding the issues at stake, exposing the Western bosses to severe blind spots. For example, when no opposing views are expressed, a Western boss may assume that he has achieved consensus when this is not the case. This is because no one in the audience wants to rock the boat and break the harmony of the group. They are also reluctant to challenge the boss or offer alternative views and opinions openly. For these reasons, more time is required at the outset to make absolutely sure that everyone understands the issues. In particular, and as mentioned earlier, private meetings and conversations must be conducted to get more feedback and to ensure that everyone agrees with the course of action to take the issues forward. Monitoring is needed to ensure that subsequent actions and behaviors are aligned with what has already been agreed upon. It is also a good way to identify possible confusion, disagreement, and resistance within the organization.

Handling Silence

As mentioned earlier, silence is particularly dangerous and difficult to interpret. What can be very unsettling for a Westerner is when after giving a carefully crafted presentation, instead of receiving immediate feedback, questions, or indeed applause, he gets stony silence. Often, he invites questions, but nobody bats an eyelid. There might be a few nervous smiles among the audience. Instead of staying quiet, the immediacy of the silence forces him into saying something, perhaps even repeating part of the presentation. The silence continues. This is where the Westerner needs to realize that rushing in to fill a silence in Asia may be considered impulsive or even emotional. What he needs to know is that if he remains silent himself, someone will eventually speak up, even if it is intended to save his "face" (discussed in Chapter 11).

It is important to realize that silence is often used as a stratagem among Asians for various reasons. To begin with, the typical Asian does not believe in the first mover advantage when it comes to speaking. Instead, he prefers to listen to what others have to say and use the occasion to size up the others before making his own views known. The problem with this approach is that everyone chooses to remain silent, waiting for the other person to speak up first.

Second, without a full grasp of what the boss wants, no one likes to stick his neck out. This is because he does not want to show that he is smarter than the boss by asking too many probing questions or offering too many views. Moreover, if the questions or views are not acceptable, he may be perceived as stupid and an irritant by the boss and his colleagues. Hence, the best option is the "say nothing and you can never make mistakes" strategy as discussed earlier.

Third, silence is a good way to ensure that the boat is not rocked. It ensures that options will remain open and that decisions are not rushed. Fourth, silence can be used to test the patience of the boss and others. In fact, it is also an effective way to determine the urgency of the matter at hand.

Finally, the typical Asian will avoid speaking conspicuously in public so as not to incur the jealousy of colleagues, or threaten the position of the boss, especially when his views are indeed profound. The last thing he wants is to cast the spotlight on himself and become a target for others to take him down. In sum, when silence occurs in a meeting, it does not mean that the audience agrees with what has been said. On the contrary, the audience may have very diverse views, except that they are not expressed. Indeed, this is where skills in handling silence at meetings become very important in order to find the way forward.

It Is about Reciprocity

One of the common traits of Asian society is that, in return for loyalty, unquestioning commitment, and reward, a leader will give unequivocal support for and protect his team members. While this very feudalistic model of reciprocity has its strengths in terms of unity of purpose and fierce team spirit, it also has its weaknesses, especially when underperforming team members are being tolerated. There is a tendency to close ranks and protect anyone who is vulnerable to external criticism. Asian leaders need to be very careful to achieve the right balance in compassion toward their employees. Often, they are able to recognize some weak chinks in the armor, but, for the sake of harmony and saving "face," they take no action. When challenged by Westerners on this, emotions can easily spill over. The interfering Westerner and, to a lesser extent, the underperforming team member become the issue. To present "face" to his team, the Asian manager has no choice but to defend the underperforming team member.

The continual retention of underperforming Asian executives presents a dilemma to Western leaders. How can they convince the Asian leader to remove any poor performers? Confrontation, especially public, is clearly not the right course. The middle way is to find some private time together to discuss the individual or individuals concerned. By stating that you have certain concerns about X and that you would like to hear the Asian manager's views first allows the Asian to describe X's strengths and needs. Some of your perceptions may not be valid. These have to be aired and discussed. Evidence needs to be presented. It may be a case of "You don't know X so well," in which case, you can request more time to have direct exposure to X to help to consolidate your opinion. However, where there is clear resistance and defensive behavior, then action must be taken. It has to be explained that personal fiefdoms, especially if they run contrary to corporate philosophy and policy, will not be tolerated. Strong, united teams under a fair but demanding leader are acceptable and encouraged. Everyone's credibility suffers if a weak team member is being protected. There is actually an opportunity to strengthen the Asian manager's "face" within the organization if he takes decisive action.

Of course, this is not just an Asian phenomenon, it happens in Western companies as well. However, the Confucian model of hierarchy and respect, combined with high family values, makes it even harder for an Asian manager to remove underperforming team members. If it is to be done, it has to be achieved with dignity and equity.

Open Secrets and Gossip

One of the biggest challenges for any Western business in Asia is keeping things confidential. Asia does not generally appear to have the same ethos regarding privacy and secrecy that exists in the West. Information is definitely power. As a result of this, and because of the relationship networking that exists across Asia, it is extremely difficult to keep a lid on most things. This is due to the distortion of the Confucian model. Self-respect and credibility are earned by access to information. If you are entrusted with useful information, then "face" has been given to you. Your "face" can be increased by sharing this information with people who may benefit from it. They, in return, are grateful for the information given and may one day return the favor. A whole labyrinth of mutual obligations is created by the sharing of information. This goes way beyond the expected loyalties of a Western organization. It is a version of "You scratch my back, and I'll scratch yours," but what makes it different is that less guilt is associated with it. If anything, it is very much accepted as part of social behavior.

Open secrets are also linked to gossip, which may indeed be the way in which confidential information is leaked out. Gossip also works at a different level, especially in developing Asia. It is a main source of entertainment. People love to talk about other people over a coffee or lunch. They often try to identify the politics that is going on in the office. If there is someone who is disliked, then stories are created against his character. Conspiracy theories are expounded. The unofficial internal communications process—gossip and coffee shop talk—ensures that information, whether true or false, is spread quickly throughout an organization and beyond.[5] When a story is told from person to person, especially if it is gossip or scandal, it inevitably gets distorted and exaggerated. In the worst case scenario, such gossip can even degenerate into unsubstantiated rumors.

Managing Sensitive Information

Recognizing that unguarded information may get out of hand, a Westerner operating in Asia needs to be more cautious when handling sensitive information. He must be careful about who needs to know what. However, he also has to accept that sharing certain information is unavoidable if he wants to build trust and credibility with his business partners or employees. At times, disclosing information, including some aspects of his personal life, will make him more human in the eyes of his partners and help to enhance the business relationship. Indeed, revealing personal snippets, sharing some internal concerns and fears, and raising issues that may come up in the future will help to draw him closer to the Asians as they appreciate his humanity (he is like one of us) and even his vulnerability. Not surprisingly, the Asians, in turn, will begin to share some of their own information. Over time, trust will be built up between both parties as well.

In the business world, one of the most damaging things that can happen is when corporate secrets leaked out through the grapevine become the content of gossip as well. This is where stern and tough action may have to be taken. Sun Zi, the great Chinese military strategist, was absolutely unequivocal about secrecy. While he greatly encouraged the use of spies and agents to access information on the enemy, he was ruthless if confidential information was deliberately leaked by his own people. The following quotation is very telling:

间 事 未 发， 而 先 闻 者， 间 与 所 告 者 皆 死。
jian shi wei fa   er xian wen zhe   jian yu suo gao zhe jie si

---

When espionage activities and secret operations have been leaked before their implementation, then the agents concerned and those whom they are in contact with must be put to death.

~ *Sun Zi Bingfa*, 孙子兵法,
Line 13.31 of Chapter 13 on Intelligence and Espionage,
用间 (*yong jian*)

While capital punishment is not appropriate in the world of business, clear and decisive action should be taken against individuals who are found guilty of leaking corporate secrets. Strong disciplinary action will send a strong message to the rest of the organization. The challenge lies in determining who is responsible for the leak. This is because in a group-oriented culture, Asians tend to protect their own colleagues. When quizzed and interrogated, they are seldom willing to attribute the source. Nonetheless, "punishment" may still have to be meted out to those individuals who are caught for spreading the news even if the primary source (main culprit) cannot be identified.[6] The key is to cultivate responsible behavior and instill a strong sense of accountability for one's words and actions.

Even though a Western company operating in Asia may detest gossip, it should be on its guard to avoid becoming a victim of gossip. It is ironic that one may find it necessary to plug into the information grapevine, especially those pertaining to the competitors and their products/services. This is because it can be a tremendous opportunity to access information, though one will have to distill the substance from the froth, the truth from the gossip and exaggeration. More importantly, if a Westerner becomes a member of the gossip loop, it is a clear signal and acknowledgment that he is now deemed to be an "insider" who can be trusted. Of course, this will only come about when he has built credibility and trust with other Asians.

Distinguishing the Substance from the Froth

Once the Westerner has become part of the gossip loop and has obtained whatever information is being talked about, he will need to distill the froth from the substance. To begin with, there is always no smoke without fire. Thus, all gossip, with the exception of rumors, is bound to be based on some truth. The challenge is to determine how much of it is the real thing. Remember what we said earlier about the Chinese—they rarely lie, but they seldom tell the truth either. Many Asians share similar behavior when it comes to gossip-spinning. It takes a very skillful person to sieve out the peripherals from the real stuff. The following is some advice we would like to share.

First, the key is determining the source of the information. You will be surprised to find out that many Asians will make remarks like, "Oh, I heard it from someone," without specifying the name of the person; "The talk is all over the company ...," without commenting on how true that statement is; "Many people are talking about it already," without justifying the number; "Oh, it's already an open secret," without feeling any guilt about it; and so on. Determining where the gossip came from (that is, the source) will provide you with some sense of the credibility of the information.

Second, knowing the person who shares the gossip with you is important. Is he someone who thrives on gaining social acceptance through gossip-spinning? How reliable is the person, especially in terms of closeness to the target of the gossip? Is he a friend or foe of the target? If the person who provides you with the gossip is someone of some stature and a well-respected individual, then you may want to pay serious attention to what you are hearing.

Finally, how does the information gained compare with those gathered from other sources? It is always very important to cross-check the credibility of what is gathered. For example, if the information collected from the different sources contains some common content, it will give you a higher level of confidence in figuring out the truth. The appropriate response can then be made.

Avoid Misunderstanding

The failure to understand that Asians generally do not express themselves directly has caused many Western managers to often misunderstand issues and consequently make the wrong decisions. Western managers must recognize that while direct communication and straight talking are commonly practiced in the West, they cannot expect Asians to do likewise. Cultural and social differences, among other things, have made them different. In order to do well in another culture, one has to adapt and adjust to that culture. The willingness to recognize the difference is a good step in the right direction. After all, awareness is the beginning of wisdom.

Endnotes

1. The custom of using the indirect approach of expression is not confined to the Chinese. Indeed, indirect expressions must be taken seriously among other Asian cultures too.

2. As an illustration, a Chinese mother-in-law may praise someone else's daughter-in-law directly as a way of criticizing her own daughter-in-law. By not referring to her own daughter-in-law directly, there is no embarrassment to the latter. At the same time, the mother-in-law avoids potential conflict as she can always claim that praising someone else does not tantamount to criticizing her own family members. However, the daughter-in-law must be smart enough to get the message in order to avoid further comparison and comments.

3. Although it is also true that some modern Chinese have become rather boastful of their capabilities and achievements.

4. *Jun zi* (君子) has been translated to mean "gentleman" here. In ancient China, the term *jun zi* (君子) was originally used to denote a philosopher-leader. It later evolved into referring to someone who has high moral character. See endnote 5 of Chapter 14 and pages 334–335 for more detailed explanation.

5. As an anecdote, Oscar Wilde, the famous Irish playwright, never traveled to Asia, but if he had, he would have been proud. His famous phrase, "There is only one thing in life worse than being talked about, and that is not being talked about" has a very strong set of believers in Asia!

6. These individuals will include those with whom the agent (who leaked the information) comes into contact.

廉 洁，可 辱 也；
lian jie   ke ru ye

If he is sensitive to honor, he can be insulted.

(Sun Zi Bingfa, 孙子兵法, Lines 8.28 of Chapter 8 on Variations and Adaptability, 九变 (jiu bian))

CHAPTER **11**

"Face"

Potential Hazard or Invaluable Value?

Myth or Reality

"Face" is a term that is commonly mentioned in Asia, especially within Chinese societies. It is frequently used in conversations or discussions when it is felt that someone's self-esteem or reputation has been undermined or enhanced by something he has done himself or by someone else. Many Westerners who come to work in Asia are typically cautioned in advance about the potential hazards of "face" if it is not managed properly. On the other hand, when it is handled effectively, it can also bring considerable benefits.

The significance of "face" is not helped by the many stories, true or false, that one may have heard over the years. These include businessmen who are able to secure loans from banks based on their "face" rather than on their credit worthiness; that credit terms are extended based on one's "face"; that someone with a "bigger face" in society will be able to get things done faster and more expediently; that people are known to commit suicide as the result of a severe loss of "face,"[1] due to business failures or bankruptcy, etc. All these stories tend to perpetuate and magnify the myth behind the concept of "face" in Asian societies, especially among the Chinese.

The concept of "face" is very much alive in Asia. While the stories cited above may seem rather exaggerated, there are elements of truth in them. To deny the existence of "face" is similar to denying the existence of *guanxi* among Chinese and Asians.[2] So conscious are they in trying to make themselves look and appear good before others that a lot of effort and resources are put into enhancing their "face." For example, among other reasons, branded products are highly desired by Asian consumers because they are used to project a better "face" for the consumers and to signal that they have "arrived." Not surprisingly, the following Chinese saying captures this phenomenon very well:

打 肿 脸 皮 充 胖 子

da zhong lian   pi chong pang zi

To slap the face until it is swollen in order to pretend to be a plump person.

Clearly, the management of "face" is something that any Westerner will have to contend with while working or doing business in Asia. It is something the smarter amongst us have learned to use with due care and diligence—a sort of Asian apprenticeship on the importance of "giving and saving face." As mentioned earlier, sometimes it can be overexaggerated as a sensitivity; sometimes, it is underestimated; sometimes, it is abused; and sometimes, it is ignored at one's peril. With time and experience, however, the

Westerner is normally able to navigate his way through the "face" minefield. Understanding, respecting, and managing "face" are key skills a Westerner must learn and execute with great care while working in Asia. This chapter will try to unravel the concept of "face" and give guidance and support on how it can be managed on a day-to-day basis.

Understanding "Face" in Asia

What exactly do we mean by "face"? "Face" is a multifaceted term, and its meaning is inextricably linked with culture and other terms such as honor, reputation, image, stature, and everything else that enhances the standing of the individual before his peers and community. In Chinese social relations, "face" has commonly been used to refer to two related concepts, namely *mian zi* (面子) and *lian* (脸). They come from the common term *lian mian* (脸面). Their exact meanings depend on the context in which they are used, and they are often used interchangeably. The following are some examples:

1. *Mei mian zi* (没面子) means "loss of 'face'" and can be used interchangeably with *mei lian* (没脸). It means deeply shameful and embarrassed to the extent of having a severe feeling of guilt and humiliation. This phrase is often used to describe oneself. For example, when someone makes very strong promises to deliver, but fails to deliver on them, then he may feel that he does not have the *mian zi* (面子) or *mei lian* (没脸) to see the person whom he made the promises to.

2. *Diu lian* (丢脸[3]) also means "loss of 'face'," though not totally. It can be used interchangeably with *shi mian zi* (失面子). In this instance, it refers to bringing shame and dishonor not only to oneself, but to the

family and other related parties as well. For example, when a highly respected professional is caught stealing, embezzling customers' funds, or committing any other fraudulent act, then his actions are considered *diu lian* (丢脸). In turn, his action(s) also cause his profession and fraternity to suffer a loss of "face," or *shi mian zi* (失面子).

3. *Shang lian* (赏脸) means "to give 'face'" and can be used interchangeably with *gei mian zi* (给面子). In this instance, it is to accord someone with respect, honor, and prestige, which he may not fully deserve. For example, when the prime minister of a country shows up at a banquet hosted by a not so prominent businessman, he is indeed "giving face" (赏脸 *shang lian* or 给面子 *gei mian zi*) to the host. His sheer presence will enhance the "face" of the host and increase his stature and standing among his peers in future.

Lian (脸) or *mianzi* (面子), in Chinese, can be used to project the confidence of society in a person's moral character, social standing, and reputation. To a Chinese businessman, maintaining "face" is important in social relations because "face" translates into power and influence, and affects goodwill. A loss of "face" would result in a loss of trust within a social network, and possibly a loss of authority and influence as well. As an example, bypassing an Asian manager and speaking directly to his boss would cause the manager a loss of "face" and great embarrassment. He will feel that he has lost his credibility in the eyes of his peers and bosses.

Gaining "face" is as important a concept as losing "face." A major objective in many Asian cultures is to increase one's "face" value or standing in society while successfully avoiding the loss of "face." The prime minister's presence at the banquet of a businessman, as cited on the previous page, will definitely help the latter to gain more "face" among his business associates.

The Importance of Face in Asia

To the Westerner who is not so well-informed, the loss of "face" is probably nothing more than having one's ego deflated, and the person should be able to get over it quickly. However, this is not the case in Asia, especially among the Chinese. The Asian concept of "face" represents an individual's entire being—body, soul, and spirit. It has a lot to do with the person's honor, reputation, image, and everything else that allows him to appear and look good before his family members, relatives, peers, friends, and the community at large. Saving "face" is important not just for the individual concerned, but also for his family and the entire community to which he belongs. As such, when a person loses "face," such as when he is severely embarrassed, insulted, humiliated, dishonored, or criticized publicly, the consequences can be very damaging and disastrous. The following Chinese sayings are very indicative of the importance of "face" in Asia:

可 杀 不 可 辱 。
ke sha bu ke ru

(You) can kill me, but you cannot insult me.[4]

豹 死 留 皮 ， 人 死 留 名 。
bao si liu pi   ren si liu ming

When a leopard dies, it is remembered for the quality of its skin that is left behind; when a person dies, he is remembered for the reputation that he has left behind.

以 名 誉 扬 天 下 。
yi ming yu yang tian xia

A person is known throughout the world
by his reputation and credibility.

Even the great Chinese philosopher Confucius alluded to
the importance of creating a reputation for oneself when
one is alive:

君 子 疾 没 世 而 名 不 称 焉 。
jun zi ji mei shi er ming bu cheng yan

The gentleman deplores dying before leaving
a reputation for himself.

~ *The Analects of Confucius*, Chapter 15, verse 20,
论语第十五篇: 卫灵公第二十节

Clearly, one cannot leave behind any reputation if one does
not gain "face" or, worse still, is often disgraced and dishonored by others around him. In order to gain "face,"
the typical Asian will go all out to ensure that he is well
perceived, respected, and looked upon favorably in his
society. Not surprisingly, this is manifested in many ways,
including the friends and business associates that he has;
the people he knows or is well connected with, especially
government officials, politicians, and well-known individuals; the kind of house(s) and car(s) he owns; the places
he patronizes, including social and golf club memberships; the products that he uses, and so on. All of these
are ways and means that are used directly and indirectly
to gain "face." At times, he may even over-stretch himself
in order to look good (that is, to project a better "face")
before others.

Face and Politics

Without doubt, "face" is a very important factor in many facets of life in Asia. It matters from the micro level of inter-personal relationships to the macro level of relationships among nations.

The Case of ASEAN Countries

In Asia, it is striking how few nations will engage in shouting matches with each other when it comes to solving disputes and disagreements. "Face" is important, and conflict can break out when one side experiences severe loss of "face." Direct confrontation is avoided. "Face" must not be lost. Everybody must feel comfortable. Cynics will argue that the "face" issue is abused as a convenient form of evasion of the main issue at stake. However, it is the quest for harmony and the need to allow the other party to preserve its honor (despite whatever shortcomings there may be) that drive much of the relationships and behavior of these nations toward each other.

Take the case of ASEAN countries.[5] Every one of its member states is fully aware of the human rights problems in Myanmar. Its abuses have been widely reported in the international media,[6] and the other nine members know that if such abuses persist, it may affect the image and standing of ASEAN in the world. However, as a group, it is not prepared to impose strong sanctions on Myanmar or to ask it to leave the group. Instead, these members continue to use subtle and behind-the-scene diplomatic means to nudge Myanmar to move toward a more acceptable position. Myanmar, on the other hand, has cleverly used the whole concept of "face" as a pretext of saying, "Don't criticize me," and that the issue is a domestic matter for the country to resolve. It is precisely the considerations of saving "face" and giving "face" to a fellow member state that has prevented the other nine countries from taking stronger measures.

Settling Territorial Disputes

Myanmar is not the only example within ASEAN. In another case, Malaysia and Indonesia were unable to resolve their long-standing disputes over the ownership of two islands, Pulau Sipadan and Pulau Litigan.[7] Resorting to strong political measures, including the use of military force, would have been disastrous. Instead, both countries finally agreed to resolve the issues of sovereignty through the International Court of Justice (ICJ) in late 2001.[8] In that particular instance, the ruling went in favor of Malaysia.

This same approach was taken to resolve the dispute between Singapore and Malaysia over the sovereignty of Pedra Branca, which houses the Horsburgh Lighthouse. When Singapore became independent in 1965, Malaysia did not raise any issue pertaining to the ownership of the little piece of rock. However, in 1979, Malaysia published a controversial map that showed Pedra Branca belonged to Malaysia. The Malaysians even called it Pulau Batu Putih. This marked the beginning of a long dispute that lasted almost 30 years. Despite the occasional exchange of words between politicians on both sides, neither country was prepared to take tough action against the other. Finally, both sides agreed to let the ICJ decide on the case. In May 2008, the ICJ ruled that Pedra Branca belonged to Singapore.

It is important to point out why nations involved in such disputes prefer to go to a third party, like the ICJ, to resolve their disputes. It is because direct negotiations are unlikely to resolve such an important issue as that pertaining to sovereignty. Neither side will want to lose. More seriously, being too forceful and direct during the negotiations may sour bilateral relations even further, especially when one side emerges as the winner, causing the other side a severe loss of "face." However, when the verdict is delivered by a third party, it allows the loser, especially, to exit gracefully without severe loss of "face." After all, it has made the best representation possible, and the third party, in this instance the ICJ, can always be made the scapegoat when the case is lost.

Looking ahead, a more interesting and complicated dispute and territorial claim awaits the international community as to how it will be resolved. It concerns the Spratly Islands. Consisting of about 200 small islands and reefs, the Spratly Islands contain rich fishing grounds and, more importantly, potentially large gas and oil deposits. At the moment, China, Taiwan, Indonesia, Malaysia, the Philippines, and Vietnam have all laid claims to the islands, with a handful of them even occupying some of the islands. While staking their claims, none of these countries has tried to occupy the islands by force. Given the strong "face" culture of these nations, it will take some time before this issue is settled. This is because none of them will want to over-rock the boat by taking any action that may cause the others to lose "face" in the process.

"Face" and the Conduct of Business

Without doubt, managing "face" plays an important part in the realm of business. As an illustration, we like to focus on the area of communication and negotiation behavior between the West and Asia, which essentially also exhibits the differences between what we call high-context and low-context cultures.

High-Context and Low-Context Cultures

The United States and other Western countries are generally considered low-context societies. Here verbal communication is often more direct, and there is very little concern or need for nonverbal cues in order for people to understand each other. People generally try to "say what they mean." They are individualistic. If someone makes a social blunder or faux pas as an adult, in most cases, there is only personal embarrassment, and hopefully a desire to correct the error with a sincere apology. Conflicts are seen as a natural part of life. People are not offended by contradiction because low-context cultures relish debate and fundamentally believe in the freedom of expression. People have a strong sense of personal responsibility and, equally, a personal sense of guilt. If there is any face, it is relatively insignificant and dealt with on an individual basis. People also tend to compartmentalize life. Personal relationships, work, and many other aspects of day-to-day life are separate from each other.

However, in collectivistic societies or high-context cultures, such as Asia, there is a significant difference. Face is extremely important. These high-context cultures are often hierarchical and traditional societies where the concepts of shame and honor are much more important than they are in low-context societies. Humiliation can be worse than death. Group harmony is absolutely essential. People in these cultures dislike direct confrontation, and, as we have seen in other chapters of this book, Asians generally avoid giving a categorical "no." It is important to keep up appearances. People will generally use avoiding, obliging, and compromising tactics to deal with conflict. This is done deliberately so as to allow the other party more space to maneuver, to draw his/her own conclusion, and, in the process, to allow him/her to save "face."

Another way to consider the difference between the opposing cultures is that in the West (low-context), people generally want to simply solve problems and move on, whilst in Asia (high-context), people want to mend and build relationships. In the West, verbal communication is almost a matter of fact, a basic process to pass on information. In most cases, it tends to be a rather dull and mundane task. However, in collectivistic cultures, communication is very carefully watched and analyzed. High-context communication is primarily concerned with maintaining face and group harmony. Many expressions of respect and courtesy are included. People literally hang on to every word. You can palpably sense this when you are communicating to a group of Asians. It is even more acute when communication is made through interpreters. We have often seen the interpreters themselves being corrected by the other party if it is felt that something we have said was not conveyed correctly in their language.

When speaking to Asians, you have to be more careful with your words than with a Western audience for at least two reasons, namely to ensure no one is unintentionally offended and to prevent the meaning of your words from being misunderstood. We have experienced many situations when, after making a short speech or presentation, an Asian manager approached us to question a certain point because, in his analysis, he had spotted another meaning or angle to what we said. In almost all instances, the assumption was wrong, and we were able to correct his interpretation. However, imagine all the possible misinterpretations that the other Asian managers might take away with them if they chose not to approach us. What might be going on in their minds?

Communication and Negotiation Behavior

Table 11-1 shows the differences between the preferred styles of communication and negotiation behavior between Asian high-context cultures and Western low-context cultures. You can see exactly how opposite the approaches to negotiation tend to be. If both sides do not truly appreciate these differences, it may lead to frustration and great misunderstandings. When dealing with a Westerner, an Asian high-context negotiator's nightmare is the loss of "face." He will, therefore, prefer to take as much uncertainty as possible out of the picture. He will try to envisage in advance every element of the ensuing negotiations in order to prevent failure. Leaping into the unknown is not an option. Many of the non-negotiable items will have been communicated to the Western team ahead of time, either directly or indirectly through messengers.[9]

The Western team of negotiators should take note of these requests and the need to guard the loss of "face" of their Asian counterparts. If they are not in agreement, it is important to deal with these items off-line in private discussions rather than in the negotiating room. If the Westerners do not get the subtle hints and decide to raise the non-negotiable items anyhow, it will cause the Asian negotiator a serious loss of "face" as he will be forced into an uncomfortable corner. As there is too much potential for humiliation and loss of dignity, his only escape is to be evasive or, in the case of insensitive pressure, change the subject to another item and come down hard on you to

TABLE 11-1: COMMUNICATION AND NEGOTIATION BEHAVIOR

Asia (High-Context Culture)	West (Low-Context Culture)
1. Create a base for mutual trust first	1. Get down to business first
2. Value goodwill and personal relations	2. Value expertise and performance
3. Negotiations are slow and tedious	3. Negotiations are fast and slick
4. Agreement based on trust	4. Agreement based on contract
5. Motives are expressed indirectly	5. Motives are stated directly
6. Communication is implicit, nonverbal, and ambiguous	6. Communication is explicit, verbal, and unambiguous
7. Prefer more formal setting	7. Comfortable with informal setting
8. Careful deliberation	8. Can be spontaneous
9. Emotionally self-controlled	9. Emotionally expressive and clear
10. Humble and modest	10. Self-promoting and individualistic
11. Long-term and goal-oriented	11. Short-term driven
12. Personal and public relationships are mostly the same	12. Personal and public relationships are mostly kept separate

recover his "face" in front of the others. He may end up using an extreme form of vagueness, pregnant with hidden meaning. It will take considerable time for the mistake to be amended. Sometimes, saving "face" can become so central an issue that it swamps the importance of the real, hard issues at stake and, if not handled with sufficient care, can generate intense conflicts, which ultimately impede progress and can eventually kill the deal.

Mutual Concern Needed

The concern for "face" is not confined to between high-context and low-context cultures. In the case of conflict resolution or negotiating between two high-context cultures, it is more likely that an attitude of concern for preserving the other party's "face" will achieve a more successful outcome than aggressive confrontation and "face-threatening" behavior. When it cannot, a mutually respected third party may be introduced to facilitate "face" issues between two parties.[10]

At times, it may be necessary to use "face-threatening" moves as a last resort if things are not going well in a negotiation. However, the chances of a successful conclusion will be higher if "face-threatening" moves are balanced by offering "face-honoring" moves as well. In other words, the other party may be offered a gracious exit route, or some other goodies, if it chooses to back off on some of the main issues. In other words, one cannot expect to have a win-lose (zero-sum) outcome when negotiating in Asia. Rather, one should always seek win-win possibilities, although the margins of winning on each side may be different. By allowing the other side to gain back some "face" in the process, one will gain greater respect. It is what an honorable gentleman in Asia would do.

Not surprisingly, communication and negotiation are very much an art in Asia. While there is always the desire to ensure the clarity of a message, one must guard against being perceived as overly aggressive, direct, and insensitive. On the other hand, if one tries to be too indirect in order to be sensitive to the other party, one may be perceived as evasive and deceptive. Worse still, the intended message may be lost, and misunderstanding may even arise. One will have to choose a good balance between these two approaches. Our advice would be that where the message is concerned, focus on the facts and avoid adding your own opinions. By doing so, you can be certain that the message will not be lost. How one should put the facts across is another matter. This is where sensitivity and a good grasp of the right timing and setting to do so become very important. For example, choosing an informal setting will desensitize how the message will be perceived. Similarly, conveying some sensitive points through a third party is always a good move.

Watch Out for the Subtle Nuances

There are many ways in which one can cause the loss of face to others in Asia. Some examples include rebuffing or insulting someone openly, not according the proper protocol befitting the person's social status, highlighting a person's weaknesses in front of others, and so on. On the other hand, an Asian may, on his/her part, feel a loss of "face" too. Some examples would include showing a very poor business performance, not being dressed suitably or prepared for an occasion, feeling inferior before others, and so on. More often than not, these can be detected without too much difficulty as the person will show signs of acute discomfort. However, at times, one may not immediately realize the seriousness of the loss of "face." The effects are only known much later. By then, it will be too late to do any damage control. Let us illustrate with an example that one of us happened to witness in China a few years ago.

Watch Your Language

A Western buyer was reprimanding his Chinese manufacturer for the defective leather jackets that were supplied to him for export into North America and Europe. His voice was loud and furious. On many occasions, he pointed repeatedly to the various flaws of several leather jackets that had been shown to him. His comments were translated to the Chinese counterpart via a Chinese interpreter. What amazed the author most was the role played by the interpreter.[11] Instead of translating verbatim what the Westerner said, which contained many scathing and unwarranted remarks, the interpreter deliberately filtered out many of the harsh comments and criticisms. In contrast to the loud and furious tone of the Westerner, the Chinese interpreter was calm and measured. Despite this, the Chinese counterpart and his team were clearly uncomfortable with the criticisms that they did receive. In fact, they behaved very humbly and were very apologetic that their products had not met the specifications. They even expressed confidence and gave assurances that the final products would meet all the specifications laid down by the Western buyer.

Satisfied that he had aired his views and gotten all he wanted, the Western buyer left in a rather elated mood. He even said a hearty "hello" to the author who was sitting at a table next to the meeting room. After the Westerner left, the Chinese counterpart and his team questioned the interpreter in greater detail over what was said about them, their leather jackets, their company, and so on. Clearly, from the Westerner's tone and mannerisms throughout the meeting, the comments could not have been limited to only what had been translated. They sensed that the interpreter was withholding some information and had not done a complete translation of what the Westerner had said. It was then that the interpreter told the truth. On learning how sarcastic and critical the Westerner had been about their products, the Chinese side decided to call off the deal unilaterally as they felt insulted and humiliated. In their own words, the Westerner gave them no "face," and they felt that moving on with such a business relationship would be meaningless.

Watch the Body Language

Tone, phrasing, and body language are extremely important in any business negotiation. Take the example cited above. Clearly, the tone and body language of the Western buyer gave his position away. Despite the efforts of the interpreter to do damage control by mellowing his tone and not doing a verbatim translation, the Chinese team was able to see through the displeasure of the Westerner. Absorbed in the pursuit of his own arguments, the Westerner did little to notice the tone and body language of his interpreter and his Chinese counterparts. What made matters worse was that his own mannerisms sent unmistakable cues to the Chinese that he was neither polite nor understanding.

This is why we often recommend that low-context communicators such as Westerners use "spotters" in their negotiating team to pick up these subtleties and pass on their observations to the lead negotiator. While what is said is still important, other nonverbal cues can be far more revealing. The little nods (is that "yes" or "no"), the little smiles (is he happy or uncomfortable), and the gestures to his other team members (is he positive or embarrassed) are all telltale signs of how well a negotiation is progressing.

At times, a smile can be very misleading. It can be used to cover embarrassment or discomfort. Reactions to something positive, on the other hand, can be controlled and concealed as Asians generally do not exhibit their feelings publicly. Other key signals are facial expressions, hand gestures, bowing, and eye contact. Touching and personal space will give you a clearer sense of how close the relationship is. The interactions among members within the Asian group will also give a strong sense of the hierarchical relationships and how that may communicate what is going on.

Managing the Deadly Silence

Worst of all, though, are the deadly silences,[12] which can leave most Western negotiators flummoxed. Have I offended him? Is he thinking out his next move? Is he being evasive? Has he not understood? Should I repeat what I have just said? There are so many possibilities when the other party chooses to remain silent. The low-context communicator needs to work overtime to sense what is going on. This can be mentally exhausting and quite stressful.

A Western friend recently shared an experience, where he met a Cambodian businessman for an introductory discussion. Everything had to be interpreted from English into Khmer. Normally, some pleasantries are exchanged before the real business starts. In this case, his opening messages were simply acknowledged with a nod or a grunt. Nothing was said in return. The next hour passed by in a similar vein. The other party said nothing, other than an occasional grunt. After the Westerner had said all he could say, the Cambodian businessman gave a final grunt, stood up, shook his hand, and made his farewell. He had said nothing for more than an hour. It was an extremely bewildering, indeed intimidating, experience for the Western businessman.

Fortunately for him, he found out subsequently that, despite his fears, the meeting had actually gone very well because his Asian colleagues, who were present at the meeting and were familiar with Cambodian culture and business behavior, gave him the thumbs up. Sure enough, a week later, a follow-up meeting was arranged. While this is a rather extreme and perhaps rare situation, it demonstrates how individuals in Asia can communicate meaningfully even when no words have been exchanged. What this Westerner did not realize was that although he heard only occasional grunts, he had failed to observe the other aspects of the Cambodian businessman's body language. There is another lesson to this episode. At the end of the day, cross-cultural communication is never confined to the rules of one's home country. Rather, there are more subtleties and nuances in communication that go beyond the verbal realm that can signal the success of a negotiation or business deal. One only has to learn to discover them.

Fatal Bypasses

One of the most common forms of losing "face" in Asia is when a Westerner, generally impatient or frustrated, decides to take things into his own hands and go straight to the top of the hierarchy, thus bypassing the ranks below. By going over someone's head, the consequences are normally disastrous, even in the more developed nations of Asia. It is unacceptable to try to bypass a step of the ladder of authority when working on a project. Most Asians will feel slighted and confused if their status is ignored. Their collectivist cultures expect, reinforce, and reward the subordination of individual interests to those of the group. Cohesive groups protect their members in exchange for loyalty and obligation. As such, when that structure's integrity is threatened in any way, they can be deeply discomforted. Yet this happens regularly because it is an easy trap for a Westerner to fall into.

In the low-context culture of the West, people expect to get straight answers and quick decisions. Therefore, when faced with the hierarchy and bureaucracy of certain Asian governments or corporations, their natural instinct is not to play the game of "working up" the decision-making tree, but to go direct to the top of the tree and then "work down." Unfortunately, this often backfires. If they are lucky enough to be granted time to discuss an issue with the top guy, but have not spent any preparatory time conditioning the lower ranks, then it can easily create a double "face-losing" scenario. The senior manager or official can be embarrassed because he may be taken off guard by the spontaneity of the Westerner's overture and may be too uncomfortable to give an adequate response. He would prefer to be well briefed by his management before such a meeting was set up. Equally, his management team will lose "face" as they have been sidelined in the process.

Managing "Face" in Asia

Without doubt, managing "face" in Asia is not a straightforward issue. As mentioned at the beginning of this chapter, one must be prepared to pay the tuition fee, and learn along the way. There are, however, possible ways to shorten this learning curve. For example, a Western company may wish to establish a matrix management approach to business relationships. Once a clear business objective and approach has been agreed internally, the Western company needs to establish a team comprising different ranks who will play the key roles of relating with the different levels of the Asian organization structure. This is particularly useful when dealing with SOEs (state-owned enterprises) in China or Vietnam, as well as family-owned companies across Asia.

Often the ground work can be established by the company's lower and middle management. The work undertaken by these soldiers should not be underestimated as it can often be critical to a particular project's success when relationships are built at the working level. They will be able to assess the general views of the Asian company's management to the proposal, identify the chances of success, root out the potential obstacles and management blockers, and lay down a refined route to achieve the overall objective. In some cases, the outcome may be different from the original proposal, especially when some "face-saving" measures may have to be incorporated.

If the relationship between both parties is strong, then the Asian partner's management team will be able to give good advice and suggest alternative solutions or approaches, which may make the task easier. It also means that the Asian management team has time to brief and condition their superiors on the proposal and sound out their opinions. This is a critical part of the process because the Asian management team will want to minimize any risk of loss of "face," not just for their bosses' sake but for their own too. The team also needs to be convinced of the merits of the proposal and that there is little downside for anyone involved. A win-win scenario must be pursued, although, as mentioned earlier, the margins of winning may differ for both sides. A win-win outcome will ensure no loss of "face" on both sides.

The matrix, or multilevel, approach can be very time-consuming but ultimately rewarding for those who are patient, resilient, and flexible. Once the doors are unlocked and opened, opportunities and new ideas start to flow both ways. Those who do not invest time, money, and resources in a multilevel relationship structure can become lost and caught in limbo, not knowing where they stand with their Asian partner and how to extricate themselves from the stalemate.

Unfortunately, many companies still get it wrong and pay the price when they finally lose patience, decide, "Enough is enough. I want answers," and make the fateful visit to the senior employee. This, as mentioned earlier, is often very damaging. Indeed, failing to treat Asians with proper respect can have severe consequences—cooperation can cease and retaliation may ensue. Saving "face" means to avoid situations in which you might reduce or are perceived to reduce someone's self-worth. "Face" is the hallmark of human relationships in Asia. Preserving the relationship is of utmost importance. As such, even when things become sour, never resort to litigation. This would certainly destroy whatever relationship there is and, worse still, cause severe loss of "face" to both sides when the dirty linen is washed in public. In fact, Confucius specifically cautioned against going to court to settle disputes:

听讼，吾犹人也。必也使无讼乎！
ting song　　wu you ren ye　　bi ye shi wu song hu

In hearing lawsuits, I am like anybody else. What is necessary is to eliminate the need for litigation.

~ *The Analects of Confucius*, Chapter 12, verse 13,
论语第十二篇：颜渊第十三节

Modesty Rules

One of the cardinal rules a Westerner should follow when working in Asia is to demonstrate restraint when it comes to describing one's own strengths or achievements. The nobler way to behave is to understate your accomplishments and let others find ways to identify them. This can take some time, but it allows you to be given face by your Asian partners or employees and also gives you the opportunity to discover their unique attributes and to give them face. It may sound like a rather slow and torturous getting-to-know-you process, especially when it is clearly visible that both parties are successful. As such, saying it straight up seems very logical. However, this is the way it is done in Asia, and it does play a critical role in building the relationship. Even Sun Zi, the great military strategist, had this to say about humility:

故 善 战 者 之 胜 也 ，　无 智 名 ，　无 勇 功 。
gu　shan zhan zhe　zhi sheng ye　　wu　zhi ming　　wu　yong gong

Thus, the person adept at warfare wins without being known for his wisdom and reputation or for his courage and merit.

~ *Sun Zi Bingfa*, 孙子兵法，
Line 4.18 of Chapter 4 on Disposition of the Army
形 *(xing)*

Westerners can often be deceived into making false assumptions about Asian businessmen because of their deference to the Westerner. When Asians play this deferential and respectful role, the Westerner must not abuse it. Rather, he should take the opportunity to raise their face through compliments, gratitude, and praise, even if they try to shake it off. Flattery can work extremely well in Asia so long as it is sincere.

One of the true leadership qualities, whether in the West or in Asia, is recognizing when you have made a mistake, and to apologize for it. As is abundantly clear, Asians place a great deal of importance on relationships. In any relationship, there will be ups and downs, successes and failures. Thus, when a Westerner admits his error and, if possible, attempts to undo the wrong, he will be greatly admired and respected. It will strengthen the overall relationship. In this instance, he may even gain more face as a result of behaving humbly and modestly.

Treat People Well

Asians look very carefully at how people issues are handled by Western companies. Therefore, the way you treat your staff, particularly those with problems, can be critical in winning the heart and soul of the organization. If you handle your staff sensitively and with dignity, then you will have the full support and loyalty of the company. If, however, these people are treated badly or unfairly, then it can badly affect the motivation and happiness of the company. As mentioned earlier, many Asian organizational cultures are like large families, and they will close ranks if there is a sense of injustice against any one of its members. Employees will start to think that they could be next, and that they could easily have been the ones who were treated badly. They will start to look after each other's interests, and it can be very easy for them to fall on the wrong side of the fence.

Generally, Asian employees want a sense of reassurance and security that, in return for hard work, commitment, and loyalty, they will be treated with respect, even if they have made a mistake or have underperformed. Saving "face" is important. Public warnings, humiliations, or dismissals will seriously undermine your leadership and their morale. They need to know that if something does go wrong for whatever reason, even if it is due to their incompetence, they will not be exposed to public shame or ridicule.

This does not mean that they will accept poor performance by one of their members. It does not mean that an individual's mistakes will be tolerated. What matters is how the issue is handled by the organization itself. The subtlety is critical. So what does this mean for the Westerner? The following is some advice:

1. Emotional outbursts, whether in anger or frustration, will rarely be respected in an Asian business environment, whatever the cause. In fact, it has a negative effect. Your own esteem and credibility in the organization will be damaged. In Asia, self-control is considered a sign of maturity and virtue. If you do feel let down or disappointed, or are simply furious, it is better to channel that energy elsewhere—take a time-out and speak to the individual(s) concerned in private. Do not disclose, however, what you have said to any other party. Keep it confidential, and the individual, no matter how badly he feels, will respect you more for it.

2. If subordinates make a decision that you have to change, you have to be careful how you go about it. When not handled properly, it can create an incredible loss of "face." Somehow as a foreigner, you have to try to establish a relationship so that they can come to you without a huge loss of "face" to admit their mistakes. Only then will you know that you have gained their acceptance and credibility.

3. In the case of incompetence or a serious breach of company policy, where you feel strongly that the individual should be fired, it is far better to discuss the matter again in private and allow the individual to resign with dignity, if possible. This does not mean that you have to be overly compassionate. It is simply a question of managing the issue while showing respect to the individual, his family, and his community. Asians, we repeat, do expect strong discipline in any organization and, if someone has clearly been at fault, they will support any action you take. Just do not make them feel ashamed in front of their peers. It is worse than death.

Conclusion

Why does the concept of "face" seem so predominant in Asia? After all, the term is rarely used in the West. In the West, reputation as a primal need certainly seems to be more diluted now than in the past. Yet, in the 18th and 19th centuries, duels at dawn were the straightforward solution to a little bit of humiliation. These days, people in the West seem more thick-skinned and individualistic; they do not seem to care what others think of them. They are able to compartmentalize these reputation issues somewhere in the "people to be loathed and ignored" file of their brain and just move on.

We think, however, that this is a Socratic Western approach to dealing with things. The deep-rooted negative feelings of hurt, humiliation, and loss of self-esteem and the converse positive feelings of honor, pride, and satisfaction are still within all of us. We have simply created an internal management system for defusing and suppressing these feelings. We actually believe every Westerner would appreciate a lot more genuine "facework." Living and working in Asia, we enjoy the respect Asians give us. We find the service culture refreshingly sincere. Asians are reciprocal in "giving and saving 'face'." Would it not be far more pleasant if all Westerners also treated each other with a little more "face"?

Treating others the way you would like to be treated yourself is something everyone aspires to. Whether Asian or Westerner, everyone wants to be treated with respect, dignity, and equity. "Face" need not be an Asian phenomenon only. It can be a basic human need within all of us. Thus, we would like to conclude with the following episode: Tzu Kung, a disciple of Confucius, asked him if there was a word that could guide a person's behavior throughout his lifetime. Confucius replied with the following time-tested and situation-tested saying:

己 所 不 欲， 勿 施 於 人 。
ji suo bu yu   wu shi yu ren

What you do not want others to do to you,
do not do to them.

~ *The Analects of Confucius*, Chapter 15, verse 24,
论语第十五篇：卫灵公第二十四节

Endnotes

1. Even up till today, Japanese business executives are known to commit suicide when they are the cause of the poor performances of their companies. The reason—they simply feel too humiliated and embarrassed to face their

colleagues, relatives, and friends. Indeed, this severe loss of "face" causes them to take their own lives.

2. Read Chapter 12 for a detailed exposition of *guanxi*, and how it affects the conduct of business.

3. It is important to point out that the word *diu* (丢) is less severe than the word *mei* (没), which literally means "don't have."

4. This saying clearly illustrates the importance of "face." When a person is insulted, he loses "face" and will not be able to face the people around him. In this instance, it is tantamount to killing him. As a result, he can turn vindictive and will not hesitate to take whatever action necessary to salvage his lost pride and ego, and to restore his "face."

5. ASEAN stands for Association of Southeast Asian Nations. It consists of 10 member countries—Brunei, Cambodia, Indonesia, Laos, Malaysia, Myanmar, the Philippines, Singapore, Thailand, and Vietnam.

6. These included the brutal suppression and arrest of peaceful demonstrators, including monks, in 2007, and the long-time house arrest of 1991 Nobel Peace Prize winner Aung San Suu Kyi, an opposition leader and human rights advocate.

7. These two resort islands are tourist attractions. In particular, they are nesting grounds for turtles.

8. The ICJ is a body of the United Nations, which was set up in June 1945. It consists of 15 judges elected by the United Nations General Assembly and the Security Council. Each judge serves a term of nine years. The ruling of the ICJ is final.

9. See Chapter 4 on the roles and importance of the messenger, especially in negotiations.

10. This, in fact, was the case in the dispute between Indonesia and Malaysia, and between Malaysia and Singapore, both of which were cited earlier in this chapter.

11. It was the first author who happened to be taking his afternoon tea in the business lounge in close proximity to where the discussion took place. Interestingly, despite knowing that there were several other guests in the lounge, the Western buyer who went into the meeting room last did not shut the door to the room. He was also extremely inconsiderate with regard to the presence of the other guests in the lounge. Perhaps he was simply too upset with the Chinese manufacturer who had failed to measure up to his expectations.

12. This topic is also discussed in Chapter 10.

故 不 知 诸 侯 之 谋 者，
gu bu zhi zhu hou zhi mou zhe

不 能 豫 交；
bu neng yu jiao

Thus, if the schemes and ploys of the neighboring warlords are not known, one should not be keen to enter into any alliances with them.

(Sun Zi Bingfa, 孙子兵法, *Lines 7.24 of Chapter 7 on Military Maneuvers,* 军争 (*jun zheng*))

凡 军 之 所 欲 击， 城 之 所 欲 攻，
fan jun zhi suo yu ji , cheng zhi suo yu gong

人 之 所 欲 杀， 必 先 知 其 守 将，
ren zhi suo yu sha bi sian zhi qi shou jiang

左 右， 谒 者， 门 者，
zuo you ye zhe men zhe

舍 人 之 姓 名，
she ren zhi xing ming

令 吾 间 必 素 知 之。
ling wu jian bi su zhi zhi

There may be armies that you wish to strike, cities that you wish to conquer, and key people that you wish to assassinate. For such cases, there is a need to know beforehand detailed information on the identities of the garrison commander, his supporting officers, the visiting consultants, the guards and patrols, and the various attendants. Your agents must be ordered to investigate these matters in great detail.

(Sun Zi Bingfa, 孙子兵法, *Lines 13.32 to 13.34 of Chapter 13 on Intelligence and Espionage,* 用间 (*yong jian*))

CHAPTER 12

Personal Business Relationships, or *Guanxi*

Necessary Evil or Part of Asian Culture?

Mining Gold Blindfolded

One of the greatest pitfalls of Westerners trying to do business in Asia is the failure to understand the need to cultivate personal relationships with their local partners and other stakeholders. More seriously, they grossly underestimate the value and power of relationships, especially those that are built upon personal ties. Often, they think that since they have a better product and are able to provide superior business terms and services, they should win any deal with ease. This cannot be farther from the truth. In Asia, and among Chinese societies in particular, socializing is often part and parcel of doing business. More importantly, typical Chinese businessmen, as well as other Asian businessmen, want to get to know their foreign partners better before having any business relationships. This is very different from the West, where the contract-based system allows business deals to go through without even the need to know the person.

Some misguided Western businessmen in Asia, upon hearing that relationships are important, go the extra mile to try and woo their local partners. Often, they are told that giving gifts would be a very good way to "buy" a relationship. As a result, many of them try to please their Asian counterparts with excessive and extravagant gifts. Ironically, this often does not yield the desired results. On the contrary, such gifts help to whet the appetites of their local partners and officials, and further aggravate the existing problem of corruption. The failure to understand the Asian concept of relationships, or what the Chinese call *guanxi*, has indeed caused much misunderstanding, confusion, and frustration. This chapter aims to provide the reader with a better perspective in understanding the concept of *guanxi*. In the process, it is our desire that businessmen doing business in Asia, in particular in China, will have a better sense of how to go about building the right kinds of ties and relationships.

Understanding *Guanxi*, or Personal Business Relationships

The Chinese characters for "relationship" are 关系 (*guanxi*). Many Western businessmen assume that the term refers to establishing business contacts, networks, or relationships. The answer is both yes and no. Business relationships are definitely part of *guanxi*, but *guanxi* encompasses much more than business relationships. This is precisely the reason why many foreign businessmen doing business in China think that gift-giving is the way to go when building business ties and relationships in that country. They tend to focus the relationships on the business itself, instead of going beyond into the personal realm.

To understand *guanxi*, one has to have some knowledge of the Chinese language. *Guanxi* (关系) in Chinese means "relationships" in the generic sense. However, it can also be used in an abbreviated form to denote many types of relationships, depending on what other Chinese characters are used before or after these two characters. For example, *guanxi* can refer to business relationships (商务关系 *shang wu guanxi*), social relationships (社会关系 *she hui guanxi*), husband-wife relationship (夫妻关系 *fu qi guanxi*), economic relationships (经济关系 *jing ji guanxi*), relationships among students (同学关系 *tongxue guanxi*), relational ties (亲戚关系 *qin qi guanxi*), etc. As such, when the term *guanxi* (关系) is used, its exact meaning will have to depend on the context in which it is expressed.

In the context of business, *guanxi* refers to business relationships (商务关系 *shang wu guanxi*) that are built upon *ren qing guanxi* (人情关系). This refers to the business relationships that are built more on personal ties, which include understanding and having concern and feelings for each other. In fact, it has a twofold meaning. The first is that of a business relationship, which is easier to understand as the relationship is built upon business transactions. The second, and subtler one, is that of a personal relationship (个人关系 *ge ren guanxi*), one that is built upon the social and emotional dimensions. It is about how two business partners relate to each other as personal friends. Such a relationship can extend far beyond the businesses that they have with each other. In fact, it is very much on a "personal-to-holder" basis. Often, the relationship even extends to the families and friends of the business partners. Taking all of these factors into consideration, the closest English translation for *guanxi* when used in the context of business would be personal business relationships.

More Insights into Personal Business Relationships (*Guanxi*)[1]

There are several subtle but important points about *guanxi* that are worth highlighting. In particular, understanding the terms *ren qing guanxi* (人情关系) and *ge ren guanxi* (个人关系) can provide key clues to the understanding and management of *guanxi*.

Guanxi *Is Built Upon Personal Contacts and Is Not Transferable*

The word *ren* (人) means "persons or people," and *ge ren* (个人) refers to the individual or person himself. This means that *guanxi* (关系) is largely built with people, is very personal in nature, and requires personal contacts. As such, the building of such a relationship cannot be delegated nor subcontracted. You have to do it yourself. It is like courting a girlfriend. One cannot depend on one's friend to woo the girl. If anything, one may end up losing the girl to the friend! Indeed, the tendency to rely on others and subordinates to build contacts is a common mistake made by many top executives doing business in China. To build *guanxi*, top executives must undertake the job themselves. Let us illustrate this with the example mentioned in Chapter 8.[2]

Recall how the American chief executive officer (CEO) in the example never used to stay more than two days on his business trips when visiting his Chinese business associates and colleagues until he attended a talk on the importance of *guanxi*. Unknown to him, a senior executive in his Chinese management team—who thought it crucial that the CEO set aside more time to socialize with his Chinese counterparts[3]—had asked the speaker (the first author) to pattern his talk to include the importance of cultivating personal business ties, and why such a job could not be left to the executives on the ground. The game plan was a simple one: to get the American CEO to extend his stay during that trip so that he could join his Chinese counterparts for an evening of drinks, food, and karaoke.

The message went out loud and clear. The CEO delayed his departure by two days so that he could spend more time with his Chinese counterparts. That same evening, the CEO, together with his executives in China, had a fantastic time dining, drinking, and singing with the Chinese team. To the surprise of the CEO, his Chinese counterparts were not as conservative, stiff, and reserved as he had thought. They were actually fun-loving people like the typical American. The Chinese took lots of pictures with him that night. Some Chinese ladies even grabbed his arm tightly during the photo shoots.

The biggest takeaway for the CEO was that in between the drinks, the laughter, the jokes, and karaoke session, he was able to resolve some of the outstanding issues that were standing in the way of stronger business ties with the Chinese. The CEO had a totally different perspective of the Chinese after that memorable evening. That event taught him that cultivating business ties in China was indeed something very personal, and, being the CEO, he had that added "X" factor that his other executives simply did not have. Building *guanxi* was an act that could not possibly be delegated to his executives to carry out.

As *guanxi* is built on a "personal-to-holder" basis, it becomes nontransferable. What has been established belongs only to the person who has cultivated it. This "personal-to-holder" relationship means only that person can cash in on the ties for any benefit or favor.[4] At the same time, wherever he goes, he takes along the established *guanxi* with him. In other words, a person with very strong *guanxi* can literally become a valuable corporate asset. It is something that is also very difficult to quantify or measure until it is needed or cashed in.

Personal Chemistry, Time, and Effort Needed in Building Guanxi

As *guanxi* is built on personal ties between people, it depends largely on the personalities, characters, feelings, and emotions of the people concerned (人情 *ren qing*). In other words, there must be chemistry between these parties. It does not mean that when you want to build a relationship with the other party, you will automatically get it. The other party also has the option of choosing the people he wants to build relationships with. In other words, you may like him, but for *guanxi* to be established, he must like you too. Viewed from this perspective, presenting gifts to someone who does not like you is tantamount to throwing stones into a wide and deep ocean. Nothing will come out of such acts. For the cultivation of *guanxi*, both sides must like each other in order to have a mutual and lasting relationship.

In the context of doing business, knowing the other person well becomes very important for any successful and sustainable relationship. If the person can be trusted and relied upon, then there is no fear that he will not deliver what he promises. Hence, whether there is a contract or not becomes less consequential. Instead, what matters is the words of that person. Not surprisingly, the Chinese word for "trust" (言 *xin*) consists of two words—person (人 *ren*) and words (言 *yan*).

Arising from the focus on trust, it becomes inevitable that it takes time and effort to develop that relationship, especially to build understanding and establish trust between the parties concerned. In addition, finding the right moment or occasion to build that relationship is important. For example, when the other party is in great need, showing concern and extending support to him will be a good way to establish the relationship.

Systems, Documents, and Procedures Cannot Replace Guanxi

It must be remembered that personal ties and relationships cannot be replaced entirely by systems, documents, and procedures. Yes, such processes are important to the conduct of business, but they cannot build the human aspects of a relationship. They cannot replace the warmth of handshakes and smiles, and the feelings and emotions that are accumulated through close interactions and socializing. *Ren qing guanxi* (人情关系) requires the human touch and personal involvement.

Guanxi *Is a Closed System of Relationships*

The word *guanxi* (关系) implies that it is a closed (关 *guan*) or exclusive system. When the relationship is based on personal ties, the building and cultivation of this closed or exclusive relationship will need time, and will be tested through different experiences. There is no way to shorten the "courting" process or to bypass it. A closed system based on personal ties operates much more on trust than on paper contracts. A saying regarding this highlights the importance of getting in before the system is closed. This means that it is always more useful and important to cultivate the relationship when the person has not yet arrived, and not when he has arrived at the position of power. This is because when he has attained the position of power, he is never certain of your intentions, actions, and behavior. Moreover, at this stage, he will also have no shortage of other parties trying to win favors from him. If anything, he will tend to view these newcomers with much scepticism.[5]

On the other hand, he will always remember those who swam with him against the tide when he was still an unknown. The Chinese idiom *yin shui si yuan* (饮水思源) provides very insightful understanding. It literally means "when one is drinking water, one must never forget the source where the water comes from." The idiom is commonly used to remind a person not to forget those who have been kind to him or her, and that there is a need to repay gratitude.

Gifts Alone Cannot Buy Guanxi

Many foreign businessmen think that gifts can remove all obstacles and open doors to new and more opportunities when they do business in China. As mentioned earlier, this is one area that is commonly misconstrued. In reality, gift-giving forms only part of the process of building *guanxi*. It is not the key component of *ren qing guanxi* (人情关系). In fact, the phrase, *ren qing guanxi* (人情关系), does not contain any words on gifts. Instead, it focuses on people relationship, and gifts need *not* be used at all. When gifts are used, they form only part of the process of building the relationship. Moreover, the Chinese typically emphasize the principle of reciprocity, whether it is in the realm of exchanging favors or gifts. This is reflected by the phrase *li shang wang lai* (礼尚往来), which means that gifts and presents that are received must be reciprocated accordingly, and when you are treated well and/or have received kind acts, you must reciprocate accordingly.

Reciprocity forms an integral part of Chinese culture as captured by the phrase *you lai you wang* (有来有往), which means that there should always be an exchange of favors and deeds. Thus, even when gifts are used, they are typically reciprocated, whether in a similar generous manner or in a lesser form.[6] In *ren qing guanxi* (人情关系), one should not be distracted by emphasizing the gifts. Rather, one should focus on understanding and showing care and concern for the other party (关心对方 *guan xin dui fang*). This is the more appropriate way to build the relationship.

Indeed, the misconception that gifts can build and/or buy *guanxi* has caused much misunderstanding and, to some extent, generated bad practices by many Western businessmen. They often buy expensive gifts, thinking that this will be the most expedient way to build relationships. Unfortunately, they typically end up spending unnecessarily large sums of money on gifts, and worse still, giving them to the wrong people, and to more parties too. The end result—more frustration, especially when they do not get the favors they want. In fact, there are several flaws pertaining to this approach of trying to build relationships through gift-giving.

To begin with, the Chinese typically consider it rude to reject gifts. Like the Japanese and many other Asians, gift-giving and gift-receiving are very much a part of Chinese culture. If anything, they will find every possible excuse to give gifts, such as on birthdays, Chinese New Year, anniversaries, births of babies, weddings, funerals, corporate opening ceremonies, etc.

Second, and as mentioned earlier, the act of receiving gifts without much hesitation is further supported by the practice of reciprocity, albeit the reciprocal act may not be as generous as the gifts received. Hence, when an act of generosity is being reciprocated, there should not be any further expectation. Sure, you may feel "shortchanged" by the smaller gift or lesser favor that has been returned. However, you made the first mistake of giving a much more expensive gift.

Third, there is no guarantee that the gift presented is the most expensive and valuable among all the other gifts received by the person concerned. Someone else could have beaten you to it by presenting a much better gift. Moreover, if the receiving party does not have a favorable impression of you, the value of your gift is discounted even more.

Finally, and also mentioned earlier, gift-giving unwittingly encourages and aggravates the problem of corruption, which currently plagues many Asian societies. Given the low incomes of government officials and politicians, the temptation to accept high-value gifts has become one that few of them can resist. In the process, the gift-givers are simply feeding the insatiable greed of these receivers, and making the conduct of business even more difficult for everyone else.

In reality, real cultivation of *guanxi* does not depend on providing gifts. Instead, it is about showing care and concern when the other party is in need. The key is not about an exchange of favors and extracting a favor immediately. For that matter, the thought may not even arise. If there is an intention to extract a reciprocal favor, it is usually targeted at the long term, something that may not be realized at all.

Managing Guanxi *Is Dynamic and a Changing Process*

As the focus of *ren qing guanxi* (人情关系) is on people, the relationship is a very dynamic one. Unlike documents, systems, and procedures, which are relatively static and predictable, dealing with people is never an easy task. This is because the moods and tastes of a person change over time and in different circumstances. People in positions of power can also be rotated, transferred, promoted, or fired. Thus, there is a constant need to track who is in, who is out, who is coming up, and who is going down. Indeed, this is one of the most challenging tasks in dealing with decision-makers in China. In a society where tremendous premium is placed on personal relationships, the departure of any key decision-maker can cause great discomfort to any company that has links with him.[7] What this means is that building *guanxi* is a continuous process, and includes spotting, developing, and cultivating potential candidates (points-of-contact) before they assume positions of power. It is definitely not sufficient to network with existing people in power alone.

Putting *Guanxi* Into Action

Real *guanxi* is about true friendship and solidarity, and not about bribery and corruption. It is very personal and cannot be delegated or transferred. This means that the corporate leader must be prepared to spend considerable time and effort to cultivate a large network of personal relationships, within and outside office hours. These face-to-face interactions will go a long way to develop the contacts that are so necessary to gain further business opportunities as well as to resolve problems and difficulties when they arise. There are several other points about *guanxi* that are worth paying attention to.

First, the concept of *guanxi*, as stated earlier, is premised on trust, and not meritocracy. A businessman who operates in a *guanxi*-based society will prefer to do business with someone he trusts, and not necessarily with the most capable person. In the deployment of people, he will, of course, choose the most capable and trusted person. However, in the absence of having someone who can be both trusted and capable, he will rely on the most trusted person. This is because such a person will never "play him out" and will always have his interests at heart.

Second, the personal relationships and ties that are developed will become proprietary and, to the extent possible, not revealed publicly, especially not to the competitors. In other words, one should not boast about the well-connected individuals within the company. Indeed, *guanxi* can become an intangible and valuable corporate asset.[8] In fact, the capable CEO should also attempt to multiply the power of such an asset in his company. This is because *guanxi*, when well established, is unique to the company and cannot be copied nor replicated by the competitors. For example, the CEO can expose his subordinates or underlings to his network of relationships, that is, help them to establish ties with his contacts or their subordinates. Such private and invisible ties can be very powerful in the conduct of business, and can be commonly seen among Japanese, Korean, and Chinese companies. However, such a strategy can also become a two-edged sword. When a well-connected subordinate leaves, he takes all his contacts with him too.

Finally, the corporate leader who is unfamiliar with cultivating *guanxi* may want to assemble a strong team of well-connected local advisers to help him build those relationships. Picking those local advisers to begin with can be a challenge. This is because there will be no shortage of people claiming strong and direct connections with key government officials and business tycoons in order to earn your fees. The challenge is not to rush in, but to take time and effort to do your own research on such claims.

Can the Contractual West Meet Asian *Guanxi*?

Given the differences between the Asian focus on strong personal business relationships and the Western focus on contracts, conflicts between the two seem inevitable. The answer is again yes and no. There will be misunderstandings and conflicts if both sides fail to find a common ground that can lead them to agree with one another. On the other hand, if both sides are determined to find common areas of interest, many successful business deals can still be struck. Thus, it is very important to find areas in which both sides can identify with.

To begin with, each side must attempt to understand why they prefer a certain mode of conducting business, that is, why the typical Western company is more contract-oriented while the typical Asian or Chinese company is more *guanxi*-oriented. Interestingly, in either approach, the end goal is to build trust so that they can conduct business together. However, the approach to building that trust is very different.

In the case of the typical Asian or Chinese businessman, the way to build trust is through socializing with the potential partner first. He has to know him well as a person and friend so as to determine whether he can be trusted. This will take time and effort, which the typical Western businessman may not have the patience for.

The focus on reliance on the person rather than a contract came about because, traditionally, many Asian countries, especially China, did not have strong legal systems to enforce contractual obligations and arbitrate business disputes. The only guarantee that the businessman had was the word of his partner. As mentioned earlier, the Chinese word for "trust" (信 xin) consists of two words, the person (人 ren) and his words (言 yan). Any business dealings will be built up on a gradual basis, and trust is further gained when the other party shows consideration and concern for the interests of his business partner. In other words, trust has to be earned over time and through circumstance. Once the trust is there, such a business relationship, which is built after the establishment of personal ties, will not be easily sabotaged or undermined by others. It also has the added advantage of flexibility as nothing is ever cast in stone in any ongoing relationship. It is about considerateness and helping each other to do better. The disadvantage of a business environment that is *guanxi*-oriented is that the most efficient and cheapest provider may not win as it is very difficult to break into existing locked-in networks.

In contrast, in a typical Western society, contracts work because they are supported by a very robust and efficient judiciary system that can enforce the fulfillment of contracts and redress any breach of contractual terms. The strong enforcing agencies also ensure that contracts are transferable and valid even if the signatories have changed or have left the company. As such, one can do business based on the best terms and best performer. The need to know who the other party is becomes less consequential. Hence, the so-called trust is built upon the ability to enforce and fulfill the contract. Over time, and as a result of the repeated fulfillment of contracts, the two parties may become good friends on a personal basis. In sum, it is business first, then friendship follows. This is in total contrast to the *guanxi*-oriented system. The contract-based system is, however, not foolproof either. It can be very vulnerable to being undermined by the next provider who is able to offer better terms for the business. At the same time, once a contract is signed, there is also very little flexibility for changes to be made.

Logic as the Bridge to *Guanxi* and Contracts

As mentioned, trust is needed to do business. In Asia, trust is built through *guanxi*, and in the West, it is enshrined in a contract. Not surprisingly, when relationships fail, the typical Asian businessman will resort to reasoning (logic) to resolve any differences. The last thing he wants to do is to take his business associates to court. Doing so would end the relationship that has been built up painstakingly over the years. At the same time, it may earn him a bad reputation too. His mode of doing business is that of relations (情 *qing*), logic (理 *li*), and then legality (法 *fa*), in that order.

On the other hand, when contracts are repeatedly fulfilled, the typical Western businessman will reason that his business partner is a nice person to know, and will then seek to establish a friendship with him. His mode of doing business is about legality (法 *fa*), logic (理 *li*), and relations (情 *qing*), which is in reverse order to that of his Asian counterpart.

Interestingly, the convergent point of the two approaches is logic or reasoning. Let us further illustrate this line of thought. In the case of a *guanxi*-based society, the purpose of establishing personal ties and relationships is to build up business networks (this is the logic for it) for the conduct of business (which will eventually lead to contracts). In the case of a legal-based society, the purpose of having contracts is to establish business relationships (the logic for doing so), which may eventually lead to friendships and personal ties (the relations component). Whether it is establishing business networks or business relationships, there is a common and very clear ultimate goal—to make as much money as possible for the participating partners. Now, making money (profits) is jargon that every businessman understands, and it is the glue that binds them together. Moreover, it is one goal that can provide win-win outcomes for all parties.

Explaining this win-win outcome in profit-making and business dealings is more important to the Western businessman trying to team up with his Asian partner. This is because Asians, especially the Chinese, tend to view the business world as a battlefield (商场如战场 *shang chang ru zhan chang*), where there are clear winners and losers. In other words, they view business as a zero-sum game. Hence, if you win, it must be at my expense.[9] This cannot be farther from the truth. A good business deal must and should always result in win-win outcomes. In fact, win-win outcomes should be the overriding guiding principle in structuring any business transaction. Thus, the challenge is to demonstrate that win-win outcomes are possible, and that the winnings are allocated in a fair and equitable manner.

Will *Guanxi* Ever Go Away?

Without doubt, countries in Asia, especially China, have come a long way in understanding the role of contracts in modern businesses. For example, after joining the World Trade Organization (WTO), China has begun to abide by international rules and guidelines even more. This includes understanding how the international legal framework operates and the need to abide by it. Our view is that over time, there will be a convergence of the East and the West in terms of how business is done. In particular, there will be greater appreciation of and emphasis on the contract as the way to formalize any business transaction. However, we are also of the view that *guanxi*, or personal business relationships, will continue to exist for a long time, especially in China. Even in other Asian economies like Japan, Korea,[10] Taiwan, and Hong Kong, *guanxi* exists in various forms today, and will continue to exist for a long time.

In the case of China, some understanding of its culture and history will provide strong and convincing reasons why *guanxi* will remain for a long time. To begin with, Chinese words and phrases are typically written, structured, and expressed in relational forms. For example, in ancient China, wood (木 *mu*) was the common medium used to make chairs (椅 *yi*), tables (桌 *zhuo*), cupboards (柜 *gui*), pails (桶 *tong*), cups (杯 *bei*), and even pillows (枕 *zheng*). As a result, the character for wood (木 *mu*) can be found in all these words. When "two woods" are placed side-by-side, they form a new word, "forest" (林 *lin*), and when "three woods" are stacked, one on top of the other two, they form yet another word, "jungle" (森 *sen*). Not surprisingly, and logically, the word for "tree" (树 *shu*) contains the word "wood" (木 *mu*). Hence, *shu lin* (树林) is used to refer to "a forest of trees," while *zhu lin* (竹林) refers to a "bamboo forest." A huge jungle is called *sen lin* (森林).

This above series of illustrations is but one of countless examples of how Chinese words and phrases are expressed not only in relational terms, but how the relationships are also reflected in a very precise and clear way. Indeed, the Chinese have a much more sophisticated, detailed, and precise manner of depicting various types of relations among family members and their relatives as compared to the West. In sum, *guanxi* has been very much enshrined in Chinese culture for over 5,000 years now, and we do not see how it can suddenly disappear overnight. If anything, one should attempt to understand how *guanxi* works while, at the same time, educate the Chinese to understand the contractual system as well. Only then can the West meet the East.

Conclusion

The patient and smart Western investor will eventually succeed, so long as expectations are not set too high and the time lines too short. Understanding who and what you are up against is half the battle. The second half is identifying a strategy, which will create a win-win situation to satisfy the majority of the critical stakeholders' motivations. Even for the more experienced, this is no easy task. Upsetting the wrong stakeholder can destroy all the painstaking progress that has been made, which may take years to recover. This is why making the invisible visible is not just for magicians, it applies to businessmen as well.

Endnotes

1. This part of the chapter is adapted largely from Wee, C.H. *Sun Zi Bingfa: Selected Insights and Applications*. Singapore: Prentice Hall, Pearson Education (Southeast Asia), 2005, pp. 224 to 227.

2. *See* Chapter 8, page 181.

3. This senior executive confided that on many previous occasions, the Chinese counterparts had wanted so much to socialize with the CEO as they deemed it to be a great honor to know him personally and to develop a stronger personal relationship with him. They could not comprehend why the CEO confined himself only to the normal business operating hours.

4. Although one can also use the *guanxi* of someone else who is very influential as leverage.

5. This is where a fundamental difference exists between the East and the West in viewing and cultivating relationships. In the West, it is perfectly normal and acceptable to cultivate relationships with top corporate executives who have reached the pinnacle of their careers. Thus, CEOs are courted relentlessly, and they do respond and trade favors accordingly. In the East, especially among the Chinese, it will be too late to network with the CEO once he has arrived. It is more important to cultivate a relationship with him before he reaches the top. This requires careful spotting and cultivation, a process that many companies doing business in China fail to realize.

6. This happens often when the receiving party is not able to reciprocate with an equally expensive gift. The focus is on the intention and that the kind act has been reciprocated, and not on the value of the gift. It is like another well-known Chinese saying, 千里送鹅毛，礼轻情意重 (*qian li song e mao, li qing qing yi zhong*). What this means is that while a person may travel one thousand miles to send a very light gift like goose feathers, the good and noble intention behind such an act is simply insurmountable.

7. There is no shortage of such examples in China. When a key official, e.g. a city mayor, is transferred or removed from office for whatever reason, it is often very difficult to enforce existing signed contracts on the new person in charge. The common excuse given for not fulfilling any previously signed contract is that it was not signed by the new official, and, as such, he is not obligated to the commitment. As a result, such contracts often have to be re-negotiated.

8. In many Asian countries, such as China, India, Malaysia, the Philippines, and Indonesia, *guanxi*, or strong personal ties, have even allowed extended families to exert a strong influence on politics and businesses.

9. Indeed, this was the mindset of the Chinese when China first opened its door to the outside world in 1978. Chinese businessmen, government officials, and senior executives of state-owned enterprises (SOEs) in the early years viewed Western investors and businessmen with much caution and suspicion. To them, the concept of profits was not well assimilated, and the idea that both sides can gain from a business deal was still quite alien, especially as they hold a war-like mentality toward business. Of course, Chinese businessmen and officials have come a long way since then.

10. Our view is supported by certain business practices that still exist in Japan and Korea today. Despite years of modernization and exposure to Western business practices and culture, discrimination against women in the workplace, the seniority system, and lifelong employment are still widely entrenched in these two countries. In fact, the inability of women to rise up the corporate ladder has caused many of them to look for job opportunities in other Asian countries where there is less sexual discrimination. Our point is that practices that are deeply rooted in culture and history will take a long time to change.

赏莫厚于间，

shang mo hou yu jian

There can be no bigger rewards than those showered on spies and secret agents.

(Sun Zi Bingfa, 孙子兵法, Line 13.24 of Chapter 13 on Intelligence and Espionage, 用间 (yong jian))

必素敌人之间来间我者，

bi su di ren zhi jian lai jian wo zhe

因而利之，导而舍之，

yin er li zhi dao er she zhi

故反间可得而用也。

gu fan jian ke de er yong ye

The secret agents of the enemy who are spying among us must be actively sought out.
Use incentives to bribe them, guide and counsel them, and then pardon and release them. Thus, they can become double agents and be used and employed by us.

(Sun Zi Bingfa, 孙子兵法, Lines 13.35 to 13.37 of Chapter 13 on Intelligence and Espionage, 用间 (yong jian))

CHAPTER 13

Gifts or Bribes

Taming the Big "C"

The Big "C"

One of the biggest dilemmas facing Western companies in Asia is the issue of bribery, which can be disguised as elaborate expensive gifts to outright payment to overseas bank accounts. Yes, bribery exists everywhere, including the West. However, the perception of it in Asia is that it occurs from the lowest to the highest levels of government; it is very widespread; and it occurs frequently, even among businesses in the private sector. As different cultural traditions meet in the marketplace and inside organizations, managers face tough choices about the values that they and their organizations live by. In order to be effective, they must find ways to deal with the different views that people hold with regard to matters such as authority, fairness, responsibility, and even the very purpose of business. Global managers need to learn to anticipate and deal with the kinds of value conflicts they are likely to face when crossing cultural borders. Western clients, partners, and friends often ask us how they should deal with the big "C" word in Asia. Many Western companies complain about corruption in Asia, stating that it is a necessary evil to expedite approvals, obtain special rights or favors from government departments and officials, sweeten business deals among companies, and bypass violations of laws, etc. As a statement, this can be used rather too liberally for our liking. Let us explain.

Pot Calling Kettle Black

To begin with, to label the whole of Asia as highly corrupt is too broad and naïve a statement to make. It fails to take into account that some Asian countries are, in fact, less corrupt than the West and that the degree of corruption varies across countries, something that is no different from the West. Let us illustrate with some statistics.

Transparency International, located in Berlin, was set up in the 1990s to help to combat corruption. It is a non-governmental organization dedicated to increasing government accountability and curbing both international and national corruption. Every year, Transparency International produces a league table of the cleanest and most corrupt countries in the world. It is called the Corruptions Perception Index (CPI). The CPI ranks countries in terms of the degree to which corruption is perceived to exist among public officials and politicians. The 2007 CPI ranked 180 countries by their perceived levels of corruption, as determined by expert assessments and opinion surveys. Scores range between 10 (highly clean) and 0 (highly corrupt). Table 13-1 shows how Asian countries fared against selected non-Asian countries in the 2007 survey.

TABLE 13-1: RANKING CORRUPTION (FROM LOWEST TO HIGHEST)

Rankings	Asian Countries		Non-Asian Countries	
	Rank	*Country*	*Rank*	*Country*
Top 50	4	Singapore	1	Denmark
	14	Hong Kong	1	New Zealand
	17	Japan	12	United Kingdom
	34	Taiwan	19	France
	43	Malaysia	20	United States
	43	South Korea	41	Italy
Middle 50	72	China	56	Greece
	72	India	61	Poland
	84	Thailand	64	Turkey
	94	Sri Lanka	69	Romania
	99	Mongolia	72	Brazil
			72	Mexico
Bottom 50	123	Vietnam	143	Russia
	131	Philippines	147	Nigeria
	143	Indonesia	162	Venezuela
	162	Cambodia	175	Uzbekistan
	168	Laos	178	Iraq
	178	Myanmar		

Source: *Corruptions Perception Index, Transparency International, 2007*

There are generally no surprises. However, it does show that one has to be very careful about generalizations when it comes to perceptions about corruption not only in Asia but elsewhere. We have already said that it is very dangerous to stereotype Asian countries as highly corrupt. Clearly, from Table 13-1, there are large variances in Asia, with some countries doing very well, particularly Singapore, Hong Kong, and Japan. They ranked among the least corrupt nations in the world. In fact, Singapore ranked very favorably. While fourth, it scored an index of 9.3,[1] which was not significantly lower than the top ranked countries such as Denmark and New Zealand, which scored 9.4. More importantly, it was ranked ahead of well-developed Western countries such as Canada (ranked 9th), the United Kingdom (ranked 12th), Germany (ranked 16th), France (ranked 19th), and the United States (ranked 20th).

On the other hand, some Asian countries performed extremely badly, especially Laos, Cambodia, and Myanmar. Perhaps it is these countries that contribute much to the stereotyping. The main concerns though would be the performance of the two big Asian economies, China and India, and the emerging markets of Thailand, Vietnam, Indonesia, and the Philippines. However, the findings also show that people who live in glasshouses should not throw stones. Italy was very close to Malaysia in terms of ranking, while Brazil and Mexico were on an equal ranking with China and India. Moreover, it is important to note that there were countries in Eastern Europe, the Middle East, and Latin America that ranked among the most corrupt countries. Hence, one must be very careful not to overgeneralize a phenomenon that is commonly found across the globe.

The West, however, may take a different and tougher approach in resolving corruption. Perhaps, the most revealing and forthright statement was made by Richard Holbrooke, the former US ambassador to the United Nations, who stated during a visit to Hong Kong: "To be sure, there is corruption and a Western version of crony capitalism in the United States and Europe as well, we grant that. Except that when it is uncovered, when it is exposed, it is not condoned and it is not justified on the grounds of some rhetoric." Yet, despite relentless efforts over the years, including the tightening of laws, increased punishment, and so on, corruption continues to occur in the West, even at the highest level. Thus, let us not continue to adopt a "pot calling the kettle black" mentality. Rather, continuous attention should be focused on how to tackle the big "C" not just in Asia, but elsewhere as well.

Chicken and Egg Problem

The debate on corruption also begs the chicken and egg question. For example, who started it? For a person to be corrupted, there must be a corrupter. A person cannot be enriched if there is no one willing to give him money and gifts. Even beggars will go out of business if no passerby is willing to drop them a penny! They are there and continue to beg because there are sympathizers who support their behavior. Let us illustrate with another piece of evidence.

A less publicized study called the Bribe Paying Index (BPI) by Transparency International commented that, among other things, multinational corporations (MNCs) operating in Asia are among the culprits that perpetuate the corruption problem in the countries that they operate in.[2] In fact, it cited that overseas bribery by companies from the world's export giants is still common, despite the existence of international anti-bribery laws that criminalize this practice. Moreover, the study found that companies from the wealthiest countries, which generally ranked well in the study, were the ones that still routinely pay bribes, particularly in developing economies. This shows the blatant demonstration of double standards—that bribing in other countries is acceptable but not on one's home turf!

Without doubt, there is as much corruption in the West as in the East, but the world media, which is controlled largely by the West, has the habit of damning the East on this score.

It is well known that former colonial powers, such as Great Britain, Spain, Portugal, the Netherlands, and France, were great perpetrators of corruption. They initiated the practice mostly in Africa, South America, and parts of Asia during the years of their occupation. This was when the shameless land grabbing and resource plundering took place across the world as local heads of clans, tribes, and provinces gave wide concessions in return for new treasures. It was not quite a quid pro quo trade as the local leaders' naiveness caused them to give away too much in return for a dramatic improvement in their wealth and also because the colonial powers used their military superiority if there was any serious resistance. It was very much a low-cost bullying tactic employed by the Western colonial powers, which rewarded a few in the local hierarchy who allowed the occupation to take place with little difficulty.[3]

Given the historical perspective, it is very difficult to point a finger at the guilty party without a good look at oneself in the mirror. Certainly, corruption was pervasive in the earlier years of history among Asian colonies, which was ironically perpetuated by the colonial masters. This issue is no different from child labor, the abuse of domestic help, and pollution. Western countries were highly guilty of such "crimes" in the past. Ironically, they are also the strongest advocates against such malpractices today. The Asian countries and leaders, however, are not blind to the pages of history.

Understanding Bribery

Definition

Bribery can be broadly defined as an attempt by one party to influence, through various incentives, another party's complicity or decision-making for his own benefit. Implicit within this definition are several important assumptions. First, there must be a proven intent to influence the action or behavior of the other party. Second, the incentive must be significant enough to cause that action. Third, the incentive must be received before the action. This is because if the incentive is received after the action, it is harder to prove the intent. It becomes even more difficult if the incentive comes several months later and is given in the form of a sizeable festive gift. In this instance, one can easily argue that it is a festive gift or a gift of appreciation, and not a bribe for decisions made months earlier to benefit the giver. Indeed, with a longer passage of time, the causal link is harder to establish, more so if the gift occurs after the decision is made. Finally, the benefit to the receiver must also be proven. Thus, if a gift is delivered to a relative or friend of the receiver, the onus of proof becomes more challenging.

Acts of Bribery

Describing what is tantamount to bribery may be much more difficult and challenging than trying to define it because of complicated ethical and moral interpretations. It is like trying to draw fine lines in the sand—on one side, a person may have a clear conscience about his position while, on the other side, another person may have feelings of doubt or guilt. For example, you might readily classify giving a gift to a low ranking government official to expedite the approval of a business application as an act of bribery. On the other hand, when you offer your child an ice cream if he behaves nicely in front of grandma, or take him on a vacation if he scores better grades in his examination, hardly anyone would classify your "manipulative" incentives as bribes.

What is the moral difference between a First World governing political party pledging extra funding to electorates where it risks losing parliamentary seats at the next election and a Western multinational funding the construction of a bridge in a Third World country as part of an unofficial deal to seek some additional corporate tax benefits? How do you expect a Third World traffic police officer to not accept a small bribe for a nonexistent traffic offence when his head of state is looting the country? Is it ethically wrong to lobby and finance a school to ensure your child gets one of the few places available for a first-class education? Is it morally correct to donate funds to a hospital to ensure a relative gets the best possible healthcare? The list can go on, but the basic message is that most people are motivated by one thing: a personal incentive, whether it is driven by financial and material gain or by a rise in self-esteem and personal status in the eyes of others.

One Man's Meat Is Another Man's Poison

Honestly, we find it very difficult to play the moral arbiter on all of the issues just raised. One way, albeit rather weakly, is to examine each of these actions in terms of scale or quantum and transparency or bluntness. It is not uncommon to find people tending toward a business approach that is soft, subtle, and involves a number of intermediaries and no paperwork to risk confidentiality. If, for the same purpose, the approach is direct, blunt, face-to-face, and could be exposed, then people will shy away from it.

Another way is to look at the issues from a legal perspective. More often than not, a nation will use the law to decide what is acceptable and what is unacceptable behavior and conduct within its society. Then again, one can easily point out countless examples to demonstrate that even when certain actions and behavior are legalized, it does not necessarily make them ethical. Moreover, what is considered legal in one country may be deemed illegal in another country. For example, moral and legal standards pertaining to matters such as abortion, prostitution, the sale of guns, the sale of drugs, gambling and casinos, and homosexuality differ significantly among nations.

The same case can be made about corruption. At what stage does one consider gift-giving as bribery? For example, in Asia, gift-giving is a practice that goes back hundreds, if not, thousands of years. In particular, the Chinese and Indians considered it extremely rude to turn away a gift that is presented to them. What you can and will usually do is reciprocate the act. The dilemma is that you cannot determine the size or the value of the gift that the other person wants to give you. It is also unfair to restrict you in your gift-giving to people you respect and love. Moreover, in Asia, there are so many social occasions when gifts can be presented—birthdays, anniversaries, weddings, festive occasions, and so on. Besides, the recipient need not be limited to you alone. It can be your wife, children, parents, other relatives, etc. Take the case of Chinese New Year. It is common practice to give and receive hampers, and to give red packets containing money during this festive season. Their value can range from a small sum to a staggering tens of thousands of dollars. The same can be said about cash gifts for occasions such as anniversaries and weddings. How does one determine if such a gift constitutes a bribe?

Roots of Corruption

Many foreign observers blame Asian values and the concept of *guanxi* (关系) as key factors influencing corruption in many parts of the region.[4] After all, they argue that Confucian values emphasize the paramount importance of personal relationships and interpersonal reciprocity. Many of the large entrepreneurial Asian firms have strong ties and networks with one another, which can create problems for those who want to use strictly market criteria when choosing suppliers and employees, and when entering into contracts. Some critics have defined this way of business, which uses the smoke screen of Asian values to obscure business practices and corporate governance, as crony capitalism.

However, we tend to believe that this is an over-simplification of the issue. As explained in Chapter 12, *guanxi* (关系) can take on many forms, and building *guanxi* cannot be based on money or bribery. In fact, gift-giving alone cannot buy *guanxi*. Then, why do Asians, especially the Chinese, seem so eager to accept gifts, you may ask. The explanation is simple. In their culture, it is considered rude to reject a gift brought by a visitor or guest. For this reason, reciprocity (有来有往 *you lai you wang*) is very much an integral part of Chinese culture, and any gift is typically reciprocated (礼尚往来 *li shang wang lai*) by another gift, although the value may not be the same. Similarly, the exchange of gifts plays an important part in building a relationship, but it cannot be used as the basis to influence behavior. Where and what then are the roots of corruption in Asia?

Unwitting Abuse of Gift-Giving to Build Guanxi

Since we have mentioned *guanxi* and gift-giving, let us begin with this somewhat misunderstood issue in Asia. The unwitting Westerner is often ill-advised to think that by delivering expensive gifts, he can easily achieve his agenda. As a result, the average official or local representative is so used to receiving all kinds of gifts that he finds it difficult to resist. Worse still, such acts unwittingly encourage and aggravate the corruption problem that plagues many Asian countries. As discussed in Chapter 12, given the low incomes of government officials and politicians, the temptation to accept high-value gifts, including cash, has become one that few can resist. In the process, the gift-givers are simply feeding the insatiable greed of these receivers, as such forms of incentives and benefits come too readily and easily. At the end of the day, it makes it more difficult for everyone who is trying to do business in Asia. More seriously, instead of cultivating *guanxi,* mindless gift-giving creates the more serious problem of corruption.

What is important is to learn the right way of cultivating *guanxi,* as outlined in Chapter 12. For example, it is important to show care and concern. Frequent business contact can foster a personal friendship, and the Chinese feel obligated to do business with their friends. This is not that different from the West. Westerners also tend to work with people they trust and like, which is only normal. Following through on promises, going the extra mile, caring for the personal well-being of your local partner beyond business issues, and treating him with courtesy and respect are some examples of how you can build a strong personal business relationship (*guanxi*) without having to resort to buying him over through bribery. The occasional personal treats to him and his family and the occasional personal festive gifts are inevitable in the building of this relationship. Such acts are also found in the Western world.

Without doubt, *guanxi* is important for doing business in Asia. Without it, one is likened to having no eyes and ears, and yet still hoping to mine gold in the dark. As a senior expatriate manager, you also risk being starved of insider information. However, one does not need to resort to bribery in order to get *guanxi*. If anything, such a method is highly risky and will also not last.

Hoping to Take Short Cuts

There are always two parties involved in corruption: the corrupted and the corrupter. Too often, companies and individuals take the short cut, rather than be patient. If foreign companies are under pressure to secure a deal, get a factory constructed, a new brand launched, or simply to survive, then they may easily find themselves in a position where they are tempted to use bribery as an accelerator or as a way out of a problem. This temptation gets bigger when the odds of not getting caught are greater than the odds of getting caught. It becomes worse when one can even bribe one's way out when caught.

Westerners often accuse Asian firms of paying bribes more readily than Western companies, and there is probably some truth to this. For example, the locals may be more comfortable with demanding bribes from other Asian companies because they are culturally closer. On the other hand, demanding a bribe from an American or British company can be awkward and embarrassing. Therefore, in some ways, the double glazing discussed in Chapter 3 acts as a half-defensive shield for Western companies. As such, there is actually more buffer for these Western companies, which need not opt for the easy way of jumping onto the fast track through bribery. In particular, Western companies that bring along large investments, important technologies, and a strong transfer of know-how, have more chips in their hands to rely on. They can afford to take the high road, and still be successful.

Transitional Nature of Asian Economies

Much of the corruption epidemic is a result of the transitional nature of Asia's economies. There are pockets of tremendous entrepreneurial vitality in an overall environment that is still subject to heavy government control. In addition, the salaries of bureaucrats, government officials, and politicians are generally very low. These create the "perfect storm" for corruption, fraud, cronyism, and nepotism. Faced with a long list of regulations, taxes, licensing fees, and fines, a manager can be overwhelmed. By drawing on close relationships with local government officials, he can often circumvent the rules. It may be as simple as a one-time bribe payment or as complex as a partnership in the business. Although it is clear that this way of operating is illegal, many will argue that without it, the private sector cannot be developed. The chances of detection and punishment are also very small. A government official who is a bribe-taker is more likely to make sure that his revenues are maximized without hurting his department or company's economic growth. He does not want to kill the goose that lays the golden egg.

The problem is aggravated by weak judiciary systems that are also susceptible to bribes. The law and order regime is woefully under-resourced and under-disciplined to act as a deterrent. Even China's most recent laws dealing with corruption are targeted more at domestic firms and individuals than at foreign companies. Asia's corruption problem is mainly the result of weak law enforcement and vague regulations that allow government officials to interpret them on a case-by-case basis. The sheer saturation of corruption through society also gives bribe-takers a sense of safety in numbers. Sure, occasionally, someone—a bigwig, a government minister, or head of a province—is made an example of, with high media coverage. Often though, the offender, while clearly guilty, has more enemies than friends and is being "taken down" because he has offended too many people or has been too open in parading his gains.

Unpredictability and Uncertainty of Doing Business

If rules and regulations are transparent and enforced, then corruption will be less obvious and carry greater risks. The economies of developing countries tend to have a high level of inefficient government regulations and state intervention, imperfect markets, imperfect information, etc. The transaction costs of doing business are thus high, discouraging investment and hence economic growth. Corruption, regretfully, although in some cases essentially, helps businesses to get around these barriers and difficulties so that companies and individuals can still conduct their business.

In some Asian countries, the private sector is largely controlled by certain ethnic groups, which are minorities that may be politically vulnerable. However, they can be very efficient, entrepreneurial, and willing to invest in business. As they are not in government, they are often forced by circumstances to pay bribes to government officials and bureaucrats in order to be allowed to operate and expand their businesses, and to secure new deals. As they are strong revenue generators, they become heavily "taxed" by corruption, which is used as a means for their political masters to augment their income, and as a means for them to have greater leverage and a greater degree of freedom to build their business empires. Ironically, this delicate situation has persisted for decades as both sides see it as a "win-win" proposition.

Handling Greasy Situations

Asia will certainly have to change before the problem of corruption worsens and foreign investment is severely affected. Meanwhile, foreign companies will do better if they are prepared to confront this issue squarely and openly, instead of pretending that it does not exist. More importantly, each company should develop its own code of conduct in handling corruption. It should also provide specific guidelines to their senior employees and staff operating in these countries on how to conduct themselves when confronted with bribery issues. We would like to propose the following for consideration.

Know Your Battleground

It would be extremely naïve for any MNC to move into Asia without realizing that corruption is a prevalent problem among many of the countries. In fact, the problem can push up the cost of doing business substantially. Intensive homework is needed before making the move overseas. Some tough questions do need to be addressed. For example, what are your corporate goals, values, and objectives of investing and doing business in a country that is known to have a corruption problem? Do you know how severe and widespread the corruption is? How strong and well prepared is your company in handling corruption? Surely, one cannot go into a war zone and expect not to be shot. The challenge is how to ensure that the bullets are not aimed at you, and if they do, what are you going to do? And what if you are hit?

Global managers often feel pressured into compromising their corporate code of ethics. Most companies' standards regarding improper payments make it extremely difficult to compete in places where such transactions are a way of life. The real dilemma is whether organizations should conform to the environment they are in, or should they export their ethical standards to those countries. More importantly, they must try to understand that the perception and practice of ethics can be very different across countries. Let us illustrate with an example.

At an Institut Europeén d'Administration des Affaires (INSEAD) Leadership Summit, held in Singapore in October 2007, one of the panelists for the "China Rising" session was Judy Leissner, the president of Grace Vineyard in China. She discussed the gap in ethical perceptions between the West and developing Asia. She recounted the story of a tractor that had been reported missing from their vineyard. The employees suspected it had been stolen and were finally able to identify the tractor's location and who had stolen it. It was a local farmer, who, when confronted with the facts, burst into tears. He denied having stolen the tractor. He had only "taken" it. When the company charged that he had not exchanged any money or goods for the tractor, he replied that he had contributed labor in moving the tractor from the vineyard to his farm! In his mind, he was morally right!

Judy Leissner continued, "That's how they look at things. It was quite shocking. If you do want to work in China, my advice would be that you have to have a sense of humor. You have to be able to laugh at things." While this example may seem unreal to many of you, especially those from the West, the truth is that it happened and is indeed food for thought. Managers operating in Asia may need to look beyond the differences in practice to the underlying principles. This "middle way" approach can often help managers to identify a strategy that respects the company's ethical code and values while resolving a particular issue. The great Chinese military strategist Sun Zi said:

凡 军 之 所 欲 击 ， 城 之 所 欲 攻 ， 人 之 所 欲 杀 ，
fan jun zhi suo yu ji   cheng zhi suo yu gong   ren zhi suo yu sha

必 先 知 其 守 将 ， 左 右 ， 谒 者 ， 门 者 ，
bi sian zhi qi shou jiang   zuo you   ye zhe   men zhe

舍 人 之 姓 名 ，
she ren zhi xing ming

There may be armies that you wish to strike, cities that you wish to conquer, and key people that you wish to assassinate. For such cases, there is a need to know beforehand detailed information on the identities of the garrison commander, his supporting officers, the visiting consultants, the guards and patrols, and the various attendants.

~ *Sun Zi Bingfa*, 孙子兵法,
Lines 13.32 to 13.33 of Chapter 13 on Intelligence and
Espionage, 用间 (*yong jian*)

Although Sun Zi was referring to war, his advice is none-theless equally applicable to the world of business. After all, doing business in countries where corruption is rampant is like fighting a battle in an economic war zone. If you are not careful, you can be "assassinated" or "killed" in the process.

Stall, Investigate, and Verify

When you are confronted blatantly with a demand for bribes, how should you respond? To begin with, always find an excuse to stall for time. Never respond immediately, even if your answer is no. For your sake and that of your company, you need to investigate and verify certain matters such as who is the person asking for the bribe, what is his background, his connection, etc. Can you afford to reject him? If so, what are the likely consequences, and can you and your company afford to bear them? Remember, giving in may not solve the problem. In fact, it may create a precedent that can lead to greater and more serious problems in the future.

It is important to note that in an environment where corruption exists, there will always be no shortage of extortionists who try to bluff you. In other words, the demands they make may not be real, and their claims highly suspicious. A vigorous investigative system in place will probably throw out at least 50 percent of such demands. In addition, you will be surprised that many of them will also back off when they know that you are running checks on them. Remember that no one asking for bribes wants to be exposed and caught. Finally, in this game, everything is negotiable, and this includes finding legal and moral alternatives, which we will discuss later.

Beware the Dracula Effect

We have always argued that paying to get things done via corruptive practices is tantamount to creating the Dracula effect. As we all know, when Dracula sucks your blood, he will only stop when you are dead. More seriously, vampires multiply and are highly infectious. In the same way, once you succumb to bribery, the person who is demanding it will not stop. You have just turned on the tap that cannot be turned off so easily. What is even worse is that corruption breeds corruption. As a result of paying this third, or outside, party, you risk corrupting people within your own organization too. For example, those who are responsible for delivering the bribes may be tempted to pocket some of the money for themselves without being detected. This is because when such payments are made, receipts are never issued or asked for, and nobody wants to incur additional risks by asking the recipient if he has received the amount in full. You may also have just created a culture where bribery is the way to go in order to get things done.

Resist the First Fall

The key to resisting corruption is to avoid the first fall. Remember that the fall of Adam began with the first bite of the apple given by Eve. We repeat, you should not give in to bribery. At all times, seek ways to avoid doing so. When in doubt, seek counsel and advice to find out how you can circumvent the problem. This may seem tough, but when you hold on to your principles, you will be surprised that you may not lose out after all. Let us cite an example.

One of us interviewed the managing director (MD) of a large MNC operating in India. The company was confronted with a sudden problem with its electricity supply, which could be fixed if a "facilitation fee" was paid. Rather than succumb to this threat, the MNC held out. It used its back-up generator to supply minimum electricity to the plant so that the factory lines could still operate. All other non-essential energy requirements, including the air-conditioning system, were suspended. The workers had to sweat it out using fans for two months until the electricity finally came back on. Throughout this ordeal, the MD explained to his workers the company's position on corruption and on being held to ransom. Somehow the message must have got back to the relevant authority and the source, and the electricity was finally restored.

As the MD stated afterwards, "Once word gets round that you pay, you're dead!" It is possible to do business in Asia without bribery, and many multinationals can attest to that. Once a foreign corporation has made it clear that it will not pay up and holds firm to this position, it is likely to be left alone after a while, and the bribery requests will stop. We hope this example will inspire other companies to hold on to their beliefs and values in such matters.

Explore Legal and Moral Alternatives of Doing Things

We must however concede that at times, it may be almost impossible to get away without some form of payment. Not every company is as lucky as the one that we have just cited. You should always seek to explore legal and moral alternatives of doing things, including meeting that demand for bribes. This is where some creativity is needed. For example, we all know that paying bribes directly into a person's individual bank account is illegal and immoral. However, if one is able to explore diligently, some other more acceptable alternatives may be found. These may include giving scholarships or donations, providing sponsorships, underwriting overseas study trips and training programs, restructuring compensation and incentive schemes, etc.

Not surprisingly, many Western companies will not admit to bribery, yet the more entrepreneurial ones among them will often find ways to pay bribes through their local partners or trusted intermediaries. In other words, they literally outsource bribery to another party that is prepared to take the fall if need be. Somehow, they tend to think that such an approach is acceptable, even though they are still paying in the end. This approach keeps them away from the corporate scrutiny of audit committees and allows them to use smoke screens to label the paperwork as consultancy services or some other banal description. Unfortunately, such an approach is very short-sighted and temporary, and carries a high risk too. This is because it does not prevent the intermediaries from blowing the whistle on them, and the intermediaries can also easily become part of the corruption chain by pocketing part of the payment. A vicious trap and cycle are now created. Once such payments are "known" (there are few secrets in Asia), the Western company will always be expected to pay. In fact, they will get nothing done without making a payment in some form. The "facilitation fees" take an alarmingly inflationary direction. Suddenly, issues that were once fairly straightforward become more complicated.

We concede that to eradicate corruption overnight in many parts of Asia remains a dream. However, a conscious attempt must be made to reduce the current volume of backdoor or under-the-counter business practices and to replace them with more subtle forms that are morally more acceptable, and within legal boundaries. Even if some form of disguised payment is made ultimately, it is important that it is done in a way that is above board. This is important not only to cover yourself, but your company too. Counsel and advice is needed to ensure that the company's code of conduct is not violated, and neither are the laws of the land, whether those of the host country or those at home. Remember, at the end of the day, seek to do things legally and morally.

Do Not Be Unequally Yoked

When operating in Asia, nothing beats choosing your local partners carefully, whether he is your joint-venture partner, agent, dealer, or local representative. When you are unequally yoked, there will only be problems ahead. More seriously, the local partner may even be using your name to do things behind your back, and end up putting the company in a bad light. It is important for Western executives working in Asia to socialize with the right company. When you are in the wrong company, you can become influenced, and vulnerability sets in. Sooner or later, you end up compromising your values and position without even realizing it.

Many Western companies tend to rush into partnership. They are often deeply impressed by the claims of the local partner—his strong *guanxi*, connections, and standing within the local community. Instead of spending more time and effort to verify such claims, and to establish his moral character and integrity, these Western companies tend to fall back on what they excel in—relying heavily on "curriculum vitae" type of information. When they discover that they have gone to bed with the wrong partner, it is often too late.

Walk Away If Need Be

MNCs operating in Asia are, in fact, in the best position to help to eradicate the problem of corruption by holding fast to their own principles instead of succumbing to local pressures. This is because these MNCs are typically in a much stronger position as they bring along not only investment, but also help to create jobs and transfer management and technological know-how. More often than not, the host country needs them more than they need the host country. It is from this position of strength that these MNCs should help to educate the host country into understanding that corruption is not just about freebies; it comes with severe costs. These costs are not purely economic, but can include social, political, and spiritual dimensions as well. They breed cynicism and disenchantment, sustaining a vicious cycle that has held some Asian societies down as well as brought down many governments.

To eliminate corruption, Western MNCs must rise above it and be on the moral high ground. To put it candidly, they should not operate in societies that are corrupt unless it is for the purpose of helping to eliminate this menace. Business leaders should set an example. As you are aware, there are two parties in corruption—the one that gives and the other that takes. Both are equally guilty. However, when there are no givers, the corrupted will need a lot of effort, including outright extortion, to get what he wants. This inevitably will increase his risks and exposure, something that only the most outrageous ones would want to attempt.

When all else fails, the MNC should simply walk away and look for a better place to invest.

You Can Tame the Big "C"

Without doubt, we are strongly against corruption, no matter what form it takes. It should be condemned and criminalized. However, we also acknowledge that it is a very complex problem that requires concerted efforts on all fronts. Pointing accusing fingers at each other will not solve the problem, nor can one simply accept it as something that cannot be eradicated. Instead, everyone should play his part. This is like keeping lawns clean. For a start, one must learn to keep his own lawn clean. When one has a lawn full of litter, he has lost all moral authority to tell others to keep theirs clean. More importantly, having kept one's lawn clean, one must not go around dirtying other people's lawns. This is precisely the challenge faced by Western countries. Without doubt, they have managed the problem of corruption at home much better than their Asian counterparts, although they have not completely eradicated it. Unfortunately, they tolerate their companies' corrupt practices when they operate overseas, such as in Asia. These actions, in turn, aggravate the existing corruption problem among Asian countries.

The corruption issue is not much different from tackling pollution. When Western MNCs set up factories in less developed countries, their tendency is to shift the lower technology and more polluted industries to these places first. In doing so, pollution is exported overseas. The home country, in turn, enjoys a better quality of air. Certainly, the home governments (almost entirely from the Western world) of these MNCs are not particularly concerned about how these polluted industries affect the quality of life of the people living in the places where they have shifted to. As long as such pollution can be localized and isolated, we do not think that these Western countries would be too bothered. It is only since global warming has become an issue in recent years that these same Western countries have begun finger-pointing at these developing countries, such as China, for causing environmental pollution.

In summary, our main message to all of you is that one need not succumb to corruptive practices in Asia. It is unnecessary and can be avoided. If you weave your way through the good parts of Asian values and avoid the pitfalls of some of the darker elements of *guanxi,* you can run a perfectly good business. In essence, as has been discussed in previous chapters, you have to demonstrate trust, sincerity, commitment, patience, and stability to your Asian partners/friends on a continuous long-term basis. When you hit obstacles or troubles, it will be these same partners and friends who will help you to identify the easiest way to overcome or resolve them. This is why it is so critical that a Westerner should devote much more time to building business relationships in Asia than he would in his home country. It may seem like heavy investment of time and resources upfront, but it can truly pay dividends later on.

Endnotes

1. Sweden also ranked fourth alongside Singapore with the same score of 9.3.
2. This 2006 study also found that many Asian countries did not fare better than the West in the handling of corruption.

3. Indeed, the practice is not much different from the large corporate takeovers of today, where the real winners tend to be the "fat cats" of the acquired company rather than its shareholders.
4. Read Chapter 12 for more details on *guanxi*.

夫 将 者， 国 之 辅 也，
fu jiang zhe　　guo zhi fu ye

辅 周 则 国 必 强，
fu zhou ze guo bi qiang

辅 隙 则 国 必 弱。
fu xi ze guo bi ruo

Now, the general is like the guardian of the nation. If the guardian is a thoughtful and detailed person, the nation will be strong and mighty. If the guardian is full of character flaws, the nation will be weak and vulnerable.

(Sun Zi Bingfa, 孙子兵法*, Lines 3.31 to 3.33 of Chapter 3 on Strategic Attacks,* 谋攻 *(mou gong))*

14

Leading in Asia

More Insights and Perspectives

The Emperor Has No Clothes

"The royal subjects applauded wildly as the Emperor paraded down the street in his new clothes. Such wild admiration had not been seen in the kingdom as all commented on the richness of the fabric, the fine tailoring, the sparkling jewels, the exquisite cut...save for a little boy who, tugging on the sleeves of his mother, shouted out, 'But Mummy, the Emperor has no clothes on!'"

Many of you will be familiar with this popular fairy tale by Hans Christian Andersen, which strikes an uncomfortable chord in many hierarchical organizations. It is a management malaise, which infects many businesses around the world. In Asia, this problem can be more pronounced and serious. Asians tend to respect and follow hierarchical superiors much more than the West. If their superiors are inept, they may feel frustrated but will remain loyal and not confront their bosses. This is because they have a high level of trust in their leaders and expect that their interests and welfare will ultimately be taken care of. In addition, when their superiors spend time and appear with them in public, they feel very honored and privileged. Many will even be prepared to work harder to serve their leaders. Asians also place more emphasis on communalism, group values, and harmony. Few would like to rock the boat, even fewer would want to challenge the decisions of their bosses. While such a system may have its virtues and advantages, which we will discuss later, it tends to breed serious flaws over time.

To begin with, as leadership is rarely challenged, insularity, paternalism, and cronyism can easily creep in. More seriously, the need to develop a strong support team for the leader is often overlooked. As the leader is rarely questioned, he also tends to develop blind spots that can severely affect his judgment and decision-making. Not surprisingly, when crises occur, Asian companies tend to collapse more as they rely heavily on their leaders only to pull them through. The failure to develop and involve more employees in the decision-making process has become an Achilles heel for many Asian leaders. It is even more troublesome for Western leaders working in Asia as they often struggle to receive genuine advice.

Enlightened Leadership

What kind of leadership is needed in Asia? How should Western leaders working in Asia behave? Who can they look to as role models? How does one exercise good leadership in Asia? We have discussed some leadership issues in Chapter 9 and elsewhere in this book. In this chapter, we provide more insights into and perspectives on leadership in Asia. We would like to propose that leadership in Asia is not about being democratic or autocratic, although one tends to witness many examples of autocratic leadership in the region. Rather, Asians typically subscribe to enlightened leadership (明正的领导, *ming zheng de ling dao*). An enlightened leader may be strong and autocratic, but he can also be benevolent and kind. More importantly, he must be able to create a better life for his followers.

It is very interesting to note that the Chinese word for "enlightened" is *ming* (明). *Ming* actually consists of two other words, *ri* (日), which means "the sun," and *yue* (月), which means "the moon." Hence, to be enlightened means to have both the sun and moon together—literally implying that there are 24 hours of light! Indeed, the Chinese call an enlightened leader *guang ming de ling dao* (光明的领导), using the word *guang* (光)—which means "light"—together with *ming* (明). Based on the two words, *guang ming* (光明), we can easily highlight several important characteristics of light, which have strong implications for leadership.

Reach Out First

It is in the nature of light to radiate outward to its environment. Light does not hide itself. It shines, and will throw itself outward readily. This implies that an enlightened leader will always reach out to his followers first, and not expect them to come to him. In Asia, this characteristic is particularly relevant. This is because Asian employees typically do not try to bother or impress their bosses unlike their Western counterparts. Take the case of behavior at meetings. The Asians will be the ones who remain silent while the Westerners will never be short of ideas to impress their bosses.

There are actually several reasons why Asians tend to remain silent. To begin with, they are very conscious of what their bosses may think of them. They are afraid that if they say something that is not in line with that of the boss, they may be perceived as "stupid" and earn a negative impression for themselves. Second, rightly or wrongly, they tend to assume that the boss should know more than them. As such, if the boss does not ask, they prefer not to volunteer answers. After all, the answer may not be what the boss wants or likes to hear. Finally, they are also conscious of what other colleagues may think of them and their answers. Talking too much may give the impression that they are trying to curry favor with the boss, something that will be detested by their colleagues. Giving poor answers or views publicly will reflect poorly on their performance in front of others. Giving brilliant answers will put others on guard and make them a threat to others—something that is not very acceptable in a culture where group norms tend to dominate. For these reasons, it is important that the boss learns to reach out to his Asian employees by learning to ask questions, and to ask the right questions. Only then will the employees be more willing to open up to him.

In addition, the Western leader operating in Asia must first seek ways and means to reach out to his Asian subordinates in order to win their hearts and trust. Only by coming down to their level, and making them talk, will the Western leader really get to know what is going on. It is always easy for the leader to reach out from a position of strength, rather than to expect his subordinates to reach him from their positions of weakness. By reaching out, the Western leader is also practicing the "walk the talk" principle that is commonly preached in the West. Nothing beats knowing the ground and listening to what the grass roots have to say.

In reaching out, a Western leader must not be concerned with only the people around him. Those farther away also need his attention. He should never fall into the "out of sight, out of mind" syndrome. The top leadership of a multinational corporation (MNC) somewhere in the United States or Europe must be concerned enough to reach out to its executives operating in Asia—whether they are expatriates posted there or locals recruited to work for the subsidiary. In turn, the Western senior executives operating in Asia must also reach out to the employees at the bottom of the organization hierarchy. You will be amazed how much harder those down the line will work when they know that the big bosses care for them.

When the Asian subordinates notice the sincerity of the Western leader in reaching out to them through his leadership style and behavior, they, in turn, will be attracted to him and be more willing to support him. Remember that the light that shines the brightest will attract the most people to it as it projects more hope and energy. Only when people are attracted to the light can it lead them to a new destination and direction. This quality of attracting people as a result of an enlightened leadership style is aptly captured by the response given by Confucius when the Duke of Ye asked him how one would know if one had governed a place well. To that, Confucius said:

近者说，　远者来。
jin　zhe　shuo,　　yuan　zhe　lai

Those who are near are pleased, those who are far away long to come.

~ *The Analects of Confucius*, Chapter 13, verse 16,
论语第十三篇：卫灵公第十六节

In essence, an enlightened leader not only earns the praise of his employees, his reputation also spreads far and wide. As a result, others will yearn to join his organization and work for him.

Stretch to Your Fullest Potential

Other than radiating itself outward, another related characteristic of light is that it stretches its distance of coverage. In fact, it will be relentless in trying to provide light to the farthest point possible. There are a few interesting implications to this. A leader must be as far-sighted as possible. This is particularly true in Asia. A Western leader operating in Asia cannot be concerned only with current issues, but also with long-term problems and issues, although they may not be very clear and discernible.[1] For example, cultivating business relationships and *guanxi* require a long-term perspective. In fact, the return on investment (ROI) of various projects in Asia is never immediate. Any company doing business in the region must be willing to take the long-term perspective, and this begins with the chief executive officer (CEO). In the words of Confucius:

人 无 远 虑， 必 有 近 忧
ren wu yuan lü   bi you jin you

Men who do not care about the future will soon have trouble.

~ *The Analects of Confucius*, Chapter 13, verse 16
论语第十三篇: 卫灵公第十六节

Sun Zi, the great Chinese military strategist, said something quite similar pertaining to the assessment of the competitive environment in war:

夫 惟 无 虑 而 易 敌 者， 必 擒 于 人
fu wei wu lü er yi di zhe   bi qin yu ren

He who lacks strategic foresight and insight and underestimates his enemy will definitely end up being captured.

~ *Sun Zi Bingfa*, 孙子兵法, Line 9.70 of
Chapter 9 on Movement and Deployment of Troops,
行军 (*xing jun*)

Leadership is about stretching one's potential.[2] Asians typically look up to their leaders as role models, not just in the workplace, but in everyday life too. As such, the personal lifestyle of the leader matters. This is something many expatriate senior executives tend to forget when they are sent to manage operations in Asia. At times, some even think that it is a "holiday" posting, and try to use their expatriate standing to boss their Asian subordinates around. They also tend to overlook their personal lifestyle. In contrast, Asian bosses and entrepreneurs know that they have to set an example to the rest of their employees. They typically lead by example and often stretch themselves at work so as to set an example for the rest to follow.[3] Leadership by example was clearly spelled out by Confucius when he replied to one of his disciples, Zi Lu (子路), as follows:

先之劳之， 无倦。
xian zhi lao zhi,   wu juan

Work yourself relentlessly before you work others.

~ *The Analects of Confucius*, Chapter 13, verse 1,
论语第十三篇：卫灵公第一节

Be Fair and Objective

Light is fair, embraces everything in its path, and shows no favoritism. In the same way, a leader operating in Asia must follow suit. This is particularly important as Asian employees tend to gloat less about their achievements but rely heavily on their bosses to judge them on their performance. In addition, they have greater trust in the "system" and expect their bosses to do the necessary. Rarely do they complain or protest in the open and directly. If anything, they complain privately among themselves and air their grievances through informal gossip and hearsay. In many ways, such behavior can become more damaging over time if bosses are not sensitive to the feelings on the ground.

We have often witnessed extremely talented Asians being misjudged in a Western organizational setting because of the bias of their Western bosses. For example, at performance appraisal meetings, Western bosses are fond of highlighting business situations where the Asian manager in question remained silent or invisible. These situations are used as evidence to indicate his indifference or lack of ambition, and to label him as a poor performer. Unfortunately, these Western bosses overlook the fact that there is plenty of other evidence to suggest that the same Asian manager has a high level of commitment and has worked very hard. Regrettably, it is not in his nature to gloat about his achievements, nor is it in his culture to speak openly and loudly at meetings. Instead, he is a silent worker who will unfortunately end up a silent sufferer too. This is because the jury, which comprises mostly Westerners, tends to use Western performance measures to judge him.

In Asia, it is important not to judge a person by his rhetoric, but by what he can deliver. You should not judge a person negatively just because he does not speak up openly or chooses to remain silent throughout a meeting. The first author almost made the same error of judgment. He has been on a particular corporate board for more than two years. Twice a year, the senior management team joins the board meeting. During these meetings, he noticed that one of the more elderly senior management members never spoke a word. At the last board meeting, he deliberately asked this member for his views on a particular project. To his pleasant surprise, the elderly management member gave the most profound and insightful argument on the project. In addition, despite looking old and weak, he was very robust and vigorous in his response, and spoke with much passion and vitality. At teatime, the first author discovered from other senior management members, including the CEO, that this elderly gentleman rarely spoke at meetings. However, when he did, he did not mince his words, and his views were always highly objective and profound. In addition, he was one of the hardest working and most highly respected members of the senior management team. Indeed, one should never judge a book by its cover.

Asians, in turn, must also take an active role in combating the problem of being unfairly judged. For example, when they are not promoted, they should not just shrug helplessly and say, "See, they are simply being biased and unfair." Instead, they should learn to manage their own career advancement by drawing the attention of their bosses to their achievements and capabilities. Excessive humility is also hypocrisy. While biases in the workplace cannot be eliminated, a career ceiling is not necessarily imposed by others. It could, in fact, stem from self-inhibiting cultural attitudes. Just as we expect Western CEOs and senior executives to be sensitive to the cultural nuances of Asia, Asians themselves must also learn to play by the rules of Western culture. Simply whining and complaining behind the backs of bosses will not solve the problem.

Beware Your Blind Spots

Light removes both blind spots and dark spots. Not only that, arising from its glow, light is able to provide hope and clarity, direction and focus. In the same way, a leader must be aware of his blind spots, be clear-minded, and learn to focus on the actual issues at stake. Take the case of the unfairly judged Asian manager again. It is very tempting for his panel of Western bosses to wish that he were more articulate and assertive in drawing their attention to his performance. In other words, he should have made his contributions known to his bosses. If possible, he should have publicized them more. Unfortunately, his repeated quiet and humble behavior at business forums, presentations, and discussions ended up creating a different picture for others, especially his bosses. This was also exactly the same impression that the first author had of the elderly senior management member of one of his boards.

It is always easier to blame the other party for any mistake, problem, or situation. As in the issue of corruption discussed in Chapter 13—blame the person taking the bribe rather than the one giving it. We all tend to carry our own social and cultural bias, perspectives, and "baggage" in our interaction with others. These, in turn, create severe blind spots that can prejudice us in judging others. Let us cite another example.

Eye contact in Western culture is very important in any conversation or discussion. Lack of eye contact can easily be interpreted as a lack of assertiveness, shiftiness, or indifference. Such a perspective can easily create severe blind spots for the Western senior manager in Asia, especially in judging the behavior of his subordinates. It is customary in many Asian cultures to cast one's eyes downward in deference. It is intended to create a sense of respect for the person in power. Direct eye contact is not always favored, especially in dealing with people you highly revere or respect.

Motivate and Energize Your Troops

Without doubt, light energizes; it removes fear and evokes courage. One tends to fear more in the dark and is also more averse to taking risks. Not surprisingly, we use phrases like "groping in the dark," implying not only the lack of focus and direction, but also the tendency to be very cautious and risk-averse. As mentioned earlier, Asian employees look much more to their bosses to provide direction. They also expect their leader to motivate and encourage them. As such, the leader must be seen to be in touch with the ground, and be accessible when the need arises.

The pivotal role played by a leader cannot be ignored. Take the case of China. It was Mao Zedong (毛泽东) who brought together a fragmented nation. It was he who motivated and energized 1.2 billion people to work together under a new regime. In the same way, Deng Xiaoping (邓小平) motivated and energized the whole of China toward economic modernization.

To motivate and energize your employees, it is obvious that the leader must be with them. Let us cite an example. The former CEO of the subsidiary of a multinational pharmaceutical company was a Singaporean Chinese who was originally posted to China in the late 1980s as the vice-president of strategic planning.[4] Despite being English-educated with very limited knowledge of the Chinese language, he immersed himself in learning the language and culture.

More importantly, he took it upon himself to be close to his subordinates, and was always there to motivate and energize them. His drive and energy, plus his superb performance, enabled him to become the CEO of the company's China operations within a few years. Despite his promotion, he stayed close to his troops. He could be seen exercising, picnicking, drinking, socializing, going to karaoke, and participating in many other activities with his employees and dealers, no matter how hectic his schedule. For example, he would fly in specially for a closing dinner and go around toasting his subordinates and dealers. He would then knock at the door of each hotel room to deliver personalized gifts after the dinner.

His leadership style and behavior won him the respect and admiration of his employees. It was amazing that they addressed him respectfully as "the boss." In sum, his interpersonal skills in motivating and energizing his employees enabled the company to become one of the most profitable joint-venture companies in China. The company even won various awards and accolades from the Chinese government. When he was asked to assume a higher office, many staff members shed tears at the thought of losing him.

Uphold Your Integrity

Light has another interesting characteristic that also applies to leadership—it travels in a straight line. In the same way, a leader must be "straight" in that he must be trustworthy, honest, and of high integrity. Such a leader will always have a clear conscience in that he has nothing to hide (no dark spots) and will be highly respected too.

Not surprisingly, there are many Chinese sayings on the integrity of leaders. Sun Zi, for example, mentioned that:

善 用 兵 者 , 修 道 而 保 法 , 故 能 为 胜 败 之 政 。
shan yong bin zhe   xiu dao er bao fa   gu neng wei sheng bai zhi zheng

---

The person adept in warfare not only cultivates his moral code but also maintains law and order. In this way, he is able to develop policies that determine victory and defeat in war.

~ *Sun Zi Bingfa*, 孙子兵法, Lines 4.25 and 4.26 of
Chapter 4 on Disposition of the Army,
形 *(xing)*

In addition, the general must also possess the following qualities, which, to a large extent, are reflective of his integrity:

将 者 , 智 , 信 , 仁 , 勇 , 严 也 。
jiang zhe   zhi   xin   ren   yong   yan ye

The generalship of the commander refers to his qualities of wisdom, trustworthiness, benevolence, courage, and discipline.

~ *Sun Zi Bingfa*, 孙子兵法, Line 1.12 of Chapter 1 on
Detailed Assessment and Planning,
计 *(ji)*

Insights from Confucius

A lot of teachings from Confucius are directed at what constitute the hallmarks of a *jun zi* (君子). This term was used in ancient China to refer to someone who held a high position and was highly respected. Over time, and in our modern day context, it has often been used to refer to someone who has a high moral character (人格高尚的人 *ren ke gao shang de ren*). As a result, it is actually quite difficult to give an appropriate English translation for the term *jun zi* (君子), without taking into account the context in which it is being used. Indeed, scholars have translated *jun zi* (君子) as a gentleman, a superior person, a master, and so on. To us, these are not satisfactory translations. A good way to understand the term *jun zi* (君子) is actually to study the analects (论语) of Confucius. Among the many other sayings of Confucius, there are nine important attributes that such a person must possess (君子有九思 *jun zi you jiu si*), all of which he highlighted They are:

视 思 明 ， 听 思 聪 ， 色 思 温 ， 貌 思 恭 ，
shi si ming   ting si cong   se si wen   mao si gong

言 思 忠 ， 事 思 敬 ， 疑 思 问 ，
yan si zhong   shi si jing   yi si wen

忿 思 难 ， 见 得 思 义 。
fen si nan   jian de si yi

In seeing, he quests for enlightenment,
In listening, he seeks comprehension,
In countenance, he considers gentleness,
In mannerism, he is concerned with courtesy,
In speech, he is aware of sincerity,

In action, he is mindful of respect,
In doubt, he thinks of questioning and probing,
In anger, he considers the consequences,
In gaining advantages, he bothers about righteousness.

~ *The Analects of Confucius*, Chapter 16, verse 10,
论语第十六篇: 卫灵公第十节

Clearly, in this context, the term *jun zi* (君子) was referring more to a leader or someone of higher authority. In fact, we would argue that the nine attributes reflect very much the qualities of a leader who is not only upright and moral, but also highly enlightened.[5] Note that the nine attributes cover various aspects of his behavior, from his thinking to his attitude and mannerism. The focus is not so much on himself, but on the sentiments, reactions, and feelings of the people that he is dealing with. As a leader and someone of great influence, he is always conscious of how his behavior and disposition affect others.

The Unobtrusive and Invisible Leader

In Chapter 9, we cited what Lao Zi (老子), another great Chinese philosopher, had to say about leadership. In fact, his comments provide a very insightful and illuminating illustration of what makes a great leader, and also provide a very succinct and appropriate conclusion to this chapter. This is because his thoughts, and those of Confucius and Sun Zi, have influenced generations of Chinese over the years. They also provide much inspiration to those who aspire to be effective leaders in Asia, especially in China. Let us quote Lao Zi again:

太上，不知有之；其次，亲而誉之；
tai shang　bu zhi you zhi　qi ci　qin er yu zhi

其次，畏之；其次，侮之。
qi ci　wei zhi　qi ci　ru zhi

信不足焉，有不足焉。
xin bu zu yan　you bu zu yan

悠兮其贵言。功成事遂，
you xi qi gui yan　gong cheng shi sui

百姓皆谓："我自然"。
bai xin jie wei　wo zi ran

The best leader governs without being known
and felt by his subjects.
The next best is a leader who is loved and praised.
Next is a leader who is feared.
The worst kind of leader is one who is despised.
Such a leader does not trust his people,
and they, in turn, are unfaithful to him.
When the best ruler's orders are accomplished
successfully, his subjects will feel as though they
have done so by themselves.

~ Chapter 17 of Lao Zi's *Dao De Jing*
老子道德经第十七章

Embedded in the quotations are many qualities that will make someone a great leader in Asia, whether in politics, business, or another arena. Such a leader is never proud. Instead, he is very humble and does not seek the limelight. He is ever ready to attribute any achievement to his subordinates and those he leads, and is not concerned that he must be admired and praised publicly.[6] It reflects the confidence he has in himself and the trust he has in others. In the process of leading, he creates a great sense of commitment and ownership among his subordinates by making them feel that any accomplishment is the result of their own effort. This will motivate and energize them even more to scale greater heights.

In essence, according to Lao Zi (老子), the ability to lead quietly, unobtrusively, and invisibly is the hallmark of a great leader. Of course, this is easier said than done. When one is highly successful in leading others, ego tends to come with it, more so when others start to praise and admire one—the temptations are simply too great to avoid and resist. Hence, it is a daunting challenge to remain inconspicuous and not let one's ego rear its ugly head.

In addition, and as mentioned in Chapter 9, to reach the stage of non-interference, the leader must be able to select the right people to join him, provide them with the appropriate training, and then trust them to get the job done through effective delegation and empowerment. Again, trusting people is not an easy task as they are very different from one another. It is always easier to set up strict control measures and evaluation systems to keep them in place.

Here, it is important to point out that non-interference does not necessarily contradict the principle of "walking the talk." The key test is a simple one. When a leader walks the factory floor, do many employees hurriedly stop their work to acknowledge and praise his presence or do they quietly continue to work with confidence as if the leader is not there? Alternatively, when another leader walks the factory floor, is his presence feared and loathed by the employees? This can happen if he has a reputation of barking at every little mistake that he sees and is not happy about. In addition, such a leader desires his employees to greet him and "salute" his visit. As mentioned by Lao Zi, when employees despise their boss, they will not hesitate to leave him to seek a better leader when the first available opportunity arises. In the business world, competition will always present a threat to any incapable leader. The mobility of highly skilled employees to move to another employer is even greater.

Interestingly, Sun Zi (孙子), the great military strategist, said something very similar about the inconspicuous leader when he describes the ultimate guru in warfare in the following way:

故 善 战 者 之 胜 也 ，　 无 智 名 ，　 无 勇 功 。
gu shan zhan zhe zhi sheng ye   wu zhi ming   wu yong gong

Thus, the person adept at warfare wins without being known for his wisdom and reputation nor for his courage and merit.

~ *Sun Zi Bingfa*, 孙子兵法, Line 4.18 of Chapter 4 on Disposition of the Army, 形 *(xing)*

Clearly, the leader-strategist adept in the corporate world can opt to remain anonymous and "invisible" by remaining in the background. He does not highlight his own achievements, or yearn for the limelight, and instead attributes his successes to his employees. Indeed, we can think of several advantages when a leader chooses to remain the unsung hero.

To begin with, as he does not expose himself readily, but remains "invisible," he is less vulnerable. His competitors will find it very difficult to guess his business strategies and plans as little is known of him. This, in turn, allows him to score more victories in a quiet and unknown manner. Second, by staying in the background, he allows his employees more room to operate and make decisions, hence staff empowerment and development can truly take effect. Third, as he is not actively involved with his subordinates, he can be more objective in assessing their performance. Finally, by remaining incognito wherever he goes, he will be able to have a much better sense of the situation on the ground. Indeed, we marvel at how a corporate leader could arrive with his entourage of assistants and make his presence loud and visible wherever he visits. Often, a very good show, and yes, it is just a show, would be put on to impress him. What happens after he leaves is anyone's guess. One thing is for sure, in Asian countries, such a leader will never get to know the truth.

The amazing fact about effective leadership is that keeping a low profile and remaining "invisible" is not necessarily a bad thing. If one is able to entrust the right people to do the job and support them with adequate resources, there is no reason to believe that more interference from the leader would increase productivity.

The Choice Is in Your Hands

It is difficult for us to prescribe a winning leadership style for one to be successful in managing employees in Asia. It is even more difficult to ask someone to pretend and behave in a way that is not natural to him. After all, many leaders tend to have big egos, and they do want to make their presence felt and be highly visible to the rank and file. Yet, we also believe that leadership styles and behavior must be adapted to the local culture in order for the leader to be successful. In many Asian societies, where humility and respect are considered great virtues, a Western leader who comes to the region cannot afford not to pay attention to them. It is the willingness to learn proactively that marks a great leader from an ordinary one. The choice is indeed in your hands.

Endnotes

1. Note that the farther the object is from the source of light, the dimmer and harder it is to discern every detail.

2. This is similar to light trying to stretch to its fullest potential by extending to the widest and farthest places possible.

3. Good examples include working long hours (going to work early and leaving the office late) and living a frugal lifestyle.

4. He has since been promoted to a higher office although, as of 2008, he is still based in China.

5. We would even argue that one plausible translation for *jun zi* (君子), as used by Confucius and other ancient Chinese scholars, could be an "enlightened leader." This is because the word *jun* (君) in ancient China was used to refer to a ruler (君主 *jun zhu*), an emperor (君王 *jun wang*), or someone of high authority (君长 *jun zhang*). The word *zi* (子) was used to refer to men who were very scholarly and intellectual, such as philosophers. Hence, *jun zi* were leaders with great knowledge and wisdom and, therefore, could be considered to be highly enlightened. As such, the term "philosopher-leader" or "an enlightened leader" would be a more appropriate translation.

6. This kind of leader ranks below that of the inconspicuous leader.

兵法：一日度，二日量，
bing fa yi yue du er yue liang

三日数，四日称，五日胜；
san yue shu si yue cheng wu yue sheng

Now in warfare, evaluation must be made as follows: First, estimate the degree of difficulty; second, assess the scope of operation; third, calculate own forces; fourth, compare forces; and fifth, establish the chances of victory.

(Sun Zi Bingfa, 孙子兵法, Line 4.27 of Chapter 4 on Disposition of the Army, 形 (xing))

CHAPTER 15

Where Do We Go from Here?
One Step at a Time and More

The Long and Winding Road

"The Long and Winding Road," a song written by Paul McCartney, became a hit for the Beatles in 1970. Based on an actual road between Kintyre and Campbeltown in Scotland, McCartney said, "It's all about the unattainable, the door you never can reach. This is the road you never get to the end of."[1] Sometimes, investors in Asia also feel this way— that no matter how hard they try, and no matter how clear and logical their plans are, things just seem to stand in the way, whichever direction they take. Indeed, we have great sympathy for these managers at the coalface who have to navigate their way through the seemingly unfathomable walls confronting them.

Pressure from the head office or investors does not help either. Trying to explain to the bosses at the head office why Plan C Version 6 is still not going to work, but you have the confidence that, somehow, you will still get there is not exactly the most inspiring and convincing approach to take. Unfortunately, your big bosses in London or New York, who hardly know Asia, are unlikely to buy your story. This is when a true appreciation of how business is done in Asia is tested to its absolute point of credibility. The moment of truth comes when a board back in London or New York has to decide whether to forget the plans, discard conventional thinking and support the team on the ground, or call it a day. Seeing no clear end in sight, frustration tends to dig in and, more often than not, they end up throwing in the towel. Unfortunately, at this point, they are actually closer to the deal than they realize, and great opportunities are simply lost unknowingly.

In reality, the frustrations can be attributed to the gulf in expectation and the opposing ways in which Westerners do things from Asians. Let us explain this further.

Western Rush for Results versus Asian Quest for Relationships

In the West, there is always a rush to get things done, especially when the plans are based on logic and economics. What is worse, today's modern pace makes it difficult for Westerners who tend to be more task-oriented. Quick decision-making is the order of the day. No one, especially the Western manager operating in Asia, likes to be seen as indecisive and lacking in judgment. With increased competition coming from their own Western world as well as that from within Asia, the aim is to score more goals, and in the shortest possible time. As a result, less attention is paid to the need to cultivate relationships and build personal networks. In the rush for results, the typical Western manager also risks losing the opportunity to listen, pause, and reflect on his relation-ship with his Asian counterpart. Often, many opportunities to learn and gather valuable feedback are lost.

As mentioned in various parts of this book, getting things done in Asia requires building up and main-taining a network of reliable connections, finding the right people to talk to when problems crop up, backtracking or sidestepping when necessary, and advancing when possible. What this also means is that one needs to be very patient and flexible. For example, we have seen deals that seemed dead being resurrected, plans getting unstuck at the final hour when they had looked like a lost cause, and projects metamorphosing into something completely different yet ultimately better than what was originally planned. As such, one must constantly remember not to take things for granted in Asia because often what you see may not be the final conclusion.

One Step at a Time

U-turns, detours, and roadblocks are commonplace when undertaking deals in developing Asia. Business plans frequently get torn up before the ink has dried, signed contracts are treated as work in progress, and very large spanners can easily be thrown into the mix at the last minute. Twists and turns in negotiations can be stretched to unbelievable limits. Handling such unexpected events requires not only great patience, but also flexibility and adaptability to the changing and fast-evolving business landscape. In fact, to excel in Asia, we would recommend that one should be long on planning and research, but swift, sure, and flexible in execution. As an illustration, we would like you to consider the following:

1. The Asian hype is well deserved but do not allow it to get to you. Rushing to deliver big business targets without due diligence can undermine your new Asian relationships in the long run, and may even place you at their mercy, especially when you overpromise on deadlines and other deliverables. Chapters 1, 11, and 12 provide more insight into this issue.

2. Create more space and time for your country management teams. Traveling to where the action is to have a feel of the situation on the ground is a necessity. However, you do not have to travel excessively. More importantly, you should free up unnecessary traveling time to create the space for you to better consider how to establish a stronger foundation for your business in Asia. You can take time to choose the right team, prioritize effort and resources, manage the portfolio of business risks, focus effort on building local talent, and, of equal importance, manage expectations at the head office. During the site visit, spend more time in discussion, not on presentations. Leave the agenda free. It is amazing what can emerge when there is nothing on the agenda! Chapter 14 provides some food for thought on leadership in Asia.

3. Interfere less and allow your staff on the ground to flourish. If you are confident you have chosen the right people to lead, let them get on with it. By interfering, you are showing that you do not trust them, or that you do not trust your own judgment. Chapters 7, 9, and 14 of this book provide some insight into this issue.

4. Allow more time for relaxation with your Asian partners. An invitation to a sporting or cultural event, an

extended dinner that includes karaoke sessions, or a game of golf will be greatly appreciated. Investing more time in getting to know each other will pay dividends later on. Chapter 8 of this book provides a detailed treatment of this issue.

We will illustrate further why it is important to take a step-by-step approach when doing business in Asia.

The Peril of Embarking on Parallel Projects

In the West, many companies, when faced with a series of critical and urgent tasks, will often divide these up into separate projects and have different teams running them simultaneously. This can also work in Asia, particularly in mature markets such as Singapore, Hong Kong, and Japan. However, when it comes to developing markets in Asia, it can become a different challenge altogether, especially if the success of these projects is strongly linked to external parties. In these cases, it is far safer to handle each project in sequence rather than in parallel fashion, no matter how tempting it may be to do the latter. This is, of course, counter-intuitive to many large corporations, but the more savvy will appreciate the importance of not pursuing multiple projects in a parallel manner.

In China and Vietnam, both communist countries, any project inevitably requires a multitude of approvals from various ministries, state-owned enterprises (SOEs), provincial councils, and people's committees. Often, this task is grossly underestimated because individual motivations, historical conflicts, philosophical arguments, inter-rivalries, and opportunities to meddle come to the fore. In fact, it is hard at times for the corporation to decipher what is actually going on, who is working for and against the project, and how to remove the many obstacles thrown across the project's path.

When one adds more layers of complexity through additional parallel projects, it becomes an absolute, invisible minefield for corporations, especially if there is inter-dependency between the various projects.

We have seen many examples of companies simply trying to do too many things at the same time, which often leads to corporate and external chaos and frustration. In one case, a foreign investor in China attempted to finalize a manufacturing joint-venture, establish a new distribution network, redesign key elements of its product range, and rationalize its expatriate workforce to reduce costs. All of this sounds perfectly plausible—demanding, but achievable in a Western market. However, to attempt to do all of these in China is to invite trouble. In many cases, the key local stakeholders of one project had visible or invisible interests in other projects. Some of the senior managers of the SOE with whom the foreign investor was negotiating the manufacturing joint-venture had vested interests in the existing distribution network. Existing distributors had been selected on the basis of personal connections, political influence, and individual "incentives," rather than meritocracy.

The redesign of the product range necessitated a fresh tender from existing and new suppliers, many of whom had historical loyalties and business relationships with the SOE. A few of the foreign investor's local employees, who had never declared their family or friendship connections with the SOE, distributors, or suppliers, wanted to grab some of the choice management positions left by the vacating expatriates. In short, the conflicting reports from various interested parties, the new "issues" that sprung from nowhere, and the unhelpful pressure from the head office led to a complete state of paralysis for the foreign company. It struggled to understand why perfectly logical proposals with win-win solutions were being knocked back, why other external parties, with little connection, started to get involved and interfere in matters, why its own employees became demotivated and silent, and why a once very sensible action plan was now in shreds.

The whole saga seemed like a hypersensitive minefield, which was impossible to navigate. One false move would not only set off an immediate explosion but also trigger other explosions on the landscape far away. Sometimes, a false move did not detonate immediately but would explode many steps later when everyone had assumed it was safe. At other times, mines would explode without the investor making any move at all. It became stressful and disorientating. The only way to untangle the mess was to painfully go back to the beginning, a rather humiliating and uncomfortable process in its own right, and start again in a linear fashion as follows:

Step 1: Finalize the joint-venture
Step 2: Create a new distribution network
Step 3: Redesign the product range
Step 4: Rationalize and localize the expatriate workforce

To break down all the planned initiatives into a step-by-step process was, of course, a much slower process. However, it was more realistic and productive than the previous approach. As the foreign investor worked its way through each stage, it discovered issues and information that made the following stages far easier to manage. It was able to root out the interdependency of relationships much better so that this could be handled more sensitively. This episode illustrates how the Western pace of doing business needs to be adapted to Asia. You cannot simply leapfrog to the end without going through the intermediary stages. Never try to work in parallel.

Do Not Sidestep Small Talk and Socializing

Most people we know in the West have come to detest and try to avoid the "small talk" that they commonly encounter in Asia. They feel it is a waste of time and effort, that it is insincere, and doubt if there is any return for their investment of time and effort. They also find it excruciatingly difficult to make small talk and are fearful of rejection. There is a lot of truth behind such concerns and hesitation, especially if one is concerned largely with short-term results.

Technology has also played a critical part in the decline of conversation. Radio, television, and the Internet are a deterrent to serious and coherent conversation. Past generations speak of conversation as a pleasurable activity, much like a modern American might speak of an evening spent browsing the Internet. The art of "small talk" is lost so the constant topics of family, the weather, Iraq, property prices, and vacations have become worn and tedious. People would rather be sitting at home watching television, playing a sport, or spending time with someone they are genuinely interested in.

When it comes to Asia, however, small talk is absolutely critical in establishing and building relationships and is part and parcel of socializing. Small talk is often used by Asians to gauge whether they feel at ease with you, trust you, or can do business with you in the long run. An experienced long-term expatriate working in Asia describes it pragmatically as follows:

> *"You have got to get the Asians to talk. The first few conversations are tentative. Begin with small talk about their families, their education, their lives, etc., before talking business—why you want a partnership, the benefits for both parties. They are still trying to decide whether they can trust you or not. The floodgates only open when they feel you are trustworthy."*

Many Western managers working in Asia try to bypass the "small talk" stage. Unfortunately, in doing so, they are likely to miss key opportunities to build strong personal ties with their Asian counterparts—something that is necessary to cement long-lasting business relationships and secure helpful friends in times of trouble. Like it or not, if your intention is to stay for the long term in Asia, skipping this important step is not something that you would want to do. Indeed, when operating in Asia, you have to get to know the people and their families. You know you are making headway when you are able to talk comfortably about your family with your Asian counterpart. When an Asian starts to ask you for advice, for example, on his child's education or career choice, then you have really made progress in the trust game.

Here is a basic refresher in the art of small talk or good conversation for those of you who are out of practice. The rules for verbal exchanges are surprisingly enduring. Cicero, the great Roman philosopher, had a sensible set of rules: speak clearly; speak easily but not too much, especially when others want their turn; do not interrupt; be courteous; deal seriously with serious matters and gracefully with lighter ones; never criticize people behind their backs; stick to subjects of general interest; do not talk about yourself; and, above all, never lose your temper. The only two cardinal rules he missed were: remember people's names and be a good listener. Small talk should be used as a picture frame around business conversations in Asia—before a meeting to open it, and after the meeting to close it. Small talk indicates a level of connection or intimacy with the individual that goes beyond the business itself, so no matter how difficult the business discussions might be, there still remains tremendous respect and trust for each other as human beings.

Insincerity and clichéd questions are easily spotted in Asia so "going through the motions" is ill-advised. Asians really do enjoy getting to know each other and to know you. Family is always a very safe subject to start a conversation. Asians are very proud of their ancestry and their children. By spending some time with their older children, you will be giving the Asian parents consider-able "face" and pride. Occasionally, they will ask you to speak to their children to give them career or business advice, especially if their children have studied overseas. They realize there is more of a common link between Westerners and their children. If the opportunity presents itself, take it. It will work wonders for the relationship. The "feel good" factor in the business relationship is essential.

Taking one step at a time also helps the foreigner. He can spend more time understanding the individual and group motivations/motives of his partners. Time is needed to build trust so rushing into relationships is unwise. It is better to spend time getting to know each other. It will become obvious when the time is ready to take the relationship to the next level. The social dimension is more important than the task dimension. Tolerance also makes an enduring relationship.

The art of small talk requires charm, courtesy, and the desire to understand the ideas and opinions of others. Authenticity and emotional commitment are essential ingredients. And, whatever the strategic objective, they will never be bad tactics, particularly in Asia. As such, the ability to observe, listen, question, and probe becomes a very important complementary skill—a subject that we will discuss in more detail later in this chapter. The key is not to dominate the talk, but to flow and immerse yourself in the subject matter in a seamless manner as if you have become one of them.

Patience, Patience, and More Patience

To move one step at a time, great patience is essential. To begin with, many Asian organizations are like large families, which require more care and attention than Western organizations. They prefer face-to-face individual discussions, either during work, or more often socially, to build a relationship of trust in the leader. A chat in the corridor, a cup of coffee in the office, or a drink after work are often more effective communication exercises than seeking feedback at group sessions, where silence often frustrates the Westerner. One-on-one communication is far more successful in Asia, but it demands more time, greater effort, and much more patience from the leader. Indeed, the slower but surer face-to-face approach helps to elicit quicker feedback on what is happening—rightly or wrongly—in the organization and demonstrates greater authenticity and credibility in the leader. Your patience will pay off when they start to come up to you willingly to share their concerns and opinions about their work and the company.

When dealing with subordinates and other people, you should not appear to be restless, aggressive, pushy, or extremely competitive. Instead, you should be good at controlling your temper and naturally predisposed toward conciliation over confrontation. This is particularly applicable when dealing with your counterparts in China. Some of you may have heard the famous words of Zhou Enlai (周恩来), Chairman Mao's premier, who was educated in France. When he was asked by a reporter whether the French Revolution had been a success, he answered in all seriousness that it was too early to tell. This illustrates how an Asian's view of time is far more long-term and patient. In the same way, when Hong Kong was returned to the Chinese in 1997, the paramount leader Deng Xiaoping (邓小平) gave it 50 years of self-rule with minimal central government intervention. For an octogenarian like Deng, this effectively meant that he would never live to see that final takeover day. However, considering a civilization of 5,000 years, 50 years is a very short time indeed.

Being patient does not mean that we should not take any action. In fact, we need to be fast when it makes sense to be so, especially when opportunities present themselves. What we are advocating is that sometimes slowing down is actually required to achieve better results. In fact, the successful completion of any business deal requires a great sense of timing, not speed. Thus, the next time you hear your Asian partner say, "one step at a time" or "let us slow down the pace," do pay close attention. There is much to digest in its meaning. It is like the well-known fable whereby the wiser tortoise won the race in the long term compared to the short-term, gung-ho hare.

Be Humble and Always Have Your Antennae Up

In the West, we have been trained to be tough and decisive. We have been taught not to show our vulnerabilities and not to be soft. Everywhere we turn, there is evidence that, in public discourse, we prize contentiousness and aggression more than cooperation and conciliation. Opposition seems to be the best way to get anything done. An argumentative culture has been created in the process, and those who excel in verbal sparring are highly respected. Humility, and giving in to the opposition, may at times be construed as a sign of weakness. Not surprisingly, at meetings and discussions, those who are more assertive and articulate will win the day. Such a culture cuts across most Western countries, especially in the United States.[2]

Unfortunately, the argumentative and assertive style is completely contrary to Asian culture. When a discussion takes on the form of a confrontational discourse, most Asians will opt out from the debate. To the Chinese, who are influenced by their ancient philosophers such as Confucius and Lao Zi, humility, compassion, and mercy are all necessary traits of a leader. Thus, one of the best pieces of advice that we can offer to a Western manager operating in Asia is to be humble and to always have his antennae up—in order to detect effectively what is going on around him, especially in picking up sensitive issues.[3]

It is important to note that amongst many people in Asia, especially in countries with strong Confucian influence, humility is considered a virtue. This has also resulted in these people not wanting to challenge the other party openly and to embarrass them, despite the fact that the latter may be wrong. If you are the boss, the situation can be worse.

Asian employees are not accustomed to contradicting their bosses openly, nor do they like to volunteer information in case they are perceived as trying to win favors.

This, however, does not mean that they will not speak up and choose to "suffer" silently. Instead, it is not uncommon to find that Asians will often ask others to intervene if they feel that they have not been heard correctly.[4] Occasionally, they may feel that the Westerner's antennae have picked up neither the verbal nor the nonverbal cues that they have given, and they want to ensure that there is no ambiguity. Often, however, it is because they fear that the Westerner has decided to disregard their opinion and follow his own route of action. If the issue at hand has no impact on them in terms of "face" or material loss, then they will tend to dismiss it as sheer stupidity and take the approach of "Let the Westerner make his mistakes and learn the hard way."[5] If the Westerner's actions risk upsetting the relationship landscape and undermining their own positions, then more drastic intervention is required. The trick, as described in Chapter 4, is identifying the right and trusted person, who might be able to knock some sense into the Westerner. This is where it becomes crucial to understand its significance when a messenger is sent to visit you.[6] Your antennae had better be functioning.

As mentioned earlier, an informal setting provides a good environment in which advice and better dialogue can be pursued. Having a coffee in a hotel lobby lounge with your Asian partners is always a good option for carrying out a discussion with them. If the subject is confidential, lunch or dinner in a private room of a Chinese restaurant is a good choice.[7] Remember to avoid being too forthright, frank, or aggressive. Have your antennae out to sense how far you can push the agenda.[8] For example, if you sense that your Asian partners are not ready, or show no interest in the subject that you have raised, do not feel frustrated or disappointed. Continue to enjoy having dinner with them. Take advantage of the occasion to build social bonds with them. You can then explore using the indirect approach of using a messenger to convey the intended message.

Refine the Art of Listening, Observing, and Asking

As mentioned earlier, the typical Western manager may have lost the art of listening and detecting the "signals" that others around him are trying to send him as a result of the Western argumentative culture. In Asia, the art of listening, observing, and asking is an extremely important skill, particularly as it is necessary to filter what is seen and heard. Often, when we come across something that does not fit into our set of beliefs, we react or overreact in a way that prevents us from discovering some new insights about the other person. We close our minds to possibilities. This is not true listening. One of the best descriptions that we have come across is from M. Scott Peck, author of *The Road Less Traveled*:

> *"An essential part of true listening is [...] the temporary giving up or setting aside of one's own prejudices, frames of reference and desires so as to experience as far as possible the speaker's world from the inside, to step inside his or her shoes."*

The most important thing in communication is not only the ability to hear what is being said, but also the ability to observe and probe what has not been said. This is why the Westerner really needs to extend his antennae in a business discussion with an Asian. He needs to unclutter his mind of any preconceived ideas or prejudices and remain totally open to alternative ways of thinking, no matter how different and surprising they may be. For this, he needs to be very tolerant of ambiguity and be willing to explore such alternatives further, while preserving his own integrity, principles, and values.

To get the most value and trust out of your Asian partner, make him feel that his opinions or views are valid and are being genuinely listened to. Listen to his ideas and experience, however mad or strange, choosing one or two ideas in the process, and be seen to act upon them. This will create much "face" for your partner and involve him emotionally in the business. This does not mean that you act dishonestly in the process. In part, it is a game, but somewhere in those long and sometimes repetitive conversations lie a few real gold nuggets or jewels of ideas that may have a very positive impact on the business. It is surprising how our minds can shut down and reject too easily someone else's ideas before they can be properly aired, discussed, and given sufficient consideration.

You should pick the brains of your Asian partners by encouraging them to talk, even if it is on simple and straightforward issues. As mentioned earlier, you may start with social topics and then gradually move on to the business topics at hand. This is where learning to ask questions and asking the right questions matter. As they respond, observe their body language, and move with the flow of their responses. You should respect them even if you think that they are too old, their English is bad, or their ideas are incoherent or badly articulated. Most of them are extremely capable and would not be in the position they are today without much business experience, wisdom, and hard work. What they lack is the ability to articulate well in your language.[9]

The main challenge for the modern global manager is to balance a portfolio of managerial and leadership skills with a thorough appreciation of and sensitivity to local culture. The "hard skills" of business tasks and the "soft skills" of interacting and communicating are so interlinked that they are indistinguishable. Today's manager must be able to successfully integrate cultural knowledge into daily work. Listening, observing, and probing skills, therefore, are absolutely essential for any Westerner wanting to succeed in Asia.

Chapter 14 mentioned what Confucius said about a *jun zi* (君子):

视 思 明， 听 思 聪，
shi si ming   ting si cong

色 思 温， 貌 思 恭，
se si wen   mao si gong

言 思 忠， 事 思 敬， 疑 思 问，
yan si zhong   shi si jing   yi si wen

忿 思 难， 见 得 思 义。
fen si nan   jian de si yi

In seeing, he quests for enlightenment,
In listening, he seeks comprehension,
In countenance, he considers gentleness,
In mannerism, he is concerned with courtesy,
In speech, he is aware of sincerity,
In action, he is mindful of respect,
In doubt, he thinks of questioning and probing,
In anger, he considers the consequences,
In gaining advantages, he bothers about righteousness.

~ *The Analects of Confucius*, Chapter 16, verse 10,
论语第十六篇: 卫灵公第 十节

Note that many of the nine attributes are relevant to what we have been saying thus far. In particular, attributes such as "In listening, he seeks comprehension" (听思聪 *ting si cong*), "In doubt, he thinks of questioning and probing" (疑思问 *yi si wen*), "In seeing, he quests for enlightenment" (视思明 *shi si ming*), and "In action, he is mindful of respect" (事思敬 *shi si jing*) are essential for the Western manager in dealing with his/her Asian counterparts.

Putting Your Cultural Dexterity to the Test

How good are your sensing and detecting skills, and your ability to adjust to the Asian environment? Let us address a common Western complaint about Asians—the frequent interruptions that can take place during a business meeting. It seems to be more acceptable in the East for participants to go in and out of a conference room, answer their mobile phone in the middle of a business conversation, or to respond to SMS messages.[10] This can be very disconcerting for the Westerner as it seems to break up the rhythm or momentum of the discussion. Depending on the importance of the meeting, it can also be perceived as bad manners by the Westerner. He can easily end up feeling that his Asian counterpart is disinterested or simply rude, when, generally, this is not the case. For those who are new to Asia, this feeling can be even more acute, especially if the Westerner is trying hard to make a positive first impression. There can be nothing worse for the Westerner than making a brave verbal pitch, only to see the Asian greet it with stony silence or by picking up a call on his mobile phone.

It is strange because this is one situation where Westerners actually do feel slighted, where their "face" has been lost, as opposed to the Asian. It seems that Asians are far more tolerant of this behavior, as if it were perfectly normal, and they do not take it so badly. Surprisingly, a deeper understanding of such behavior will enable you to realize that this is not so much a "face" issue to the Asians. In fact, these interruptions reflect the greater importance Asians place on relationships. Answering the cell phone or responding to an SMS message, no matter what inconvenience it causes, at whatever time or in whatever situation, recognizes the importance they place on that relationship. It would almost be a sign of disrespect if they did not answer.

These behavioral responses are the result of the extended relationship matrix and the inherent values of trust, obligation, and politeness, hence the interruptions. The irony is that in order to maintain harmony with others, they may disrupt the flow of their own lives. Their presence at the meeting already guarantees the opportunity for them to respond, but a missed call or message may result in greater damage.

Handling Interruptions

How then should a Westerner respond to these interruptions? If it is within his organization, then rules can be established to prevent such issues arising. Most Asians will conform if they are working in a multinational corporate culture. Mobile phones and Blackberries can be switched off, punctuality can be enforced, and meetings conducted with minimal disruption.[11]

If, however, it is with external partners, then the Westerner should simply respect and tolerate the constant interruptions with patience and a good sense of humor. He should be willing to expect disruptions and allow enough time for these. There are some hidden benefits to this as well. It does create some extra reflection time in negotiations, for example, to reconsider one's position, or even to have a side discussion with colleagues. If the interruptions are considerable and the meetings are delayed, it can sometimes lead to an invitation to lunch or dinner. The Asian partner will feel indebted to the Westerner for his patience and will want to reward this in some other small way. This is a great opportunity for the Westerner to strengthen his relationship with his Asian partner. In fact, if you are skillful enough, you may even be able to commend him for making every effort to maintain strong relationships with all of his business associates.

Endnotes

1. Interestingly, "The Long and Winding Road" actually contributed to the breakup of the Beatles due to acrimony over who should play which instruments and how.
2. One only needs to witness the 2008 presidential campaigns in the United States. From the nomination process of the respective parties to the final election, which lasted more than a year, all the candidates were characterized by their strong debating and articulating skills.
3. This may be very difficult for many Western managers as, over the last 150 years, Western civilization, trade, commerce, politics, culture, etc., have dominated the world. Western superiority has been firmly established in the minds of many generations of Westerners. It will take some time to adjust to a new and emerging Asia, especially that of a new and strong China.
4. *See* Chapter 4 on using the messenger.
5. Effectively, this means choosing to remain silent.
6. By the way, this also works in reverse if a Westerner feels his message is not being properly considered.

7. Remember that when dealing with confidential matters, privacy is the key. Never discuss such issues in public/an open area. Not surprisingly, in China today, there is no shortage of private dining rooms in all major restaurants.
8. Read Chapter 10 for more details on how to minimize misunderstanding by learning to decipher the true message.
9. Imagine how awkward and clumsy you would feel if you had to speak in Mandarin (the Chinese spoken language).
10. At times, they may even request tea or coffee.
11. However, if there are senior local counterparts at the meeting, such rules may be difficult to enforce, and the occasional interruptions may still have to be tolerated.

故 明 君 贤 将，所 以 动 而 胜 人，
gu ming jun xian jiang   suo yi dong er sheng ren

成 功 出 于 众 者，先 知 也 。
cheng gong chu yu zhong zhe   xian zhi ye

Thus, the enlightened ruler and the capable general are able to secure victories for their military campaigns and to achieve successes that far surpass those of many others. The reason is because of foreknowledge.

(Sun Zi Bingfa, 孙子兵法, Lines 13.8 and 13.9 of Chapter 13 on Intelligence and Espionage, 用间 (yong jian))

必 取 于 人，知 敌 之 情 者 也 。
bi qu yu ren   zhi di zhi qing zhe ye

This foreknowledge must be obtained from men (and women) who have knowledge of the situation of the enemy.

(Sun Zi Bingfa, 孙子兵法, Line 13.13 of Chapter 13 on Intelligence and Espionage, 用间 (yong jian))

CHAPTER 16

Moving Forward

Building Bridges for a Better Future

Congratulations! You have finally reached the last chapter of this book. Our journey of exploration has come to an end, but your journey is just beginning! With the insights gained from this book, you can now start improving how you work and live in Asia. Hopefully, you can now interrelate with Asians with a fresh, open mindset and start appreciating their way of thinking. You can practice the best elements of both cultures and be successful.

The core to success in Asia lies primarily with people and relationships. It is as simple and basic as that. Doing business in Asia requires a heightened self-awareness and awareness of others, an emotional intelligence that can sense and respond appropriately to issues and concerns on a wide radar screen. A Westerner, if not thus inclined, will need to go the extra mile on the social and personal front. Westerners will need to lengthen their timelines and horizons. They need to believe that the more they give, the more they will receive. They need to be patient and persevere. And they need to show that they are committed to a deep and lasting relationship. Relationships keep the engine going when times get tough. They are the "X" factor that can move a boulder uphill whilst doing business in Asia.

The prospect of identifying, developing, and forging a business relationship in Asia might seem a rather daunting and lengthy process. However, to be successful, it is important to recognize that it often boils down to the human factor and how good you are at relating to people. Western companies are generally too impatient and have too short-term a perspective. Persistence and patience are absolutely necessary virtues for anyone conducting business in Asia, especially with the Chinese. It can be a slow, grinding process, and learning to take things one step at a time will definitely help. One should never be overly ambitious at the outset and attempt to accomplish too many things within a compressed time frame, no matter how competent your company is or how attractive your offer may be to the Asian counterpart. Adapt your mindset and stance to that of the Asians, and have your antennae up always so as to detect anything that may be for or against you.

More often than not, the process requires you to be flexible, to compromise, and to do things that meet your Asian counterparts half-way. Finding the "sweet spot," the right balance between all of these dimensions, really challenges and indeed torments many organizations. Versatility and adaptation are necessary, so too are listening, observing, and probing skills. All of these will enable you to adopt style-switching and to use a broad and flexible behavioral repertoire of cross-cultural skills that are appropriate to a given situation.[1] If you can master these, then at least half the battle is won. As for the other half ... well, you still have to pay personal tuition fees as you go along your journey to the East.

At this stage, it makes sense to briefly review the chapters you have read and highlight the key messages. We will follow the natural flow of the chapters, starting at the very beginning.

Chapter 1—The New Asian Challenge: Myth or Reality?

Key Lessons: It is undeniable reality. The new Asia is rising at a faster rate than ever imagined. This firmly shifts the global center of gravity toward Asia for the next 50 years at least. At the same time, there is a growing confidence among new Asian minds that their day has arrived. The West is generally ill-prepared for both the challenge and opportunity of the new Asia. It will need to understand and know how to manage the ambiguity, paradoxes, and contradictions of working in Asia. Most significantly, it will need to be more open and prepare for a two-way exchange of values, ideas, investments, business practices, and people between the East and the West. It will need to start thinking like Asians to better understand how to be successful in the future.

> ***Key Message:*** *Having interpersonal skills attuned to cultural differences in Asia is no longer simply a matter of proper business etiquette, but a critical competitive advantage.*

Chapter 2—*Sun Zi Bingfa*: Unlocking the Mindset of the Asian Strategist

Key Lessons: The Chinese military classic *Sun Zi Bingfa* is one of the most influential books that has significantly impacted the mindset of Asian corporate strategists. It is used in Asian countries as an authoritative text on business strategy. The Chinese view business as warfare but also believe that war should only be embarked upon as a last resort when all other alternatives have been exhausted. Instead, one should win by strategizing—a nonviolent approach to resolving conflicts. The people factor cannot be discounted in corporate strategic planning. The use of intelligence gathering is also essential. One should know oneself from an outside-in approach. By knowing the other side first (including the competitors), one can understand oneself better. It is always good to be proactive by adopting the concept of first/early mover advantage.

Key Message: *Understanding and studying* Sun Zi Bingfa (The Art of War) *can give the West tremendous insight into how to unlock the mindset of the Asian strategist. By adapting these strategies, the West can be more competitive in Asia.*

Chapter 3—Double Glazing: Why Are We Different?

Key Lessons: Westerners and Asians look at each other through double-glazed windows, which few are willing to open completely as they are held back by their comfort zones. This therefore creates a superficial world, an almost pseudo community of people linked only by the cause of work and very little else. Without doubt, Asians and Westerners respect and acknowledge each other. However, they have not displayed the confidence or the desire in themselves to go the extra step. This is in large created by being descendents of two very distinct philosophical and behavioral influences: Aristotle in the West and Confucius in the East. Greek logic and philosophy taught the West to be largely linear-oriented. It created people who tend to think of themselves as unique individuals with distinctive attributes and goals. In Asia, and especially in Chinese society, there is a cultural inclination toward harmony, a preference for internal cooperation, and a sense of belonging to a community. The Chinese are comfortable with discipline and following instructions. Asians, especially the Chinese, tend to see a world filled with changes and contradictions. They are better able to discern relationships between events than Westerners are. To a typical Chinese, every event is related to another event. Because of these different cultural orientations, one derived from Aristotle, the other largely from Confucius, it is no wonder that confusion and misunderstanding exist in business between Westerners and Asians.

Key Message: *Blending Western individual leadership with Asian collective harmony, a fascinating fusion, requires courage and perseverance from both sides, and can lead ultimately to a very powerful organization.*

Chapter 4—Using the Messenger: Achieving What You Cannot Do

Key Lessons: Most Westerners understand the danger of miscommunication between business partners, particularly in Asia. Westerners generally prefer face-to-face communication but Asians often prefer a less direct style. Realizing the differences, the smart Westerner will use messengers to develop trust between him and his Asian partner, thus ensuring a smoother path to business success. Messengers are used much less frequently in the West but can be very effective in Asia if you know when and how to use them, especially when dealing with negotiations, expectations, personal sensitivities, and performance-related issues. Unfortunately for Westerners who are not attuned to the nuances and subtleties of Asian culture, they may miss out on a golden opportunity to use one of the most useful tools in improving their negotiation strategies and winning more business deals and contracts.

Key Message: *Maintaining a regular, casual exchange of information, asking trusted third-party groups to convey information, and anticipating problem areas are ways to improve giving feedback and receiving feedback to/from Asian partners.*

Chapter 5—Moving Goalposts: Concealing Intentions or Testing Your Patience?

Key Lessons: This chapter deals with the challenges Western companies face when undertaking negotiations with their Asian partners. Both sides have a totally different approach. There are many rules outlined in this chapter that a Westerner should follow in order to avoid negotiation problems, a bad deal, or, even worse, no deal at all. In general, Asians tend to obscure their plans and intentions. Do not be overly forthcoming and trusting until you have won your Asian counterparts over. Revealing too much candid information upfront puts you in a vulnerable position. Negotiation can be a long, grinding process, and persistence and patience are absolutely essential. It is a mind battle, but both sides will come to appreciate and respect each other through the process. In Asia, you are dealing with civilizations whose cultures, traditions, and norms date back a few thousand years. The Asian way of thinking and approach to business can be more sophisticated than you may imagine. Often, appearances in Asia do not reflect reality. Many of the real relationships are invisible to the outsider. One of the hardest challenges any Western company faces in China, but also in much of Southeast Asia, is learning how to navigate through the complex web of relationships to get a deal concluded.

Key Message: Westerners should remember that Asians are skilled in the art of indirectness and concealment. Managing negotiations requires careful planning, a smart use of resources, and considerable patience.

Chapter 6—Forgiven But Not Forgotten: Less Scope for Mistakes

Key Lessons: There are considerable differences in attitude between the West and Asia toward mistakes. There are many real-life examples of situations in which Asian companies harbor resentment toward their Western counterparts for mistakes made long after the incident happened. In the West, the assumption is that human nature is prone to making mistakes. Instead of condemning a person, one should be quick to forgive and give him a second or third chance. This allows the person to learn from the experience and come out of it stronger and wiser. In Asia, the concept of forgiveness tends to be less generous, in particular with regard to serious mistakes. Once a major mistake has been made, it is difficult for the relationship to return to the way it was before. There is rarely a second chance once trust and confidence in a person have been lost. In a typical Asian's mind, it is always better to cut one's losses and bet on the certain returns of what one already has than to bet on something with uncertain returns. This explains the inherent risk-averse nature of Asian culture.

This chapter also explores the "dos and don'ts" of behavior in the company of Asians and, in particular, how to deal with confrontation and silence. Never take advantage of the other side just because he has a quiet nature, appears to be very complying, and has a poor command of the English language. Asians use silence to mask many things. Threats and ultimatums should never be used on Asians; they are not accustomed to such rough tactics. Above all, minimize the use of lawyers as this strongly suggests a lack of trust and confidence in each other.

Key Message: *Being in control of one's emotions while minimizing business mistakes and public gaffes are essential to being successful in Asia. Westerners should try to establish their credibility and reputation early in the game.*

Chapter 7—The Expatriate Phenomenon: How Valuable Are They to Building Businesses?

Key Lessons: This chapter explores some of the critical issues Western companies need to address in developing people—both local and expatriate—in Asia. Expatriates are expensive, and they need to be managed carefully to ensure that they deliver maximum benefit to the company, to the local community, and also to themselves. Regrettably, the success rate is pretty poor—expatriates can be categorized into three types: the legacy builder, the colonial missionary, and the hibernator. The chapter presents a number of suggestions on how to better manage expatriate assignments and measure their success to ensure there are more legacy builders.

One of the most consistent and vociferous complaints regarding Western companies is the frequent changes in the senior and middle management. In Asia, many people and organizations will not take you seriously until you have shown your intention to stick around. The "revolving doors" policy of Western companies needs to stop. The Westerner approaches business like running a 4 × 100 m relay race: sprinting then passing on the baton to a number of successors. The Westerner wants to start and finish the race as fast as possible. The Asian, on the other hand, views business like a marathon. He prefers a partner who can convey an image of stability, reliability, loyalty, and long-term commitment. It is a case of friendship first, business later. The process is more about feelings and emotions, followed by logic and reasoning, and finally by legality and rules.

Asians should be more forthright, speak up, and provide truthful feedback. They should not play the victim. Asians have an obligation to think about their own prospects by dropping the old colonial victim mindset and moving on.

Key Message: *Western companies can learn to transform their Asian businesses through people by actively*

> *managing diversity and stability in their organiza-*
> *tions, accelerating the development and appoint-*
> *ment of Asian leaders, and constantly challenging*
> *the quality and legacy of their expatriates.*

Chapter 8—Handling Nocturnal Activities: From Drinking Binges, Karaoke to Making Speeches

Key Lessons: Socializing with your Asian partners can sometimes seem rather daunting, excessive, unnecessary, and even damaging to one's health! This chapter explains how important it is to build relationships during these social occasions and offers some practical tips and strategies on mitigating the harmful consequences.

Building relationships is part of helping an Asian develop his business, which can benefit the Westerner down the road with reciprocal rewards. In Asia, these social events present opportunities to truly relax and enjoy oneself. With foreigners in particular, they also serve as opportunities to assess personality and character. Westerners should show their colleagues that they are also human and have inadequacies, whether it is a low tolerance to alcohol or an appalling singing voice. By participating in relaxed social activities, Westerners can make their Asian colleagues feel more comfortable and, over time, win their trust.

There is a powerful Chinese saying: "When you drink water, remember the source." The Asian culture stresses the importance of never forgetting those to whom you owe your success and those who lent a helping hand when you were in need.

Key Message: *Investing in social activities with your Asian partners, while more time-consuming than in the West, helps to build trust and confidence in each other. New insights will be gained and foundations laid for a long-term relationship of support, obligation, and friendship.*

Chapter 9—The Industrious and Adaptable Asian: Going the Extra Mile and More

Key Lessons: Westerners can often fall into the trap of misjudging their Asian employees but Asians may also behave in a way that give others the wrong impression. Generally, Asians are very industrious. They may give the impression that they work 24 hours a day, 7 days a week, 365 days a year while Westerners work 8 hours a day, 5 days a week, 230 days a year. Asians appreciate the need for discipline and a clear strategy, but they desire the freedom to adapt, take risks, and seize opportunities. They prefer not to be constrained by role profiles or job descriptions. Western human resources (HR) models often strangle the potential energy and lateral thinking of their Asian talent. Asians, like most human beings, respond well to the personal touch. They are extremely good at influencing people and communicating ideas, especially after 11 p.m. on weekdays or on weekends. In dealing with ambiguity, you require unconventional managers who think laterally and have a street-smart attitude, and determination to come up with and implement solutions. Asians prefer to be judged by their results and not by the verbal and visual diarrhea that can take place in corporate life.

Key Message: *The more successful Western companies in Asia will strive for the right balance between control and flexibility. Not only will this attract, motivate, and retain the best Asian talent, it will deliver success faster in the marketplace.*

Chapter 10—Deciphering the True Message: The Key to Removing Misunderstanding

Key Lessons: This chapter deals with some of the challenges Westerners face in decoding the truth. Often they will not receive a direct answer—yes or no—to a question, which can create confusion and misunderstanding. Asians often speak in euphemisms and in a roundabout way. This is especially true when they speak humbly. They don't want to rock the boat. The best way to distinguish between "yes" and "no" is not to believe everything one hears in a public forum. It is always better to have a private conversation with the individual(s), as this is the most common way of communicating to facilitate learning and "face-saving." A different challenge for any Western business in Asia is keeping things confidential. Western protocol protecting privacy and secrecy does not apply in the East. Sun Zi was absolutely unequivocal about secrecy. While he greatly encouraged the use of spies and agents to access information on the enemy or competition, he was ruthless if he found his own people leaking confidential information to the enemy.

Key Message*: Never accept what is being said in Asia at face value. Always probe further either on a personal level or through messengers to ensure you are clear about what is being agreed or disagreed upon. Peripheral vision is essential to identify possible confusion, disagreement, and resistance in the organization.*

Chapter 11—"Face": Potential Hazard or Invaluable Value?

Key Lessons: The Asian concept of "face" represents an individual's entire being—body, soul, and spirit. Saving "face" is important not just for the individual concerned, but also for his family and the entire community to which he belongs. Direct criticism may give the appearance that a person does not respect and honor the other person's status and rank. When speaking to Asians, you have to be more careful with your words than with a Western audience for two reasons: first, to ensure no one is unintentionally offended, and, second, to prevent your words from being misunderstood. Sometimes, saving "face" can become so central that it swamps the importance of the real, hard issues at stake and, if not handled with sufficient care, can generate intense conflict, which can ultimately impede progress and kill both the relationship and the deal. It is important to attempt to read between the lines. While what is said is important, it is the nonverbal cues that reveal much more. One of the most common situations in which an Asian loses "face" occurs when a Westerner, generally impatient or frustrated, decides to take things into his own hands and goes straight to the top of the hierarchy, thus bypassing the ranks below.

This is termed "the fatal bypass." This should be avoided at all cost. In this situation, Westerners should use the stakeholder-matrix management approach, with managers working at different levels with their prospective partners. Westerners should never feel bad about eating humble pie and apologizing; it will definitely help to regain some of the lost trust.

Key Message: *Treating others the way you would like to be treated yourself is something everyone aspires to. Whether Asian or Westerner, everyone wants to be treated with respect, dignity, and equity. "Face" need not be an Asian phenomenon only; it is a basic human need within all of us.*

Chapter 12—Personal Business Relationships, or *Guanxi*: Necessary Evil or Part of Asian Culture?

Key Lessons: The failure to understand the Asian concept of relationships, or what the Chinese call *guanxi*, is the root of much misunderstanding, confusion, and frustration. *Guanxi* refers to business relationships (商务关系 *shang wu guanxi*) that are built upon *ren qing guanxi* (人情关系). In Asia, business relationships are built on personal ties that involve understanding, mutual concerns, and emotions. The building of such a relationship cannot be delegated or subcontracted. As *guanxi* is built on a "personal-to-holder" basis, it is also nontransferable. In a society where tremendous premium is placed on personal relationships, the departure of any key decision-maker can cause great discomfort to any company that has dealings with him. What this means is that building *guanxi* is a continuous process, and includes spotting, developing, and cultivating potential candidates (points-of-contact) before they assume positions of power; it is not enough to just network with people in power. A Westerner should not boast about the well-connected individuals he knows as Asian business relationships form a closed and proprietary system. This system is based on personal ties, operates on trust, and is not revealed publicly.

Key Message: *Identifying a strategy which will create a win-win situation that satisfies the majority of the critical stakeholders is essential to success in Asia. The Western leader must invest significant time in developing* guanxi *with his business counterparts.*

Chapter 13—Gifts or Bribes: Taming the Big "C"

Key Lessons: One of the biggest dilemmas facing Western companies in Asia is the issue of bribery. Global managers will often feel pressured to compromise their corporate code of ethics in many of Asia's developing countries. There are always two parties involved—the corrupted and the corrupter. Too often, companies and individuals take the short cut, rather than be patient. Many foreign observers blame Asian values and the concept of *guanxi* as key factors encouraging corruption in many parts of the region, but this is not always true. Corruption can be avoided in Asia. It is totally unnecessary. If you are able to demonstrate trust, sincerity, commitment, patience, and consistency to your Asian partners/friends on a continuous long-term basis, then, when you encounter obstacles or troubles, it will be these same partners and friends who will help you to identify the easiest way to overcome or resolve them. This is good use of *guanxi*. You do not have to pay anyone to solve your problem if you allow your network of contacts to make use of the Asian system of favors and obligation to assist you.

Key Message: *Do not succumb to corruption. Be patient and resolute. It can be avoided. Optimize your network and those of your personal and related contacts to find solutions to the problems you face.*

Chapter 14—Leading in Asia: More Insights and Perspectives

Key Lessons: Seeking genuine feedback from employees and partners in Asia is a herculean task for both Western and Asian leaders. Asians tend to respect and submit to their superiors, regardless of their behavior. If their superiors are incompetent, they will feel disappointed but will largely remain loyal and not confront them. Likewise, they will feel honored and privileged if they publicly enjoy a special relationship with their bosses. However, this often creates an environment of insularity and obligation. Westerners need to be more active in communicating one-on-one with their Asian employees, as this helps to elicit quick feedback on what is happening in the organization and demonstrates greater authenticity and credibility in the leader. Identifying and working closely with the key influencers in the organization is also very effective. In many cases, the real reason an Asian does not speak up, particularly in a group situation, is that he does not want to be seen as presumptuous in front of others or risk looking like a fool if his view is knocked down or ridiculed. Silence is therefore the safest option. Asians must take an active role in combating this problem. Shrugging helplessly or disengaging is not an empowering approach to career management. Westerners, on the other hand, should try to better understand the Confucian values of their Asian employees, test and wear these values, and ultimately use them to gain greater trust, support, and unity for the business objectives that have to be achieved.

Key Message*: Westerners must accept the need to understand and respect the positive elements of the Asian collaborative or family culture. They should use innovative ways to influence and communicate with their employees. Asians need to realize that their personal branding, for all its strengths, also has its flaws. They need to speak up.*

Chapter 15—Where Do We Go from Here?: One Step at a Time and More

Key Lessons: This chapter deals with the Western businessman's need for patience in Asia. Many companies working in the region face significant challenges. Sometimes, no matter how hard you try, no matter how clear and logical your plans are, things just seem to be standing in the way no matter which direction you look. With no end in sight, frustration can easily set in, and, more often than not, the Western businessman throws in the towel. U-turns, detours, and roadblocks are common when you are dealing with developing Asia. You need to have a high tolerance for ambiguity. Companies should avoid doing too much at the same time—running parallel projects creates chaos amongst external parties—and hold back from micro-managing their teams. Objectives should be set for the medium to long term. Building relationships with local partners can enhance emotional commitment and the Westerner's authenticity in the Asian partner's eyes. When you hear your Asian partner say, "One step at a time," pay attention. There is much to digest from its meaning. Asian culture promotes listening to people's views. It is a sign of respect. Westerners can learn the virtues of listening and keeping quiet from Asians. Westerners will find their relationships deteriorate if genuine advice is rebuffed. By ignoring or not listening to wise counsel, you risk being labeled a bull in a china shop. When you receive pieces of advice through third parties, or messengers, you should be on the alert, as this demonstrates your Asian partner's heightened level of concern. To an Asian, answering the phone, no matter what the inconvenience, time, or situation, recognizes the importance they place on a relationship. Although this may irritate Westerners, they should understand that it would be a virtual sign of disrespect if their Asian partner did not answer the call.

Key Message*: Versatility and adaptability are required as key skills to be successful in Asia. The best companies allow space and time for their country teams to become successful and listen carefully to the advice of local partners. Westerners should always make their Asian partners feel that their opinions or views are valid and are being genuinely listened to. They should be tolerant of interruptions and work with their Asian partners through conciliation and cooperation rather than confrontation and aggression.*

Epilogue

Before we close, there have been two recent major events that we feel compelled to mention. Together, these two events may accelerate the process in which the center of gravity may shift toward the East faster than we think. More importantly, it also means that there is an urgent need to bridge the differences between the East and West in order that we all can experience a better world in future. Let us highlight these two major events.

Financial Tsunami from the United States

When Lehman Brothers, the 158-year-old and fourth largest investment bank filed for bankruptcy on September 14, 2008, it set up a financial tsunami that hit the financial markets around the world. Prior to the bankruptcy of Lehman Brothers, the serious problems that plagued the financial institutions in the United States were already brewing by the day. It began with investment bank Bear Stearns, which started to fold in July 2007 as a result of overexposure to the collapsing sub-prime investments. Bear Stearns was subsequently sold to JP Morgan in March 2008, for US$2 per share. Fannie Mae and Freddie Mac, two mortgage financiers, were next to face financial collapse. In an effort to prevent further disaster, the US government bailed them out by injecting US$200 billion into both companies.

Unfortunately, the whole financial system of the US market was already heavily poisoned by the sub-prime crisis. Following the collapse of Lehman Brothers,[2] AIG, the largest US insurance company, also almost went under in mid-September 2008. It was in severe shortage of liquidity, having incurred losses in excess of US$18 billion over a three-quarter period. To prevent further catastrophe, the US government had to pump US$85 billion into AIG. That was not all. Merrill Lynch, the largest brokerage company in the United States, was also facing severe cash problems. It hurriedly sold itself for US$50 billion to the Bank of America in mid-September 2008, a deal that was reportedly concluded within 48 hours. During this tumultuous third week of September 2008, Britain's largest mortgage lender, HBOS, was rescued by Lloyds Bank of Britain with a US$22 billion takeover. At the time of finishing this book, there were rumors that other US financial institutions were also in trouble and fast becoming targets of acquisitions and takeovers. The list of vulnerable targets included Washington Mutual, Morgan Stanley, and several others.

What caused the whole financial fiasco and collapse can be attributed to several reasons. First, it was sheer lack of financial discipline and governance. After the US government deregulated the banking and brokerage industries in the 1990s, many of these institutions managed to keep many loss-making investments, especially those pertaining to sub-prime mortgages, off their balance sheets. As such, investors were left in the dark as to the actual risk exposure of these institutions. Meanwhile, regulators were simply too slow in responding with tighter new rules.

Second, financial products became more complicated and complex. Mortgages were repackaged as investment products that paid higher returns. They were sold and re-sold as sub-prime investments. This does not pose any problems so long as there is no default of loan payments, and the property market kept booming. Indeed, this was the case as property prices in the United States soared, almost doubling during the ten-year period from 1996 to 2006. The problem was compounded because of cheap and easy credit that was created by lower interest rates.[3] Indeed, it was a super bubble waiting to be burst. In the pursuit of greed and instant wealth, all precautions were thrown out of the window. These included poor risk management by banks on their borrowers, failure of rating agencies to keep up on the risk assessment of lending institutions, and the incessant presence of speculators who borrowed heavily against numerous properties with the hope of cashing out at higher property prices. Unfortunately, when property prices began to fall in 2007, and when borrowers started to default on their loan payments, the whole credit crisis escalated out of hand.

Finally, and ironically, what aggravated the crisis even more was the insatiable greed of short sellers. Sensing that there was money to be made in a falling market, many short sellers drove down the prices of already weak financial stocks.[4] In doing so, they weakened the ability of the financial institutions even more. This is because they literally denied these institutions one important means of survival, which was to sell their shares in order to raise cash. Indeed, short selling was so prevalent and damaging that the US government was forced to ban it in the third week of September 2008 as a means to curb the financial carnage. Several other Western countries also took similar measures.

As of late September 2008, the actual damage caused by this latest financial turmoil and tsunami was still unknown, although various estimates placed the figure at anything between US\$600 billion to US\$1.5 trillion. Moreover, it is still too early to assess how this financial tsunami will spread to Europe and the rest of the world. Several lessons, however, are fast becoming clear to the eyes of the rest of the world.

First, the West, as typified by the United States, is used to "lecturing" the East on how to manage their businesses, economies and other matters. In fact, during the 1997 Asian financial crisis, there was no shortage of Western critics, analysts, and financial gurus who tried to offer all kinds of advice and lessons to the East on how to put their houses in order. For example, when then Malaysian Prime Minister Dr. Mahathir banned foreign exchange speculation and short selling, he was heavily criticized for intervening in the smooth functioning of the market. Today, Western leaders are doing exactly what Dr. Mahathir did, and more.

Second, transparency, proper governance, adequate risk management, etc., were concepts and principles that were heavily advocated by the West, and touted to be widely practiced. Regretfully, these were found to be sadly lacking as evidenced by the unfolding of events that arose from the September 2008 crisis.

Third, greed knows no boundaries nor is it culturally bound. The September 2008 crisis was caused largely by the insatiable appetite of certain Western bankers to get rich fast and, unfortunately, all principles were compromised along the way. More seriously, it drove people to become very short-sighted, and no consideration was given to the longer-term consequences of their actions. For example, the senior executives and chief executive officers (CEOs) of these financial institutions paid themselves millions of dollars in annual compensation, some of them even tens of millions. Yet, despite such high incomes, it did not stop them from going for more, nor did it stop them from compromising their ethical standards and practices.

Finally, this episode also showed the East that the once mighty institutions of the West can be vulnerable, despite their history, reputation, and seemingly vast resources. Indeed, we would not be surprised if the control of one or more of these once mighty institutions may fall into the hands of the East sooner than you think possible. If anything, the East will gain more confidence in dealing with the West from now on.

The Dragon Has More Than Awakened

In Chapter 1, we mentioned the awakening of the Asian giant, China. In fact, China has more than awakened. The Beijing 2008 Olympic Games can, indeed, be viewed as a watershed event that may signal the beginning of the changing shift of economic power from the West to the East. Prior to the Olympic Games, many human rights and lobby groups were trying to apply pressure on China.[5] Calls on Western leaders were even made, and some of them were tempted to boycott the opening ceremony of the Olympics. However, having witnessed the grandeur and the spectacular performances at the opening and closing ceremonies, and the amount of effort that was put into organizing the Olympics, any astute Western observer would have been overwhelmed by the whole episode and experience. China spent at least seven years preparing for the Olympics, having been awarded the 2008 Games in 2001. Having put in so much effort and investment into the event,[6] any attempt by any party to torpedo or sabotage it was likely to be met with dire consequences in the long run. This is because the event was designed as a showcase to the world, and to bring China closer to the world, and the world closer to China. Undermining and humiliating them openly by boycotting the opening ceremony would have caused a severe loss of "face" to the Chinese, something that would never be forgiven. Fortunately, just prior to the opening ceremony, most leaders of the Western world decided to grace the occasion.

Indeed, what the Chinese demonstrated at the Beijing 2008 Olympic Games was an eye-opening exercise for the whole world, as it demonstrated what the Chinese are capable of doing and achieving, To begin with, the performances at the opening ceremony were filled with modern gadgetry that were interspersed with significant references to its glorious past. For example, the opening performance showcased ancient Chinese history and culture, and the lighting of the Olympic cauldron was one that skillfully exploited modern technology and human creativity. The scale and magnificence of every well-choreographed performance caught the imagination of the audience in the Bird Nest stadium as well as those watching live on television. Many were overwhelmed by the effectiveness and efficiency in which such large-scale performances can be carried out, and marveled at their creative presentations.[7]

What is important to note is that the 2008 Olympic Games demonstrated to the world the new China, one that is not just modern and progressive, but one that is very much proud of its history, culture, and traditions. In addition, it signified to the Western world that China is ready to engage them, and is unlikely to be sidelined easily as evidenced by the history of the last 200 years. Already, based on its foreign exchange reserves, China is number one in the world today. In contrast, despite its military might and economic prowess, the United States is the biggest debtor nation in the world. In addition, and as mentioned earlier, the September 2008 financial turmoil and tsunami caused by the failures of financial institutions in the United States are likely to increase the confidence of the Chinese in dealing with the West.

Of course, this does not mean that China has overcome all its problems, and that its industries are free from malpractices.[8] If anything, the Chinese still have a long way to learn from the West. However, our plea is that given the fast development of recent events, there is an increased need and urgency that the East and the West must meet, and that they have much to learn from one another. The West must forsake its superiority complex that it has gained over the last 150 years. The East, as typified by the Chinese, must not live in the past nor be blinded by its recent economic surge of successes. Each must be prepared to reach out to the other. Only then will the 21st century be a better world for all mankind.

Learning from One Another to Improve Understanding

It is never easy to unmask the East, especially China, when it has a civilization that dates back several thousand years. However, this does not mean that it cannot be done. Rather, to do business in Asia, and especially in China, one must really spend time and effort to understand the people and not assume that what works at home will work everywhere else. Interestingly, it was Lao Zi (老子), one of the well-known Chinese philosophers, who said the following regarding how to overcome misunderstanding, avoid mismatched expectations, and build harmony:

故 以 身 观 身;
gu   yi   shen guan shen

以 家 观 家;
yi   jia guan jia

以 乡 观 乡;
yi   xiang guan xiang

以 邦 观 邦 ;
yi bang guan bang

以 天 下 观 天 下 。
yi tian xia guan tian xia

吾 何 以 知 天 下 然 哉 ？ 以 此 。
wu he yi zhi tian xia ran zai   yi ci

Thus, to understand a person,
live with that person;
To understand a particular family,
live with that family;
To understand a particular community,
live with that community;
To understand a particular nation,
live with that nation;
To understand the world,
live with the world;
How can one live with the world?
By accepting it.

Chapter 54 of Lao Zi's *Dao De Jing*
老子道德经第五十四章

Indeed, Chinese philosophy teaches that endings are contained within beginnings. We sow what we reap. A potential relationship, if carefully tended, can transform into a strong and cohesive match, producing mutually satisfactory results in the long run. Now is your chance. It is never too late. Start by making connections, then work at nurturing and enlarging them until you finally become a master of your network. This is the secret to unlocking the future in Asia. Perhaps, the following two quotations, one from the West and one from the East, serve as useful reminders of our journey ahead.

*"Courage is what it takes to stand up and speak;
courage is also what it takes to sit down and listen."*

Winston Churchill

三 人 行， 必 有 我 师 焉。
san ren xing　　bi you wo shi yan

择 其 善 者 而 从 之， 其 不 善 者 而 改 之。
ze　qi shan zhe　er cong zhi　　qi　bu shan zhe er　gai　zhi

When I am in the company of three persons, there is
surely a teacher among them.
I will learn from their strengths, and use their
weaknesses as lessons to correct myself.

~ *The Analects of Confucius*, Chapter 7, verse 22,
论语第七篇:述而第二十二节

We wish you every success.

Endnotes

1. One has to always remember that style differences between
    the East and the West, whether it be a result of differing
    social or religious practices, different languages or, indeed,
    different geography, have their advantages and their
    limitations. Neither the Eastern nor Western approach to
    business is necessarily correct in its own right. The correct
    balance of ingredients—sweet and sour—is what makes
    the recipe a success.

2. Lehman Brothers subsequently managed to sell off its core
    investment banking operations to Barclays Bank of the
    United Kingdom for only US$250 million. Barclays had
    earlier walked away from buying Lehman.

3. Interest rates were basically controlled by the US govern-
    ment. Since July 2007, the US government has lowered
    interest rates by 250 basis points, or 2.5%. This has made
    credit and borrowing very cheap.

4. Short selling is a practice of selling away stock that one does not own. Through massive selling, the sellers will drive down the prices of such stocks much lower. They then buy them back at much lower prices and, in the process, make huge profits from such activities.

5. In fact, the journey taken by the Olympic torch was interrupted by protests and demonstrations. In Paris, the torch was almost snatched from a handicapped lady in a wheelchair.

6. Various sources estimated that the Chinese government invested at least US$65 billion into organizing the Olympics.

7. Having witnessed the events ourselves, we would argue that no other country will be able to surpass the kind of shows put on by the Chinese for the opening and closing ceremonies of future Olympic Games.

8. As late as in mid-September, Chinese milk products were found to be tainted with the chemical melamine. Several babies in China died after consuming milk powder produced by some manufacturers. The fiasco caused a call in the West to ban Chinese milk products. Many Asian countries also took similar stern measures to ban Chinese milk products, including removing all existing products from the shelves. This episode occurred barely a year after Chinese toys and children's clothing were found to contain toxic materials. Indeed, it will take China quite some time to reach the manufacturing safety standards of the West. To begin with, it needs to step up its monitoring and regulatory enforcements.

Bibliography

Ambler, T. and M. Witzel. *Doing Business in China*. UK: RoutledgeCurzon, 2004.

Bhargava, V. and E. Bolongaita. *Challenging Corruption in Asia. Case Studies and a Framework for Action*. Washington DC: World Bank Publications, 2003.

Chu, C.N. *The Asian Mind Game: Unlocking the Hidden Agenda of the Asian Business Culture—A Westerner's Survival Manual*. USA: Rawson Associates Scribner, 1991.

Church, P. *Added Value: The Life Stories of Leading South East Asian Business People*. Sydney: Murmeli Pty Ltd, 1999.

Clissold, T. *Mr China*. London: Constable & Robinson Ltd, 2002.

Fernandez, J.A. and L. Underwood. *China CEO, Voices of Experience from 20 International Business Leaders*. Singapore: John Wiley & Sons (Asia), 2006.

Fine, D. *The Fine Art of Small Talk*. USA: Hyperion, 2005.

Fishman, T.C. "China Inc." *How the Rise of the Next Superpower Challenges America and the World*. New York: Scribner, 2005.

Griffith, S.B. *Sun Tsu: The Art of War—The New Illustrated Edition*. London: Duncan Baird Publishers, 2005.

Gundling, E. *Working GlobeSmart: 12 People Skills for Doing Business Across Borders*. Palo Alto, California: Davies-Black Publishing, 2003.

Hall, T.E. *The Silent Language*. USA: Anchor, 1973.

Heider, J. *The Tao of Leadership: Lao Tzu's Tao Te Ching Adapted for A New Age*. Atlanta: Humanics New Age, 1985.

Hoff, B. *The Tao of Pooh*. New York: Penguin, 1982.

Hofstede, G. *Cultures and Organizations: Intercultural Cooperation and Its Importance for Survival*. UK: McGraw-Hill, 1991.

Hyun, J. *Breaking the Bamboo Ceiling: Career Strategies for Asians— The Essential Guide to Getting In, Moving Up and Reaching the Top*. USA: HarperCollins Publishers Inc., 2005.

Irwin, H. *Communicating with Asia: Understanding People and Customs*. Australia: Allen & Unwin, 1996.

James, O. *Affluenza*. UK: Vermilion, 2007.

Kale, S. *Bright Ideas: Communicating with Asian Customers—It's a Question of Context*. Article from www.urbino.net. Retrieved in September 2001.

Kidd, J.B. and F-J. Richter. *Fighting Corruption in Asia: Causes, Effects and Remedies*. Singapore: World Scientific Press, 2003.

Kynge, J. *China Shakes the World: The Rise of a Hungry Nation*. Great Britain: Weidenfeld & Nicolson, 2006.

Levitt S.D. and S.J. Dubner. *Freakonomics: A Rogue Economist Explores the Hidden Side of Everything*. Great Britain: Allen Lane, 2005.

Mahbubani, K. *Can Asians Think?* Singapore: Marshall Cavendish Editions, 2004.

Mann, R. *The Culture of Business in Indonesia*. Jakarta: Gateway Books, 1994.

Marinoff, L. *Plato not Prozac! Applying Eternal Wisdom to Everyday Problems*. USA: HarperCollins Publishers Inc., 1999.

Nisbett, R.E. *The Geography of Thought: How Asians and Westerners Think Differently and Why*. UK: Nicholas Brealey Publishing, 2003.

Peck, S. *The Road Less Traveled*. USA: Simon & Schuster, 1978.

Rosinski, P. *Coaching across Cultures: New Tools for Leveraging National, Corporate and Professional Differences*. UK: Nicholas Brealey Publishing, 2003.

Ting-Toomey, S. *Communicating across Cultures*. USA: The Guilford Press, 1999.

Walker, D., T. Walker, and J. Schmitz. *Doing Business Internationally: The Guide to Cross-cultural Success*. USA: McGraw-Hill, 2003.

Wang, W. *The China Executive: Marrying Western and Chinese Strengths to Generate Profitability from Your Investment in China*. UK: 2W Publishing, 2006.

Wee, C.H. *Sun Zi Bingfa: Selected Insights and Applications*. Singapore: Prentice Hall, Pearson Education (Southeast Asia), 2005.

Williamson, P.J. *Winning in Asia: Strategies for Competing in the New Millennium*. Boston, MA, USA: Harvard Business School Publishing, 2004.

"Reaching for a Renaissance—A Special Report on China and Its Region." *The Economist*. March 2007.

"Joint Ventures in China." *The Economist*. April 2007.

"The Art of Conversation." *The Economist*. December 2006.

Philosophers

Aristotle, 384–322 B.C.

Confucius (Kung Fu Tzu), 551–479 B.C.

Buddha (Siddhartha Gautama) 563–483 B.C.

Sun Tzu, circa 4th century B.C.

Lao Tzu, circa 6th century B.C.

Index